D1716199

APHASIA HANDBOOK

for Adults and Children

Seventh Printing

APHASIA HANDBOOK

for Adults and Children

By

ALEEN AGRANOWITZ, A.B.

Director, Lakewood Speech Clinic
Long Beach, California

Formerly
Chief, Aphasia Clinic
Veterans Administration Hospital
Long Beach, California

and

MILFRED RIDDLE McKEOWN, A.B., M.A.

Chief, Aphasia Clinic
Veterans Administration Hospital
Long Beach, California

With a Foreword by

J. M. NIELSEN, M.D.

Professor of Clinical Neurology
University of California at Los Angeles
Consultant in Aphasia
Veterans Administration Hospital, and
Lakewood Speech Clinic
Long Beach, California

CHARLES C THOMAS · PUBLISHER
Springfield · Illinois · U.S.A.

Published and Distributed Throughout the World by

CHARLES C THOMAS • PUBLISHER

Bannerstone House

301-327 East Lawrence Avenue, Springfield, Illinois, U.S.A.

© *1964, by* CHARLES C THOMAS • PUBLISHER

ISBN 0-398-00017-4

Library of Congress Catalog Card Number: 63-15419

First Printing, 1964
Second Printing, 1966
Third Printing, 1968
Fourth Printing, 1970
Fifth Printing, 1971
Sixth Printing, 1973
Seventh Printing, 1975

With THOMAS BOOKS *careful attention is given to all details of
manufacturing and design. It is the Publisher's desire to present books that are
satisfactory as to their physical qualities and artistic possibilities and
appropriate for their particular use.* THOMAS BOOKS *will be true to those
laws of quality that assure a good name and good will.*

Printed in the United States of America

R-1

FOREWORD

THIS BOOK BY Mrs. Agranowitz and Mrs. McKeown is founded on the work done at the United States Veterans Administration Hospital at Long Beach, California. It is a worthy addition to the literature on speech rehabilitation. I have observed and to some extent supervised their work and have seen their methods bear fruit. I am pleased to recommend their book to anyone giving speech retraining to aphasics.

J. M. NIELSEN, M.D.
Consultant in Aphasia to the
Veterans Administration Hospital
and the Lakewood Speech Clinic

PREFACE

THE APHASIA HANDBOOK evolved from a collection of therapy materials and techniques used by the authors in the Aphasia Clinic at the Veterans Administration Hospital, Long Beach, California, where more than a thousand aphasics were treated in the decade following World War II. In response to many requests for help from aphasic adults not eligible for admittance to the Veterans Hospital and from parents of brain-injured children, the authors published an experimental edition of the *Handbook* in 1959 The present edition is a revision and expansion of the original.

Part II, Aphasia in Children, is the outgrowth of seven years' experience and research at the Lakewood Speech Clinic under the direction of Mrs. Aleen Agranowitz with Mrs. Gladys Gleason as assistant director.

The *Aphasia Handbook* has been designed for anyone who may encounter the problem of retraining an aphasic—professional therapists, teachers and family members. It provides orientation for college students of speech therapy and for professional people working in related fields of specialized education and rehabilitation. While prepared primarily for adults and children with aphasia, many of the techniques are suited to the retraining of the hard-of-hearing, the cerebral palsied, the laryngectomized, the mentally retarded and those delayed in speech.

Some of the material is the outgrowth and accumulation of experimenting and testing by the following with whom the authors have been associated in clinical work in the Veterans Administration and at the Lakewood Speech Clinic and to whom they wish to give grateful recognition: Helen Giedt, Marria Lennon Corbin, Marion Ruff Dossi, Arthur Terr, Daniel Boone, Gloria Galvin Seacat, Helen Smith, Don Ellis, Clark Harada, Barbara Bohannan and Gene Schroen. Charles Mason, Ph.D., Clinical Psychologist, and Charles Rhodes, Ed.D., Counseling Psychologist, at the Veterans Administration Hospital have been helpful in the sections dealing with hypnotherapy and testing. Jack Holmes, Ph.D., Professor of Education at the University of California at Berkeley, and J. J. Thompson, Ph.D., Director of the Speech Clinic at Long Beach State College, Long Beach, California, provided valuable suggestions from the viewpoint of experts in reading, pedagogy and speech. The authors are indebted to many writers and teachers who have contributed to the literature on the subject of aphasia in both adults and children, and who are cited extensively in footnotes and in the bibliographies. Special recognition is due Joan Waltz who retyped and assembled the revised manuscript, to Joan Schutz for sketches and illustrations and to Gladys Gleason for contributions of original ideas devised for therapy with children in her position as senior therapist at the Lakewood Speech Clinic.

The clinical experience of the authors has been greatly enhanced throughout the years by the supervision and teaching of J. M. Nielsen, M. D., at the Veterans Administration Hospital Aphasia Clinic. Dr. Nielsen, Professor of Clinical Neurology at the University of California at Los Angeles and Consultant in Aphasia for the Veterans Administration, was instrumental in setting up the national Veterans Administration program for aphasia retraining and has been with the Aphasia Clinic since its inception in 1946. His personal and professional guidance in regularly scheduled conferences at the Veterans Administration Hospital and his encouragement have been of inestimable value.

The repetition which will be found throughout the *Aphasia Handbook* is intentional. A handbook such as this seldom is read from cover to cover; the user refers to sections relevant to the particular disability he is dealing with at the moment, the description of its symptoms, and the suggested treatment; consequently, repetition must be made wherever the information is needed.

ALEEN AGRANOWITZ
MILFRED RIDDLE MCKEOWN

CONTENTS

PART I

APHASIA IN ADULTS

General Orientation

PART II

APHASIA IN CHILDREN

(Prepared with the assistance of Gladys Gleason)

Orientation

    Group Projects
    References
27. THERAPY MATERIALS 247
    Teaching Materials
    Play Therapy Materials
    Materials for Building Concepts
    Catalogs for Therapy Materials
    Records
    Teaching Helps
28. TRAINING FOR VISUAL RECOGNITION 253
    Introduction
    Training for Non-Language Visual Recognition
    Visual Verbal Recognition
29. TRAINING FOR AUDITORY RECOGNITION 271
    Introduction
    Non-Verbal Sounds
    Auditory Verbal Recognition
30. NAMING 275
    Techniques
    Materials for Naming
31. FORMULATION 279
    Spontaneous Speech
    Questions
    Action Words
    Pictures
    Story
    Use of Prepositions
32. ARTICULATION 285
    Introduction
    Basic Techniques
33. READING, WRITING, ARITHMETIC 288
    Reading
    Writing and Spelling
    Arithmetic
    References for the Therapist
34. SAMPLES OF CHILDREN'S WORK 296

    Appendix
    Bibliographies 305

Contents   xv

Pilgrim Psych. Center
Speech & Hearing Clinic
Bldg. 23-6
West Brentwood, N.Y. 11717

APHASIA HANDBOOK

for Adults and Children

Pilgrim Psych. Center
Speech & Hearing Clinic
Bldg. 23 - 6
West Brentwood, N.Y. 11717

Part One

Aphasia in Adults

GENERAL ORIENTATION

Chapter 1

QUESTIONS COMMONLY ASKED REGARDING APHASIA

I. WHAT IS APHASIA?[1]

T HE SIMPLEST DEFINITION of the term aphasia is a loss or impairment of language due to some type of brain injury. The injury may be incurred by a direct blow such as a war wound, an industrial accident or traffic accident, or by a stroke, tumor or disease. It is important to remember that asphasia is not the result of involvement of the tongue, teeth or lips where sounds are formed. However, some aphasics do choke on food, cannot purse the lips to whistle or to blow, or cannot protrude the tongue. This is a disability other than aphasia and is called an apraxia[1] of the mouth region, while aphasia is a non-functioning of the association areas of the brain which interferes with the transmission of the necessary messages to the organs of speech.

There are many ways in which a language loss may be manifested. For example, one patient may think of the word "dog" but his tongue, teeth and lips do not get the message from the brain telling how to pronounce this word. Another patient may not be able to understand the word "dog" when someone else says it. He does not have a hearing loss, but the word sounds like a foreign language to him. Still another patient may see a dog and recognize that it is a dog, but may not be able to recall the word "dog." This is much like the frequent experience of forgetting the name of a familiar friend, except that the patient will have forgotten the names of almost everything. Perhaps when he tries to speak, many words will come forth but they will not be the right ones.

The difficulties are not only with speaking. A patient may not be able to read, to write, to do arithmetic, or to comprehend spoken language. Rarely has a patient only one or two of these defects; more commonly he will have a combination of them.

II. WHAT SOURCES ARE AVAILABLE FOR APHASIA TREATMENT?

Aphasia patients are referred for treatment to Veterans Administration Clinics (if veterans' status exists), to college and private clinics, and to private speech therapists. These referrals are usually made by attending physicians. If the initial referral or suggestion for treatment comes from other sources, a medical clearance should accompany the application for treatment. Most

1. See Terms, *Appendix.*

private agencies or therapists require a medical referral. Certainly if veterans' status exists, the patient should apply to the Veterans Administration clinics[2] since they are amongst the best equipped and staffed in the country in addition to having a background of long experience. These clinics may be attended without charge. Almost all other facilities require payment. Many colleges maintain speech clinics which require a moderate charge commensurate with course fee. There are agencies which sometimes subsidize private treatment such as state rehabilitation programs, fraternal organizations, and civic and local club scholarships.

III. HOW ARE APHASICS RETRAINED?

The process of retraining is not unlike the original learning of language as a child. However, the adult aphasic has retained his concepts and experiences but needs to relearn the language with which to express them.

One of the prominent theories today is that both hemispheres of the brain are capable of functioning for speech. As individuals learn to talk, they use one side of the brain much more than the other (generally the left side); however, there are indications that language patterns are formed on both sides. In any case, clinical observation bears out the fact that other areas are capable of being trained to take over the language function.

IV. HOW LONG WILL RETRAINING TAKE?

The length of time required to relearn language depends on the severity of the damage, the patient's physical condition, his age, the extent of the language loss, the patient's previous study habits or ability to apply himself, his former language abilities, and his attitude toward recovery. With all these factors to be considered, one can not usually predict with any kind of accuracy how long retraining will take.[3] Some patients make an excellent recovery in a year or two even to returning to their jobs; others never completely regain their speech but improve; a few never show any noticeable improvement.

V. WHAT OTHER TREATMENT MAY BE HELPFUL?

Often the aphasic patient has a paralysis or weakness of the limbs of the right or major side. This indicates the need for physical and corrective therapy for activities of daily living and for walking. Occupational therapy will be helpful in providing exercise for the disabled limbs and for facility with the minor side. Many patients experience pleasure and success in making

2. Devins, George, *et al:* Activity and aphasia therapy, *Journal of Physical and Mental Rehabilitation,* Vol. 4, No. 5, October-November 1950.
   Nielsen, J. M., and McKeown, Milfred: Summary of a decade in the aphasia clinic of a veterans hospital. *Bulletin of the Los Angeles Neurological Society,* Vol. 25, No. 3, September 1960.

3. Eisenson, Jon: Prognostic factors related to language rehabilitation in aphasic patients. *Journal of Speech and Hearing Disorders,* Vol. 14, No. 3, September 1949.

attractive and useful articles as prescribed in an occupational therapy situation.

As the patient improves he should extend his activities to include some type of vocational training such as manual arts shop, clerical work, or reorientation commensurate with his former interests. A full program which will include activities other than language retraining, provides a patient with a well-balanced daily schedule. Such community resources as YMCA and YWCA gymnasiums and swimming pools usually are available.

If emotional problems are somewhat severe, a psychologist is an important adjunct to the retraining team. (See Chapter 3, Emotional Problems.)

VI. HOW MUCH BETTER WILL THE PATIENT GET?

The answer to such a question must of necessity be, "No one can tell." To be sure, the doctor may have certain indications as to the physical prognosis of a patient, but language retraining progress can seldom be predicted, only accepted as it occurs. It is helpful to set goals for immediate aims in speech therapy and to appreciate small gains as they are made. Many patients will never return to normal so far as their speech and physical condition are concerned, but even moderate gains will lessen frustrations of both the patient and his family. Progress does not necessarily stop with the cessation of language retraining therapy but may continue for many years.

VII. HAS THE PATIENT BEEN MENTALLY AFFECTED?

Unless the damage has been very wide spread or there are other contributing factors, the personality of the patient remains essentially the same. He has not lost his judgment, his reason, or his thoughts—he has lost the means of expressing them with language. One should not lose sight of the fact that being deprived of speech is a very serious blow. As the patient attempts to express himself and fails, he becomes frustrated and angry at himself and at the world around him. Because he cannot talk about his troubles, he expresses himself in other ways such as outbursts of temper, often directed towards family members or other people he is fond of. It is helpful for family members to be as objective as possible during difficult times. When the ability to talk is taken away, the barriers of behavior are lowered. Conversely, a return of speech often brings about the resolution of many emotional problems.

VIII. HOW MUCH HELP SHOULD THE PATIENT BE GIVEN?[4]

It is a very human desire to want to extend as much help as possible when the patient is struggling to say a word or is impeded in his movements by hemiplegia. Even in a clinic situation, there is a tendency to be overhelpful. In general, it is wise to let the patient do as much as possible for himself un-

4. Turnblom, Martha, and Myers, Julian S.: Group discussion with the families of aphasic patients. *Journal of Speech and Hearing Disorders*, Vol. 17, No. 4, December 1952.

less he becomes too frustrated, or indicates that he wants help. The patient will usually appreciate one's respect for his desire for independence.

IX. WHERE CAN ADDITIONAL HELP BE SECURED?[5]

The aid of speech therapists, teachers and psychologists may be secured by referring to organizations and agencies as listed below. National organizations of the various therapies publish directories with names and addresses of qualified therapists in all parts of the United States and in foreign countries. However, immediate help often may be found in the yellow pages of the telephone directory under such titles as speech therapy and physical therapy.

1. Speech Therapists—Journal of the American Speech and Hearing Association Directory, 1001 Connecticut Avenue, N. W., Washington, D. C.
2. Veterans Hospitals and Regional Offices (for veterans of the armed forces only).
3. College and University Speech Clinics.
4. Public Schools—Elementary Teachers.
5. Adult Education Department of Public Schools.
6. Psychologists—Consult the Psychology Department of a near-by college or Directory of American Psychological Association, Executive Secretary, 1333—16th Street, N.W., Washington 6, D. C.
7. Physical Therapists—American Physical Therapy Association, 1790 Broadway, Room 310, New York 19, N. Y.
8. American Association for Rehabilitation Therapy—P. O. Box 34, Lemay Branch, St. Louis 25, Mo. (Manual Arts and Educational Therapists).
9. Occupational Therapists—American Occupational Therapy Association, 250 West 57 Street, New York 19, N. Y.
10. Corrective Therapists (for walking and activities of daily living) — Association for Physical and Mental Rehabilitation, 1472 Broadway, New York 36, N. Y.
11. Mental Hygiene Clinics.
12. Private hospitals and speech clinics.
13. National Society for Crippled Children and Adults, Incorporated, 2023 West Ogden Avenue, Chicago 12, Ill.
14. Rehabilitation Centers Today—Henry Redkey, Report on 77 centers in U. S. and Canada, Office of Vocational Rehabilitation, U. S. Dept.

5. The Aphasia Foundation of Oklahoma, 811 N. W. 23 Street, Oklahoma City, Okla., has published a leaflet entitled *All Want the Facts about Aphasia.* This leaflet, produced and paid for by the Northwest Kiwanis Club, Oklahoma City, is a fine example of community interest in aphasics.

Health, Educ. and Welfare, Supt. of Documents, Washington, D. C. $1.00

X. WHY IS IT THAT SOME APHASICS DO NOT MAKE PROGRESS EVEN AFTER A PERIOD OF RETRAINING?

In case of severe brain injury, lesions may be so diffuse that the extent of the damage cannot be accurately determined and the prognosis for retraining remains doubtful.

When damage has been sustained to language areas of both the left and right hemispheres of the brain, the remaining cortical areas may be insufficient for retraining.

Native ability, of course, still plays a large part in the learning process. Just as all children do not make the same rate of progress in school, so it is with aphasics. Aptitudes vary from person to person. Many skilled in mathematics are poor grammarians and the literary-minded often are poor in numbers. Some aphasics are not interested in pencil-and-paper work and are not adept at study.

Although the aphasic may faithfully put in an appearance at retraining classes, for various reasons he may not be mentally attentive. He may be bored, depressed, worried, or ill. Occasionally in the case of a neurotic personality, he finds it to his advantage to remain handicapped.

When a minor lesion in the major hemisphere is not sufficiently severe to cripple that area completely but will not permit a transfer to the minor side, the major side limps along ineffectively, actually hindering the patient's progress.

Even if a patient appears to have made no progress in language, he *has* made progress if he has become a happier person, has accepted the disability and continues to be socially adjusted.

XI. WHAT ARE SOME OTHER MANIFESTATIONS OF BRAIN DAMAGE ENCOUNTERED IN LANGUAGE THERAPY?

In working with patients with brain damage, the therapist sometimes encounters speech and language problems which are not strictly aphasia defects, and frequently comes in contact with disabilities other than the language problem resulting from brain damage. Among the latter are inappropriate and excessive laughing and crying, retrograde amnesia and epilepsy.

A. Inappropriate and Excessive Laughing and Crying[6] accompanied by slurred and thick speech. These patients sometimes choke on foods and liquids and often cannot cough or blow on command although they do so

---

6. Nielsen, J. M.: *Textbook of Clinical Neurology.* Paul B. Hoeber, New York, N. Y., p. 154 (pseudobulbar palsy).

involuntarily. The most noticeable manifestation is the inability to control crying when, actually they do not feel like crying, and conversely, they laugh in excess when they do not intend to do so; it is a matter of lack of control rather than a breakdown of the emotions. Usually it is best to disregard such outbursts, providing the patient an opportunity to regain his composure unnoticed.

B. Retrograde Amnesia[7] is a loss of memory back to a point of time from the accident. Traumatic cases often have no recollection of the accident which resulted in the language loss. In some patients the amnesia is a matter of minutes, while in others—from surgery, for example—it has been known to be permanent. Those who recover in a matter of weeks usually can resume language retraining with success.

C. Epilepsy[8] is a convulsive seizure which sometimes accompanies brain damage. Seizures take various forms, one form of which is petit mal. A patient subject to petit mal seizures may suddenly become silent, stare straight ahead or to one side, and perhaps drool and smack his lips. He "blacks out" without falling or being aware of the seizure. When he recovers, usually in a matter of seconds, he is able to continue with his work. The entire subject of seizures should be discussed with the doctor for suggestions on the management of the problem.

XII. WHAT ARE THE REQUIREMENTS FOR ENTERING THE FIELD AS A PROFESSIONAL APHASIA THERAPIST?

Students of speech therapy, psychology majors, nurses, physical therapists and others often request information about qualifications of an aphasia therapist and about the work as a profession. Basic requirements usually include a four-year college course with majors and minors in speech therapy and psychology. Although state requirements vary, the trend is toward a Master's degree or equivalent plus two-hundred clock hours of clinical practice. While membership in state and national speech therapy organizations may not be mandatory, such affiliations are helpful in keeping the therapist abreast of late trends and conversant with new research projects and with recognized authorities in the field.

Clinical certification in the American Speech and Hearing Association is an excellent recommendation for speech therapists. Requirements for such certification may be found in the Annual Directory of the American Speech and Hearing Association, 1001 Connecticut Avenue, N.W., Washington 6, D. C.

---

7. Nielsen, J. M.: *Memory and Amnesia.* San Lucas Press, Los Angeles, Calif., 1958, pp. 53, 56.
    ————: *A Textbook of Clinical Neurology,* page 548.

8. ————: *Memory and Amnesia,* pp. 94, 108.

Clinical practice *with aphasics* is extremely important. Many backgrounds from allied professional fields such as teaching, nursing, occupational and physical therapy, and psychology provide good experience.

In considering private practice, one should be aware of the range of problems existing. In most cases long term therapy is required which will involve expense to the family unless subsidy is used. The private therapist will find himself faced with the general management of the entire problem—aside from the language problem—necessitating referrals and consultations to many other agencies.

It is wise for the private therapist to require a medical referral in each case and to consider the importance of adequate insurance to cover the treatment of patients in a private situation.[9]

An aphasia therapist should be temperamentally geared to work at a very slow rate and must be able to tolerate much repetition. He must be willing to accept small degrees of progress as the result of many painstaking hours of work both on his part and on that of his patient.

XIII. IS SPEECH RESTORED THROUGH HYPNOSIS?

Published reports[10] indicate that losses in expressive and receptive language have not yielded directly to hypnotherapy. However indications were that both attitude and motivation improved following hypnosis, consequently language improved with the increased application to the task of retraining. Cases of mutism as distinguished from aphasia have been known to begin vocalizing after hypnotherapy.

XIV. REFERENCES

1. Boone, Daniel: *An Adult Has Aphasia.* Western Reserve University, Cleveland Hearing & Speech Center, 11206 Euclid, Cleveland 6, O.
2. Danzig, Aaron L.: *Handbook for One-Handers.* Federation of the Handicapped, 211 West 14 Street, New York 11, N. Y., 1957.
3. Fink, Stephen L.: The clinical psychologist evaluates aphasia rehabilitation. *ASHA,* Vol. 3, No. 6, June 1961.
4. Jones, Morris Val: Rebuilding language in stroke patients. *Journal of Rehabilitation,* March-April 1956.
5. Longerich, Mary C.: *Helping the Aphasic to Recover His Speech-A Manual for the Family.* College of Medical Evangelists, School of Medicine, Los Angeles, Calif.

---

9. Private Practice in Speech Pathology and Audiology. *ASHA,* Vol. 3., No. 11, November 1961.

10. Kirkner, Frank J., Dorcus, Roy M., Seacat, Gloria: Hypnotic motivation of vocalization in an organic motor aphasic case. *Journal of Clinical and Experimental Hypnosis,* Vol. 1, No. 3, July 1953.
   Mason, Charles F.: Hypnotic Motivation of Aphasics. *International Journal of Clinical and Experimental Hypnosis,* Vol. 9, No. 4, October 1961.
   Rousey, Clyde L.: Hypnosis in Speech Pathology and Audiology. *Journal of Speech and Hearing Disorders,* Vol. 26, No. 3, August 1961.

6. Nathan, Ruth: How you can help someone with aphasia. *Science Digest,* 200 East Ontario St., Chicago 11, Ill., December 1959.

7. Ritchie, Douglas: *Stroke, A Study of Recovery.* Doubleday & Company, Inc., Garden City, N.Y., 1961.

8. Smith, Genevieve W.: *Care of the Patient with a Stroke.* Springer Publishing Co., Inc., 44 East 23 Street, New York 10, N. Y.

9. Taylor, Martha A.: *Understanding Aphasia, A Guide for Family and Friends.* Patient Publication No. 2, 1958, Institute of Physical Medicine and Rehabilitation, New York University, Bellevue Medical Center, 400 East 34 Street., N. Y. 16, N. Y.

10. Wood, Nancy E.: Helping the Aphasic Adult. *Journal of Rehabilitation,* January-February 1956.

Chapter 2

BASIC CONCEPTS OF APHASIA

T HE BASIC CONCEPTS of aphasia presented briefly in this chapter have been derived from lectures and writings of Dr. J. M. Nielsen,[1] Consultant in Aphasia for the Veterans Administration, and from clinical experience.

I. LANGUAGE DEVELOPMENT

The language retraining of the aphasia patient who has sustained a language loss as the result of brain injury, parallels somewhat the language development of the child. The child first gains an auditory recognition of words by hearing the constant repetition of such familiar words as "mama," "baby," and others. He learns to repeat some of the words he hears most commonly. In the beginning he may repeat these words without association but gradually he learns their meaning and uses them appropriately. As his language develops over a period of years, he learns to formulate in sentences, gradually acquiring a high degree of development in oral language.

In learning to read, the child's earliest contact with letters is often his blocks. At this time he makes no distinction between a picture on one side of the block and a letter on the other—they are both *objects* to him. Often he recites the letters by rote unaware of their symbolic significance. Later he is taught letters as symbols which have equivalent sounds. Gradually he recognizes combinations of letters as words and begins to understand words in context. At the highest development of reading he comprehends the semantics of complicated written language.

As the child learns the significance of letters and words in reading, he learns the symbols of writing. At first he copies letters. Later on when he has learned to think of the letters as symbols, he usually learns to associate the sound with the symbol. Gradually he learns to spell. As formulation is the highest development of oral language, it is also the most complex step in writing.

At the peak of development of his language the adult has at his command the diction and semantics of both spoken and written language. While language functions do not develop independently of one another in the retraining process of aphasics, functions frequently return in the order of their

---

1. Nielsen, J. M.: *A Textbook of Clinical Neurology*. Paul B. Hoeber, Inc., New York 16, N. Y.. Third Edition, Chapter X.

————: *Agnosia, Apraxia, Aphasia*. Hafner Publishing Company. Inc., New York, N. Y.

original development: comprehension of spoken language, motor speech patterns, naming and formulation, reading and writing.

It is interesting to note that retraining in English has brought about a parallel return of a second language in cases of some bilingual patients.

II. AREAS OF THE BRAIN WITH RELATED LANGUAGE FUNCTIONS

Brain injury may arise from many types of accidents such as trauma and cerebral-vascular accident or from malignancy and disease. Since resultant lesions in cortical areas, or lesions causing dissociation between cortical areas, give rise to language defects, the following areas can be associated with these functions:

1. Wernicke's Area of the temporal lobe (areas 41 and 42 of Brodmann)[2] is associated with the recognition of spoken language. Understanding of spoken language is developed in the temporal lobe in areas 21 and 22. A destructive lesion in these areas results in an *auditory-verbal agnosia*.[3]

2. Broca's Area in the frontal lobe (area 44) contains the engrams for the memory of the motor patterns of speech. A lesion in this area causes a *motor aphasia*.

3. Area 37 and the posterior part of area 21 of the temporal lobe are related to the recall of names and words, and also to language formulation. Lesions in these areas may cause *anomia, amnesic aphasia* and *formulation defects*.

4. Angular Gyrus (area 39) of the parietal lobe is associated with the visual recognition of the symbols of reading, writing, arithmetic and others. A lesion in this area may result in varied combinations of alexia, agraphia and acalculia.

---

2. See diagram.

3. See Terms, Appendix.

III. DIAGRAM SHOWING AREAS ACCORDING TO BRODMANN
WITH RELATED LANGUAGE FUNCTIONS

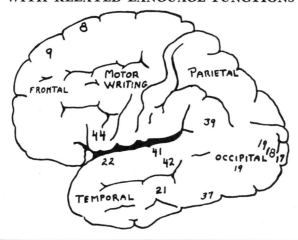

Area	Function	Language Defects Caused by Destructive Lesion
41 & 42 Wernicke's Area	Recognition of spoken language	Auditory Verbal Agnosia
22 & 21	Recall and Interpretation of spoken language	Loss of Verbal Recall
44 Broca's Area	Memory of motor patterns of speech	Motor Aphasia (speech)
37	Recall of names and words; language formulation	Anomia Amnesic Aphasia
39 Angular Gyrus	Symbols for reading, writing and arithmetic (letters and numbers)	Alexia Agraphia (Spelling) Acalculia
8 & 9 Exner's Writing Center	Knowledge of how to make movements of hands and fingers in writing	Agraphia (Motor)
17 & 18	Visual perception and recognition	Visual-Verbal Agnosia without agraphia (caused by subcortical lesion between 17 and 39)

Chapter 3

EMOTIONAL PROBLEMS

A RETRAINING MANUAL for aphasics would be incomplete without a discussion of the emotional problems which usually attend aphasia. A complete or partial loss of speech has its peculiar frustrations for the aphasic patient. He is suddenly faced with extensive changes in family life, in social relationships and in economic circumstances. Without the ability to sublimate his feelings in language, he must express his despair in overt acts and non-language ways—often a departure from a previously restrained manner. The extent to which these problems can be met plays a major part in language retraining and in general rehabilitation. In fact, it is doubtful how much can be accomplished without some resolution of these difficult emotional problems.

Usually the best management of emotional problems is a combined effort of family, speech therapist, allied therapists, doctor and consulting psychologist or psychiatrist who work together in a concerted program. Other individuals are helpful: understanding family friends, the pastor, those who have sustained similar accidents, and people interested in rehabilitation. Group psychotherapy and group retraining with other adult aphasics provide therapeutic situations. Family counseling does much to help family members meet the problems which arise and to handle them more efficaciously. In this section observations are made on some aspects of the emotional problems, and how they may be met in part by the speech therapist and the family.

I. FRUSTRATIONS OF LANGUAGE LOSS

The sum total of the patient's knowledge and experience remain his except for his inability to translate them into language. As a result of this he may be isolated from the world around him. It is possible that he is not able to understand what is said to him. He may be further circumscribed by being unable to communicate his thoughts, feelings and desires in oral or written language. A skilled therapist can often make the patient feel he understands the basis of his frustration if not his communications. An aphasic patient will usually do better if he senses that the listening individuals are relaxed and not in a hurry. If it is not practical to "hear him out," a well-tested approach is the use of questions to which the patient can answer "yes" or "no." This, at least, usually reveals the subject matter the patient wishes to discuss. Sometimes a simple direction, "Show me what you mean," will allow the patient to demonstrate or indicate what he is attempting to say.[1] Some patients are adept at sketching their ideas. Sometimes, when all measures fail, it is necessary to resort to such statements as, "The minute you think of it, come tell me." There are times when it is desirable to aid the aphasic in communicating with others; again, he may need the independence of carrying out his own communication, no matter how difficult the task. A sense of humor is a valuable asset both to the patient and to those around him, creating appropriate moments for them to laugh together at language errors.

II. DEVIATIONS IN BEHAVIOR

The patient's inability to dispose of problems through speech and conversation frequently results in outbursts of anger, or even in physical violence, often directed toward those he loves the most. Profanity is a common mode of expression.[2] This departure from a previous mode of behavior is frightening and embarrassing to the aphasic as well as to his family. The reasons for these outbursts should be explained to the patient and his family. It should be noted that the patient usually remains essentially the same individual he was before the injury and that behavior accompanying extreme frustration is not an indication of a change in basic personality.

However, when these areas are involved, a patient's behavior may be less inhibited. Acceptance and understanding by family and friends of his behavior often enable the patient to handle his difficult situations more successfully. The therapist and family can be helpful in preventing situations which are especially traumatic for the patient.

Depression in various degrees of severity often accompanies aphasia. This is especially noticeable in patients without severe auditory verbal agnosia who are acutely aware of their own errors. It is most discouraging to feel useless and in the way. The patient's tendency to dwell on the disability only deepens the depression. Sometimes psychological or medical help must be sought, but a busy daily schedule[3] to occupy the patient's attention leaves little time for dwelling on the infirmity. A most fortunate situation for everyone concerned is one in which a patient is sufficiently well motivated to carry out some purposeful activity. Sometimes such activity may be in the nature of helping around the home.

---

1. Picture dictionaries offer many pertinent illustrations: Guild, Marion: *Words, A Picture Dictionary*, Maxton Publishing Corp., New York 6, N. Y.; Lessing, Wayland W.: *Silent Spokesman, an Aid to the Speechless*, Hospital Topics, 30 W. Washington St., Chicago 2, Ill.

2. It should be noted that expressions of profanity are not related to propositional language as such, nor are they indications that the patient can formulate any other language.

3. See A Daily Clinic Schedule, Chapter 6, Section III.

Hobbies such as stamp albums, coin collections, painting, tropical fish culture, puzzles and so on are helpful. The aphasic who can follow sports events on the TV is a fortunate arm-chair sports enthusiast. Such activities as simple carpentering and painting provide good sublimation of feelings.

III. THE PROBLEM OF THE HEMIPLEGIA[4]

An aphasic patient frequently has an involvement of an upper and lower limb (usually the right) resulting in partial paralysis. The curtailment of physical activity immediately presents a problem. It may mean temporary confinement in a wheelchair, use of hand and foot braces, the cessation of such activities as driving, and a change or modification of occupation. As the patient recovers, he finds it frustrating not to be allowed to carry on certain activities because those in attendance are beset with fears—fearful of an accident, fearful to leave the patient unattended, fearful that he will feel neglected, fearful that he will not do the job as well as he did before the injury.

Physical therapy, corrective therapy and occupational therapy are important adjunctives in the rehabilitation of hemiplegia. Here the patient has the support of trained people who understand his physical problems, together with the satisfying feeling that he is attempting as much physical return as possible.

With the doctor's approval, the patient should attempt to resume normal activities as soon as possible. Certainly he should be allowed to take a walk around the block when he has demonstrated the necessary strength and the use of his cane with reasonable skill. Of course, those in attendance should keep in a convenient location all the equipment a patient uses daily so that it is within his reach, thus enabling him to be as self-sufficient as possible. This would include study materials such as pencil, writing paper on a clip board (so that the paper will not shift as the patient attempts to write) ; his toilet articles, towels, washcloths, and shaving equipment; his cigarettes or pipe, matches and ashtray; the daily paper. A Shu-Lok shoe or shoes equipped with elastic shoe strings[5] or Velcro Fastener tape[6] ease the problem of shoe lacing and tying. The radio and TV should be placed to his advantage. An orderly and consistent arrangement of articles prevents the unnecessary frustration created by disorder.

---

4. Smith, Genevieve W.: *Care of the Patient With a Stroke.* Springer Pub. Co., Inc., 44 East 23 St., New York 10, N. Y.
   Danzig, Aaron: *Handbook for One-Handers.* Federation of the Handicapped, 211 West 14th St., New York, N. Y., 1957.

5. Flex-O-Lace Elastic Shoe Laces, Cecil Corporation, Box 654, Evanston, Ill., 50c.

6. Laufer Company, 50 West 29 St., New York 1, N. Y. Black or Beige.

IV. CHANGES IN FAMILY LIFE, SOCIAL RELATIONSHIPS, AND ECONOMIC CIRCUMSTANCES

An adult aphasic frequently finds drastic changes in his family life. A man, the head of his household, is often reduced to a dependent person, with no duties, responsibilities or authority. A woman may be relegated to the role of an invalid deprived of her former status and duties. It is most therapeutic, as soon as the aphasic is capable, to include and consult him in family problems. If he cannot contribute to a discussion, he can frequently indicate his opinions and feelings. As soon as he has gained some return in arithmetic, he can often keep household expense books, sign checks, and carry out simple banking procedures. As soon as a woman aphasic is up and about the house, she can do certain household chores as outlets for physical activity and interests. In any case, husbands and wives can do much to help the psychological well-being of their aphasic partners by gradually allowing them a return to their former status. Good marital counseling is often indicated in reestablishing marriage relationships.

Just as family life is disturbed, so are social relationships changed. No longer capable of a round of golf or a long evening of bridge, many an aphasic finds friends drifting away. Friends and acquaintances are often puzzled as to how to approach the patient's lack of communication and the language problem. Here active interests often help. The avid gardener, stamp collector or checker player will find some basis of communication in the activity of the hobby, even though formal language is not present. Small group functions including friends who are able to see that their aphasic friend is still his "old self" are most helpful. Sometimes frank orientation on the part of doctor, therapist or family member helps a few close friends understand the situation.

Frequently the presence of aphasia alters the economic situation considerably. Often an aphasic must resign his job or change his type of work. Prolonged illness makes inroads on family finances. This sometimes must be offset by adjustments in living. An investigation of the patient's benefits under prevailing laws of Social Security, his insurance, and retirement plan should be made. The many community resources such as Red Cross, family service groups, National Society for Crippled Children and Adults, and church affiliations should not be overlooked. Community rehabilitation industries (a type of sheltered workshop) now growing more numerous in many communities often provide a way back to self-sufficiency.

V. THE ROLE OF THE THERAPIST

When the speech therapist becomes cognizant of strong emotional problems in his patient, he should suggest further counseling, and psychological referrals when indicated. He often finds himself confronted with a patient displaying emotional lability resulting from brain damage. Although he understands this undue emotion and can accept it in a matter-of-fact manner, he should interpret its true meaning to the patient and to his family. Since progress in language retraining is necessarily slow, the therapist plays an important role in offsetting discouragement on the part of the patient. As the patient gains insight, he realizes the fact that many problems in the gradual process of rehabilitation cannot be solved immediately. The therapist can do much to restore the patient's feeling of status by reassuring him of his good qualities and accepting him as an interesting adult who has had, and still has, much to offer the world.

VI. REFERENCES

Biorn-Hansen, Vera: Social and emotional aspects of aphasia. *Journal of Speech & Hearing Disorders*, Vol. 22, No. 1, March 1957.

Longerich, Mary C.: *Aphasia Therapeutics.* Chapter IX, Psychological Aspects of Aphasia.

Travis, L. E., Editor: *Handbook of Speech Pathology.* Psychological factors in aphasia, page 463; Psychotherapy in adult aphasia, page 474.

Turnblom, Martha and Myers, J. S.: Group discussion program with families of aphasic patients. *Journal of Speech and Hearing Disorders*, Vol. 17, No. 4, December 1952.

RETRAINING APHASIC ADULTS

Chapter 4

HISTORY AND LANGUAGE EVALUATION
Testing for Agnosia, Apraxia and Aphasia

I. INTRODUCTION

A̲ₙ EFFECTIVE PROGRAM of therapy for an aphasia patient cannot be undertaken without the complete knowledge afforded by a history and a language evaluation. The history includes personal data, neurological and medical summaries, and psychological status. A language evaluation encompasses testing for agnosia, apraxia and aphasia. The more information that is known about the patient, the better the plan for the alleviation of his problems. All the information may not be obtainable during the initial examination, particularly if the patient fatigues or if other tests such as audiometric and psychological have been indicated. This information should be inserted when test results come in or when the therapist has had ample time to ascertain all the facts.

II. HISTORY[1]

A. *Personal History*

Name: _____   Date tested: _____

Address: _____   Nearest of Kin: _____

Phone: _____   Address: _____

Birth date _____   Phone: _____

1. Family background (handedness of family members, speech handicaps)
2. Educational background (grade completed, age, where)
3. Cultural background (native language, fluency in other language)
4. Language background (skills whether in literary, clerical, mathematical or other fields)
5. Occupational background (past and present occupations)

B. *Neurological Data*

Date of trauma _____

1. Etiology of cerebral defect
   (CVA, trauma,[2] tumor, other cause)
2. Visual (glasses, hemianopia,[2] diplopia (double vision)
3. Auditory
4. Motor weakness (left or right paralysis, upper or lower extremities)
5. Spasticity or ataxia
6. E.E.G. (electroencephalographic findings, if available) [3,5]

---

1. This information sheet is an approximation of Case Report, VA Form 10-2526, used at the Veterans Administration Aphasia Clinic in Long Beach, California.
2. See Terms, Appendix.
3. See Terms, Appendix.
5. Tikofsky, Ronald S., and Kool, Kenneth A.: Electroencephalographic findings and recovery from aphasia. *Neurology, 10:*154–156, Feb. 1960.

7. Other physical defects

C. *Psychological Status*
    1. Interest in recovery
    2. Emotional state
    3. Intelligence (psychological test summary)

III. NON-LANGUAGE AGNOSIAS AND APRAXIAS

Non-Language Agnosias

Although many non-language agnosias exist, they are not commonly seen clinically.[4] However, when agnosias are present, they affect language performance and must be considered. An agnosia is an inability to recognize by one sense organ only. The non-language *visual* agnosias include losses in visual recognition of the body scheme and laterality, loss of visual recognition of animate and/or inanimate objects, of matching colors, of geometric shapes, of cardinal directions (north, east, south, west), and of pictures.

Non-language *auditory* agnosias include loss of recognition of sounds ordinarily heard in the environment such as the ring of the telephone, footsteps, the cry of a baby, and of pitch and melody.

Tactile agnosia, sometimes referred to as astereognosis,[3] involves loss of recognition by touch.

Visual Agnosia (Nonverbal)[6]

In evaluating visual agnosia, a distinction must be made between optical disturbances and visual agnosia. An optical disturbance concerns eyesight or visual perception without any attempt to interpret what is seen. Often the services of an ophthalmologist are needed for refractions, prescriptions for glasses or other recommendations.

Sometimes an aphasic has vision in only the left (or right) half (or quarter) of each eye, or he may have double vision. If he covers one eye or closes it as he shifts his paper about in an attempt to read it, indications are that he has double vision. If he writes to the middle of the line, then returns

---

4. Detailed discussions on Agnosia may be found in the following references: Nielsen, J. M.: *Memory and Amnesia*, San Lucas Press, Los Angeles, Calif. 1958, pages 132–143.
    Nielsen, J. M.: *Agnosia, Apraxia, Aphasia*, Hafner Publishing Co. Inc., New York, N. Y., Second Edition, Chapter IV.
    Nielsen, J. M.: *A Textbook of Clinical Neurology*. Paul B. Hoeber, Inc., New York, N. Y., Third Edition, Chapter X.

6. Boyle, D. G., and McKeown, Milfred: Case of alexia and visual agnosia for objects. *Bulletin of Los Angeles Neurological Society*, Vol. 23, No. 2, June 1958.
    Nielsen, J. M., *et al.*: Visual agnosia and irreminiscence for animate objects. *Bulletin of the Los Angeles Neurological Society*, Vol. 26, No. 2, June 1961.

to the left to start a new line, he likely has only half vision to the right and thinks he has reached the edge of the paper.[7] The same holds true in reading; he may read to the center of the line, then begin a new line, thinking he has completed the line. A patient may have to cope with such annoyances for a long time—at any rate, he should not wait for a clearing of the disability before beginning to use his eyes for study unless so recommended by his doctor.

An appraisal of the patient's visual recognition, or lack of it, can be made almost incidentally as the examiner first comes in contact with the patient. If he indicates by facial expression, a nod or a smile, that he is aware of the examiner, it can be assumed that visual recognition for the animate is probably intact. If he lights a cigarette, picks up a pencil and makes marks on the paper, for example, he no doubt recognizes the inanimate. A few simple questions directed to him, or indicated by accompanying gesture or example, will satisfy the examiner as to the patient's visual recognition of directions, pictures and colors. If he can imitate the examiner in identification of certain parts of his body such as holding up the corresponding thumb, putting his hand on his head, touching his right knee, pointing to his left foot, indications are that he recognizes body parts by sight.

Coping with Visual Agnosia

Since an agnosia is a loss of recognition by one sense organ only, substitute senses must be used for identification purposes. By running his hand around the form of a cup, by tracing with his fingers the outline of a picture of a house, or by handling utensils, tools and small objects, the patient aids visual recognition by the tactile sense.

The sounds produced by the jingle of keys, the rattle of a newspaper, the dial of the telephone, help him cultivate visual recognition through the help of the auditory sense. He also learns to identify people he cannot recognize on sight by the sounds of their voices. Visual recognition of many items such as foods and flowers is greatly helped by taste and/or smell.

To *test* for visual agnosia, the patient must identify by vision only. In *therapy* for visual agnosia, the patient is encouraged to identify objects by bringing into play all other senses: outlining with the finger, touching, smelling, hearing, tasting.

(1) Pairing Identical Items

Place a number of identical items before the patient. Show him how to pair up several, then direct him to follow suit.

Suggested items: two pencils, two safety pins, two matches, two cups, two

---

7. See Samples of Patients' Work, Chapter 19.

socks, two hair pins, two paper clips, two cigarettes, two spoons, etc.

(2) Matching Identical Pictures

Secure identical pictures cut from colored magazine advertisements. Mount them on tag board. Instruct the patient to lay them out on the table, then pick them up in matching pairs.

(3) Matching Items with Pictures

Continue as in exercises (1) and (2) using items and pictures. Suggested items easily accessible include: package of cigarettes, colored advertisement of the same brand; bar of soap and the identical duplicate of it from an advertisement; cameras, fountain pen, ballpoint pen, toothpaste, etc.

(4) Pairing Unlike Pictures of Like Items

Make up a file of two pictures, *not* identical, of the same person or thing. Follow the same technique as above, directing the patient to pick up pairs (or even more than two) of the same items. Suggested pictures: two pictures of the President of the United States, two pictures of Ford cars, two or more pictures of Collie dogs, horses of the same color, apples, television sets, etc.

(5) Sorting Pictures of Like Items, Not Identical

This exercise is similar to exercise (4) except that the pictures are in the same category but are not identical. For example, a Collie dog and a poodle dog, a Buick and a Chevrolet, two men (not the same person), a yellow apple and a red apple, two houses, two flowers, etc.

(6) Matching Geometric Outlines

Draw two copies each of such geometric outlines as a square, a triangle, a circle, a rectangle, an octagon, etc. Direct the patient to match them.

(7) Identifying the Form that is Different

One form in each group of four is different. Direct the patient to draw a circle around the one which is not the same. (Any other groups of four may be drawn.)

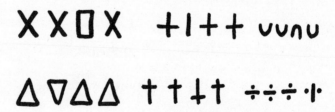

(8) Selecting the Alphabet Letter or the Number that is Different

Circle the alphabet letter or the number that does not match the group.

AAAB TYTTT PXXX BPBBBB RRRPRR JJJL WWWWMWW
2228   68666   99996   779777   444404   5505   6866666

(9) Recognizing Identical Words (Verbal)

Connect identical words with a straight line. (*Recognizing* identical words is more important here than stating their meaning.)

cat	cap	dog	god	chair	cheer
	car		dog		chain
	can		day		share
	cat		dry		chair

1. Lesson Plan

This lesson is based on parts of the exercises in this section which presumably have already been worked out by the patient.

Lay out before him a sampling of the items and pictures he has already used over a period of time. For example: pictures of a man, a horse, a cup, a cigarette, a pencil.

(1) Draw a stick figure of one of the items, say a man, and see if the patient can select the appropriate picture from the items to correspond with the drawing.

(2) Draw a cup and see if the patient will pick up the cup before him to indicate his visual recognition of the drawing of the cup.

(3) Pantomime the act of smoking. See if the patient will indicate the cigarette on the table before him. Also pantomime the act of writing to see if he will take up the pencil or point to it.

2. Auditory Agnosia

Recognition of ordinary sounds and music appears to be stored in both the left and the right hemispheres of the brain, therefore, if a patient has sustained injury to one hemisphere, he continues to recognize through the other, and consequently suffers no loss.

3. Tactile Agnosia

If a patient cannot identify an object in one hand (with eyes closed), very likely he can do so by the other hand. Of course, if a patient is hemiplegic, one hand is impaired.

Non-Language Apraxias

An inability to perform intended motor acts is termed an apraxia. The presence of apraxias which have nothing to do with language per se, but which interfere with the motor performance of it are revealed when a patient cannot protrude his tongue, purse his lips or blow, or when he cannot handle a pencil. The incompletion of an idea involving more than one motor act also is a form of apraxia.

1. Testing for Apraxias

	THE TEST	EXPLANATORY NOTES
(a) Apraxia of the mouth	Direct the patient (by oral command or by pantomime) to protrude his tongue, to place his tongue on his upper lip, on his lower lip, against his inner cheek on either side. Light a match and direct him to blow it out.	The patient may make every effort to comply but still may not be able to do so. (If medical records indicate a paralysis of the tongue, this test should not be used.)
(b) Apraxia of the hand	Place a small item such as a pin before the patient and direct him to pick it up. Ask him to button his shirt, or to light a cigarette. Notice how he handles a pencil.	The finer finger movements may fail to function, even though the hand as a whole has function.
(c) Ideokinetic apraxia[8]	Ask the patient to carry out such a command as, "Put this pencil over your left ear," or, "Take the pencil from behind your ear," or, "Sit down in this chair." (He may fling his arm and hand around in the air attempting to reach the pencil, or shuffle about the chair searching for a way by which to sit down.)	Even though it is evident that the patient has the command clearly in mind the disruption between his idea and the motor action necessary to carry it out, may interfere with his performance.
(d) Ideational apraxia[8]	Ask the patient to carry out a command composed of several individual acts such as, "Go to the table, pick up a cigarette, then sit down in your chair and light the cigarette."	The patient can likely do each separate act, but he may not be able to carry out the entire command to completion.

2. Basic Reference Index for Dealing with Non-language Apraxias

Function affected	*Typical behavior from the defect*	*Basic training needed*
(a) MOUTH Intended movements	Patient cannot protrude tongue, purse lips, blow, etc., even though his tongue is not paralyzed.	Directed exercises for placement of tongue, lips, blowing, etc.

8. See Terms, Appendix.

(b)

| HAND Intended hand and finger movements | Hand and fingers fail to carry out intended movements even though patient knows the movements he wishes to make. (Dr. Montessori's Own Handbook by Maria Montessori). | Physical and Occupational therapists provide training for hand and finger movements through their many modalities. Use of adaptive materials similar to the Montessori Self-Care Board with zippers, buttons, buckles, lacing, snaps, etc. |

(c)

| Intended motor acts. (Not completed because of inability to carry out motor patterns.) IDEOKINETIC | Patient maintains the idea clearly in mind, but he fails to make the appropriate movements because movements do not coincide with the intended acts. (Note: A patient who is *not* paralyzed may be able to carry out an intended act readily with the other hand.) | This condition often clears with the carrying out of the usual activities of daily living. |

(d)

| Carrying a long-range plan to completion. (Patient fails to keep the plan in mind.) IDEATIONAL | Patient appears to be extremely absent-minded. He may perform perfectly any single element of a plan which he has in mind at the moment, but fail to continue the entire plan to the end. | This type of disability often resolves with medication or as the patient's general physical condition improves. |

Many patients will exhibit by their initial behavior abilities precluding the necessity of testing for non-language agnosias and apraxias. However, an individual competent in language areas may be subject to non-language agnosias and apraxias. If severe disabilities exist in non-language areas involving agnosias and apraxias, much help will be secured in training for daily-living activities, in physical therapy and in occupational therapy as well as by inclusive and incidental practices which can be used by the speech therapist.

IV. THE MENTALLY RETARDED, NON-READERS, SENILE DEMENTS, AND MUTISM

The speech therapist sometimes receives referrals for patients whose primary need is psychological or psychiatric treatment rather than speech therapy. In this case such a referral should be made.

If mental retardation is suspected after a period of unsuccessful speech therapy, it may be well to secure school records and to investigate premorbid levels of achievement for a better understanding of the case and for more effective methods of coping with it.

The presenile dement has poor prognosis for language retraining because of poor retention and general disorientation. This type of patient is not necessarily old in years, however, he lives and thinks in the past and is contented to do so.

The manifestations of agnosia, apraxia, and aphasia as seen in the patient with organic lesions are often simulated in the patient with functional disorders. If malingering is suspected as in the case of patient who appears to have mutism, the help of a psychologist is indicated.

V. EVALUATION FOR APHASIA DEFECTS

A. Aphasia

A disturbance of language itself.[9] An evaluation of the patient's language defects is imperative before a program of therapy can be initiated. The purpose of the evaluation is to determine the language areas affected and to provide a starting point for language retraining. On the basis of the findings of the evaluation, initial therapeutic procedures are determined.

Several excellent tests for aphasia are listed in the references at the close of the chapter. They are comparable in structure and provide about the same type of information. Actually, most aphasia tests describe what the patient *can* do rather than what he *cannot* do, so that remaining functions rather than defects are tested.

A useful evaluation of aphasia patients includes an investigation of four primary areas:

1. Perception and recognition of language (auditory and visual).
2. Performance of motor functions pertaining to language (speaking and writing).
3. Ability to use language symbols in reading, handwriting and arithmetic.
4. Formulation and comprehension of propositional language (oral and written).

An evaluation of aphasia defects attempts to establish to what extent the patient with brain damage has sustained impairment to these four functions. The agnosias and apraxias which do not pertain strictly to language should also be considered since these defects may interfere with a patient's performance in the language examination. From the moment the patient enters the testing area, he is revealing clues which provide a basis for further evaluation. His recognition—or the lack of recognition—of the testing situation, his response to greetings and directions, his handling of paper, pencils, books, the ash tray, all provide clues which the discerning examiner will make use of as the evaluation progresses. If the patient fails to take notice, and if the examiner cannot get his attention or establish rapport in a reasonable length of time, there may be involvements other than aphasia, or the patient may still be too ill. In this case, there would be no need to attempt

---

9. See definition of aphasia under Terms, Appendix.

to carry the examination further at this time. More medical advice may be indicated; often the patient needs more time to improve before a second, and more successful evaluation can be undertaken. The mental fatigue factor must also be considered when testing aphasics. The new patient tires quickly necessitating frequent rest periods between questions; a few seconds will often suffice.

Emotional lability (laughing and crying) is not infrequently present in aphasics, especially in the period immediately following the trauma. Since this is not necessarily an indication of true feeling, often the examiner may disregard these outbursts. Such breakdowns are not to be construed as the signal to end testing unless the patient appears to be truly uncomfortable.

Any answer the patient gives to test questions should be accepted outwardly with no attempt to point out errors or to make corrections. If a patient is exceedingly nervous and distraught in the testing situation, the examiner may proceed in a casual and less formal manner keeping in mind observations for later notation on the test sheet.

Testing for complicated language functions such as oral and written formulation of sentences is not indicated if the patient has already demonstrated that the lower levels of language—the use and understanding of *individual* words—are not operating.

During the entire testing, caution must be taken not to provide clues which will reveal an answer through a sense other than that being tested. For example, in a command such as, "Sit down in the chair," given to test the patient's understanding of oral language, the examiner must take care not to offer the chair, not to point to it, or to nod to it. The patient must not be allowed to read the command. In other words, the patient must not have the benefit of visual clues when being tested in the auditory area. When testing a patient for visual-verbal recognition, the examiner must not provide auditory or kinesthetic clues by speaking the words or by inadvertently allowing the patient to watch the pencil movements as the test letters and words are being written.

The identical letters, words and items given in the accompanying test need not be used. Other items of a similar type corresponding with the patient's age, his educational level, interests, and background may be substituted.

Some examiners prefer to test patients by copying the test items on a pad or on the blackboard at each examination. Others find it expedient to make up a set of permanent cards for repeated use in testing. In this case the following suggestions are offered:

    1. Use of 3 x 5 cards.
    2. Number each card to correspond with the test item.
    3. Use of the Cado Flo Master pen or a ball point pen.

4. Use of over-size letters, words and numbers.
5. Print or write only one item on a card. (Ascertain which the patient reads the more readily, cursive writing or printing.)

B. The Aphasia Test

	Test Items	Explanatory Notes	Remarks on Performance[10]
	VISUAL RECOGNITION AND COMPREHENSION		
1. ALPHABET LETTERS	Does the patient recognize alphabet letters by sight? A M t L v r O (One at a time)	He has indicated recognition if he can read them aloud or point them out as the examiner reads them.	
2. INDIVIDUAL WORDS	Does the patient recognize individual words by sight? CUP SING RED TEACHER MAN APPLE CAT (One at a time)	He has indicated recognition if he can read them, point to them as examiner reads them, match them with objects or pictures, or pantomime their meaning.	
3. SENTENCES	Can the patient read silently and carry out WRITTEN commands? Button your coat. Open your mouth. Give me the pencil.	Caution: Do not give a hint by gesture or demonstration of any kind. He must button his coat. To read the statement is not recognition of its meaning.	
4. NUMBERS	Does the patient recognize numbers? 5 2 7 25	He has demonstrated recognition if he reads them, points to them or holds up appropriate number of fingers.	

AUDITORY RECOGNITION AND COMPREHENSION

| 5. COMPREHEN-SION OF SPOKEN LANGUAGE | Can the patient carry out SPOKEN commands? Hand me the book. Close your eyes. | Do not make any gesture which might give a clue. Patient must not be permitted to read the commands. |

MOTOR FUNCTIONS

| 6. PRONUNCIA-TION OF IN-DIVIDUAL WORDS | Can the patient produce words in imitation? AH! MAMA PIPE SEVEN WINDOW MASSACHUSETTS | Let him pronounce each word after the examiner. |
| 7. PRINTING

8. LONGHAND | Can the patient write or print? He is to copy a few words in longhand or in printing. | Patient may protest if he has recently become hemiplegic necessitating use of his minor hand; however, with guidance, he probably will comply. |

LANGUAGE FUNCTIONS

9. RECALL OF NAMES	Can the patient name items pointed out to him? THUMB PENCIL LAMP PAPERCLIP	Patient must *name* them, not merely point them out as he hears them named.
10. ORAL LANGUAGE	Appraisal of patient's spontaneous speech. Does he use wrong words, distorted words, block, etc?	Examiner ascertains this from language used in the entire examination or from such a request as: Tell me about your work.
11. SPELLING	Can the patient spell? CUP HOUSE MONDAY HOME	Patient is to write the words as the examiner pronounces them or shows an object.
12. WRITTEN SENTENCE FORMATION	Can the patient compose and write a sentence unaided?	Examiner may suggest various *topics.* but must not dictate *sentences.*

ARITHMETIC

| 13. BASIC ARITHMETIC | Can the patient do the basic arithmetic processes? 45 25 23 +15 −15 x 7 2) 26 | Patient may work these orally or on paper. |

Following the testing, the examiner's notations in the right-hand column indicate both the patient's language assets and his liabilities. It is by means of the assets that the therapist works to eliminate the liabilities; in other words, the "a-bilities" are used to eliminate the "dis-abilities." A starting point for the retraining therapy is outlined in the Basic Reference Index below followed by beginning lesson plans for three broad categories of aphasia:[11]

   The "Global" aphasic—marked losses in all areas of language (VI, A below) .

10. Notations as: no loss, marked loss, moderate loss, minimal loss.
11. It must always be borne in mind that practically all aphasics have a *combination* of defects because of the interruption of the association pathways of language. No two cases show exactly the same defects, therefore it is impossible to describe a course of therapy which will fit every case.

The Amnesic aphasic—losses in Test items 5, 9, 10, 11, 12 (VI, B below).

The Motor aphasic—loss in Test items 6 (VI, C below).

Writing loss—Test item 7, 8, 11 (Chapter 33, Section II, III, IV)

For losses in Arithmetic, Test items 4 and 13 (VI, D below).

For losses in Reading, Test items 1, 2, 3, and 4 (VI E below).

For losses in Understanding Spoken Language, Test item 5 (VI A, 1 below).

C. Basic Reference Index for Beginning Language Therapy

Aphasia Test Item	Language Function Affected	Typical Behavior from the Defect	Basic Retraining Needed	Chapter
4, 13	Arithmetic (acalculia)	Patient cannot count or recall numbers; cannot do the four basic processes.	Counting, copying numbers, recognition of numbers; addition, subtraction, multiplication, division.	17
7, 8	Handwriting (motor agraphia)	Patient has lost the memory patterns for movements of handwriting.	Motor patterns of handwriting.	16
11, 12	Written Spelling and Sentence Formulation (amnesic agraphia)	Patient cannot spell or formulate sentences in writing.	Written spelling and sentence formulation.	16
1, 2, 3, 4	Reading (alexia)	Patient cannot recognize letters or words; cannot understand simple or complicated written statements.	Recognition of alphabet letters and words; silent reading for comprehension.	15
9, 10	Recall of Language (anomia and amnesic aphasia)	Patient cannot recall words and phrases on intent. He is often heard to say, "I know what it is, but I can't tell you."	Associating names with objects, people, and places; formulating language.	10
5	Auditory Recognition of Spoken Language (auditory-verbal agnosia)	Patient has no hearing loss, but does not recognize or understand spoken language. He often does not detect errors of his own speech; therefore, unknowingly uses the wrong words (paraphasia and jargon).	Auditory training; recognition and comprehension of individual sounds, words and sentences.	9
6	Ability to Pronounce Sounds and Words (motor aphasia)	Patient cannot recall the placement of the organs of speech (tongue, teeth, lips, etc.) in pronouncing sounds and words. He *knows* the appropriate word but cannot form it.	Practice in making individual sounds and words. Drills before mirror and in imitation of the therapist.	11

VI. BEGINNING THERAPY FROM TEST RESULTS

A. The "Global" Aphasic

The patient who "fails" almost the entire test, Section V, B, above. Occasionally the therapist is confronted with an aphasic whose test sheet shows "marked looses" in practically all thirteen items of the test. Yet his general affect convinces the therapist that the patient is not senile or a victim of dementia. Acknowledging greetings, successfully carrying out such intended acts as putting on his spectacles, handling a pencil, being alert to the ring of the telephone, lighting a cigarette and smiling appropriately are reassuring clues. A "global" aphasic is in much the same position of an American in a foreign country. He does not know the foreign alphabet by sight or by sound; he cannot read orally or comprehend a single word he hears or sees; he cannot count or compute in the foreign tongue, yet he is rational and retains the sum of his experiences and his judgment. This is true of the "global" aphasic; he is cut off from virtually all communication.

1. Auditory Training

The "global" aphasic first has to work for understanding and comprehension of language just as the baby first learns the meaning of the words he hears. For example, the baby cannot say COME as yet, he can't read it or write it, but he early learns by sound (frequently accompanied by gesture) what to do when he hears the sound which is interpreted as the word, COME. Unlike the baby, the "global" aphasic—assuming he is not also beset with non-language agnosias or apraxias—may also take advantage of the opportunity to see and to study the appearance of the words written or printed before him. He can copy them and can learn their meaning.

a. *The use of gesture and imitation* is a most helpful technique in retraining aphasics to understand such words as come, go, smile, smoke, eat, drink, stand up, sit down, write, read, open, close, drive (a car), telephone, shave, bathe, goodbye, hello, shake hands, up, down, here, there, this, that, no, yes.[12] Pantomime these words and repeat them, one at a time, with the action to reenforce sound patterns. Repeat them day after day and many times during the day.

b. *Objects used in every-day living,* the name of which the patient will hear many times in conversation, provide further help in auditory training. Use of training kits (Chapter 5, Section IV,C) for drill is convenient for this type of work. At meal time, ask the patient to pass items of food such as butter, pepper, salt. Refrain from gesture as soon as the patient begins to comprehend; that is, don't reach for the article of food asked for. Avoid confusing the patient with too many words. For example, the word butter is less confusing to him at this stage in his retraining than a request, Will you please pass me the butter. Continue with such words as knife, fork, spoon, plate, coffee, cake, etc.

---

12. Strange as it may seem, no and yes are very confusing for many aphasics; they are often uncertain as to which is which and frequently misuse them as they begin to speak. It is helpful to the patient as well as to friends and surrounding personnel when he masters these all-important words.

Add items of clothing, furniture, toilet articles, hobbies, sports, the family car, etc. For example, when the patient is dressing, refer to his shoes; repeat the word as he puts on his shoes. Let him repeat the word if he can.

c. Body Scheme. (Note: Many aphasics have lost their recognition of body scheme. If the patient is unable after some practice, to identify the body parts, he may have an agnosia in this respect, and it would be more practical to postpone this type of exercise.)

Ask the patient to point to such body parts as nose, eye, ear, mouth, hand, foot, etc. Help him by pointing to your own nose, eye etc., as you say the words. If he progresses rather well, add short commands such as, Open your mouth, Close your eyes, Hold up your thumb, etc.

d. The Bed Patient or the Patient in a Wheelchair. In case the patient is not yet ambulatory, small objects or pictures clipped from magazines mounted on tag board provide good study material. For example, use a set of pictures of fruits, sports, animals, family snapshots, or other categories of some interest to the patient. Present pictures of a dog, a car, a ball game. Ask the patient for one of the pictures, say the ball game, then the picture of the dog, etc. Continue laying out more pictures, asking for one at a time and keeping the request simple. As soon as feasible, complicate the exercise by asking for two pictures at a time out of the three displayed. The Dolch Cards are convenient to use in this exercise. (Dolch Materials, Expression Co., Magnolia, Mass.)

The same procedure may be used with small items which can be placed on a lap board, bedside table, or in the lap.

e. Phrases, Questions and Short Sentences. As soon as the patient begins to recognize the individual words he hears, it is time to retrain for auditory recognition of phrases and short commands as suggested in Body Scheme under paragraph c. Short oral commands and questions testing and training his ability to understand should be given slowly.

Take off your glasses.	Are you wearing a red tie?
Open your mouth.	Is it raining?
Give me the apple.	Have you had your breakfast?
Put the apple in your pocket.	

Note: It is useless to ask the patient questions to which you do not know the answers in order to test his understanding of oral language, for he may say yes or no whether he understands or not. For example, if the examiner says "Do you have a headache?" the patient may say "yes," when he has no headache at all.

f. Additional exercises for auditory training may be found in Chapter 9, Auditory Recognition. Make use of the material in Patient's Personalized Notebook (Chapter 7) as soon as practicable.

2. Speaking

Seldom is one modality or technique in the retraining work used completely in isolation—techniques involving other senses are called upon to help. For example, in retraining for auditory recognition, it is helpful for the patient to voice the words he hears if he can do so. On the other hand, he may be so seriously handicapped that intensive oral work before a mirror or with the Moto-kinesthetic method must be undertaken. In retraining specifically for oral language, the patient may find it helpful to copy the words as he practices pronouncing them.

a. Working before the mirror for motor speech pattern practice. Sit before the mirror with the patient. Indicate to him that by imitation he is to open his mouth, protrude his tongue, touch his upper and lower lips, switch his tongue from side to side. Then purse the lips to say oo; pull the lips back to say eeee. Then indicate to him as he continues to watch in the mirror the mouth movements for P, F, M. Protrude the tongue for TH, close the mouth for M. See if he can emit an air stream for the S sound and perhaps sound CH and SH.[13]

If he can move his mouth at will and can do some or all of these sounds, present an object or a picture of a simple object such as a magazine advertisement illustrating the word pie or pipe which will be easy to pronounce. Again go through the position of the mouth to form the p sound and add the ah-ee to complete the word PIE. Continue with other words easily seen on the lips such as pipe, arm, thumb.

For additional exercises see Chapter 11.

b. If the patient has an apraxia of the mouth, he may have difficulty with the above exercises because he cannot perform intended motor speech acts. In this case, use of the Moto-kinesthetic method is recommended. (See Chapter 11, Section IX).

3. The "Global" aphasic may perform slightly better in some areas than in others, for example in numbers. By all means, emphasize the skills he does the best so that he may experience a feeling of some success, small as it may be. Perhaps he can write numbers in series, maybe he will discover that he can count spontaneously up to five or ten, he might even be able to copy and add the simplest combinations such as $1 + 1 = 2$. He might be able to draw or paint. If he has to switch handedness because of a paralysis of his major hand, he should try copy work.

The therapist can well afford to be patient in awaiting results as actual samples of patients work testify. (See Chapter 19). Neither need the therapist

---

13. See: Motor Speech Patterns, Chapter 11.
    Reference Chart for Teaching Consonant Sounds, Chapter 11, Section VIII.

be apprehensive about imposing repetitious work upon the "global" aphasic, for he seldom recalls what he wrote yesterday, but when he does begin to learn, he is usually pleased to see the progress repetition has brought about.
4. The global aphasic may have retained some understanding of money. If so, make use of it in auditory training and in oral and written exercises. See Chapter 17 for additional exercises.
5. It is often helpful to provide the patient with a notebook, although he is far from ready to undertake assignments or study on his own. If it is merely a record of what has been attempted within the confines of the day, it often provides the patient with a feeling of having accomplished something. Even if he cannot read, he recalls the use of records and notebooks. (This leads up to later work with the Personalized Notebook, Chapter 7.)

As soon as the patient acquires some visual-verbal recognition, the early notebook may contain a reference of early, often more readily acquired items such as colors, days of the week, names of family members, simple expressions of greetings.
6. Tests for the global aphasic may be found in Additional Testing, Section VII, this Chapter.

B. The Amnesic Aphasic

The patient who shows losses in Test Items 9, 10, 11, 12, Section V, B, above. In addition to marked losses in Items 9, 10, 11 and 12, the amnesic aphasic probably will show varying degrees of loss in Items 3 and 13. He may show no loss in items 5, 6, 7 and 8.

This type talks around the subject, often cannot recall the names of objects, places and people, uses the wrong words, transposes word order, and experiences varying degrees of reading, spelling and formulation losses.

1. Training for Auditory Recognition

If the amnesic aphasic has an auditory-verbal agnosia (Test Item 5) which indicates that he has losses in understanding and interpreting the language he hears, he must begin intensive retraining in auditory recognition as described above for the "global" aphasic. Also see Auditory Recognition, Chapter 9.

2. Training in Naming People, Places and Objects

The inability to name objects (Test Item 9) is one of the most common defects in the amnesic aphasic. He usually recognizes the name of an object, for example an apple, when he hears it spoken and often can correctly select the word from a list, but if he is presented with an apple or a picture of one (or tastes or smells one), he cannot recall and say apple. He may be able to say all manner of things about an apple, such as it is red, is good to eat, makes good pie, and so on, but he still fails to recall and say the one word, apple.

Start the retraining work by naming individual items used in daily living which can be put to practical use in sentences later on.

C. The Motor Aphasic

The patient who shows losses in Test Item 6.

It must always be remembered that an aphasic practically never has only one aphasia defect. The motor aphasic probably will have failed several test items besides Item 6 which will also have to be dealt with. However, the fact that he failed Item 6 necessitates a special type of retraining. The amnesic-type patient fails Test Item 9 because he cannot think of the words; but the motor-type aphasic fails Test Item 6 because he does not know how to place his lips, tongue and teeth in order to form the word.[14]

The motor aphasic has to relearn word motor patterns. He needs to sit before the mirror with the therapist and watch, for example, the formation of the M sound by closing the lips, or the formation of the F sound by placing the lower lip under the upper teeth. Some motor aphasics can imitate by watching only, others need the help of manual manipulation. In severe cases a great deal of the Moto-kinesthetic method must be used.

1. Refer to Chapter 11, Motor Speech Patterns.

2. The Moto-kinesthetic method of speech training is described in Chapter 11, Section IX.

D. Losses in Arithmetic and Numbers

Test Items 4 and 13, Section V, B, above.

Obviously a patient who fails Test Item 4 need not attempt to cope with Test Item 13.

Counting; Numbers in series: Oral counting is helpful for both amnesic and motor aphasics, and copying numbers and writing them in series is good beginning therapy.

Many aphasics who can count in series cannot name an isolated number correctly, therefore practice in writing numbers from dictation and in identifying them, or naming them in isolation is an important part of retraining.

Recovery of basic processes is a matter of paper and pencil drill. Ascertain by giving the patient sample problems in the basic processes where he begins to make errors. An elementary workbook is useful in this type of arithmetic. If an inability to comprehend written language exists, a patient should not be given written problems beyond his reading ability.

---

14. In this explanation, it is assumed that in neither case does the patient have auditory-verbal agnosia. See Terms, Appendix.

Many patients, severely handicapped in language, excel in mathematics. This is an excellent avenue for providing success in advanced areas. Some may be able to do algebra and geometry without being able to spell the most elementary words. Cultivate the advanced skills along with the basic.

See Arithmetic, Chapter 17 for further therapy in arithmetic and numbers.

E. Losses in Reading

Test Items 1, 2, 3, 4, Section V, B, above.

Patients who show losses in Test Items 1, 2, 3, and 4 have a visual-verbal agnosia and/or alexia (inability to read with comprehension). Almost all aphasics experience some degree of reading loss. The patient who comprehends a simple sentence like Button your coat, may become completely confused with a printed paragraph. He fatigues out, loses the thought, is confused by prepositions, connectives, and by interrogative and relative pronouns.

1. Chapter 15, Reading Recognition and Comprehension, contains exercises applicable to patients with reading losses from comprehension of individual words to interpretation of intermediate and advanced reading material. A combination of oral work, writing and reading is helpful in the beginning: *say* the word, *write* the word, *identify* the word from the printed page.

2. A technique often helpful for the beginning reader consists of writing down his own formulation whether only a word or two or a paragraph. This may be a description of his job, an experience, something about his home, family, etc. Necessary words may be filled in for the patient. If the ideas written down are his, this often aids his recall of the words used, thus facilitating reading.

VII. ADDITIONAL TESTING[15]

Since the therapist is frequently asked about the progress patients are making—and indeed, questions himself about it—it is important that he keep some records to substantiate a subjective appraisal of his patients. Such records consist of dated samples of patients' work, tape recordings and test scores. Few tests have been devised or standardized especially for adult aphasics. The Harada Elementary Scale for Aphasics has been validated by paired comparisons against clinical judgment and gives a numerical co-

---

15. Projective techniques and tests of intelligence are usable with aphasics only if the examiner is well acquainted with the language restrictions of the aphasic patient being tested.

2. A Scale for Measuring Language Abilities and Progress for Male Aphasics, Clark Kohei Harada, thesis for Master of Arts Degree, University of Southern California, June 1960, Los Angeles, Calif.

efficient for an overall test score and for subtests. This scale was devised by Clark K. Harada at the Veterans Administration Hospital Aphasia Clinic, Long Beach, California. Several standard tests described below are adaptable and serve well as waymarks in measuring patient progress.

A. The Harada 1000-Point Elementary Scale for Aphasics by Clark K. Harada

Ten language skills are tested, each one rated at a possible 100 points. The total score of correct responses such as 45, 300, 895, serves as a measure of performance and also as a basis for further comparison. The scale should be administered when the patient begins therapy and at intervals of from four to six months. The language skills tested include: (1) naming, (2) oral reading, (3) reading recognition, (4) writing, (5) oral formulation, (6, 7) written formulation, (8) written arithmetic, (9) oral arithmetic, (10) understanding spoken language. The test can usually be administered in approximately one hour.

B. Non-Language Tests

A few non-language tests can be used successfully with aphasics. The element of auditory-verbal agnosia must be considered if the test is administered by oral directions. Often the completion of a non-language test serves as a successful experience for the aphasic. In administering these tests, the time element seldom should be considered, and any interpretation of an aphasic's untimed score based on norms established on a timed basis is not a fair evaluation. These tests show whether or not the patient can reason and think apart from the language problem; they provide objective evidence of his general capacity for visualization and intelligence functions and emphasize residual ability. In order to carry out the tests, the patient has to call upon a fund of knowledge accumulated previous to the accident which robbed him of his language, but which is still operating regardless of language losses. Therefore, the tests emphasize the residual ability and focus on the positive assets. There is also the psychological value of affirming the positive features the patient still retains.

Such objective tests either confirm or challenge the therapist's estimate of the patient's capabilities. A repeat testing provides an indication of the patient's ability to learn, and also establishes some measure of his recovery.

1. *Chicago Non-Verbal Examination:* A. W. Brown, The Psychological Corporation, 304 East 45th St., New York 17, N. Y. This examination is composed of ten tests consisting of symbols, blocks, pictures, and geometrical designs. The patient must be able to copy numbers. A convenient numerical

score for recording or for purposes of comparison may be arrived at by computing the percentage of correct answers.

2. *Revised Beta Examination:* C. E. Kellogg and N. W. Morton, The Psychological Corporation, 304 East 45th St., New York 17, N. Y. Six tests consist of mazes, symbols, drawing, geometric designs and numbers. The patient must be able to copy numbers. The percentage of correct answers serves as a convenient score for recording purposes and for making comparisons.

3. *The Peabody Picture Vocabulary Test:* Lloyd M. Dunn, American Guidance Service, Inc., 2106 Pierce Avenue, Nashville 12, Tenn. This test is composed of 150 pages, each page containing four drawings. The patient is to select the one drawing which best illustrates the word orally pronounced by the examiner. A patient with an auditory-verbal agnosia cannot take this test unless he can read the word list. In this case, he may match the printed word with his choice of picture.

A convenient percentage score can be arrived at by using the patient's ceiling item and his raw score.

C. Achievement Tests

Results achieved from the administration of all or parts of achievement tests often help place a patient in a group compatible with his ability and also serve as a guide post for planning an individual program of work. A high grade placement established by use of achievement tests is encouraging to an "advanced" patient who may have been in doubt as to the status of his language problem. Some aphasics score far above high school in some areas, say in mathematics and, at the same time, make an elementary grade placement in spelling or in grammar. Others score more or less consistently throughout the entire test.

    1. California Achievement Tests, 5916 Hollywood Blvd., Los Angeles 28, Calif. Devised by Ernest W. Tiegs and Willis W. Clark.

        a. California Achievement Tests; Complete batteries.
            —Primary Battery, Grades 1-3.
            —Elementary Battery, Grades 4-6.
            —Intermediate Battery, Grades 7-9.
            —Advanced Battery, Grades 9-14.

        b. California Arithmetic Test; Primary, Elementary, Intermediate, Advanced.

        c. California Basic Skill Test.

        d. California Language Test; Primary, Elementary, Intermediate, Advanced.

e. California Reading Test; Primary, Elementary, Intermediate, Advanced.

VIII. REFERENCES

Ammons, R. B., and Ammons, Helen S.: *The Full-Range Picture Vocabulary Test.* Psychological Test Specialists, Box 1441, Missoula, Mont.

Dunn, Lloyd M.: *Peabody Picture Vocabulary Test.* American Guidance Service, Inc., 2106 Pierce Avenue, Nashville 12, Tenn.

Eisenson, Jon: *Examining for Aphasia and Related Disturbances.* Psychological Corporation, 304 East 45th Street, New York 17, N. Y. Second Edition.

Halstead, Ward C., and Wepman, J. M.: *Aphasia Screening Test.* The Department of Medicine, University of Chicago, Chicago 37, Ill., 1949.

Longerich, Mary C., and Bordeaux, Jean: *Aphasia Therapeutics.* Macmillan Company, New York, N. Y.. Chapter V, Section C.

Minnesota Test for Differential Diagnosis of Aphasia—Research Edition. University of Minnesota Press, Minneapolis, Minn., 1955.

Schuell, Hildred: Diagnosis and prognosis in aphasia, *Archives of Neurology and Psychiatry,,* Vol. 74, page 308, 1955.

Schuell, Hildred: Relationship between auditory comprehension and word frequency in aphasia. *Journal of Speech and Hearing Research,* Vol. 4, No. 1, March 1961.

————: Short examination for aphasia. *Neurology,* Vol. 7, No. 9, page 625, September 1957.

Sklar, Maurice: Aphasia evaluation summary. *Western Speech,* pp. 89–94, Spring, 1959.

Travis, L. E., Editor: *Handbook of Speech Pathology.* Appleton-Century-Crofts, Inc., Chapter 12, 1957.

Wepman, Joseph M., and Jones, Lyle V.: *Studies in Aphasia: An Approach to Testing.* Language Modalities Test for Aphasia. Education-Industry Service, 1225 E. 60th Street, Chicago 37, Ill., 1961.

Chapter 5

ATTITUDES AND TECHNIQUES APPLICABLE IN RETRAINING APHASICS

I. INTRODUCTION

ALTHOUGH LANGUAGE retraining for aphasics has been likened to teaching language to children, there are actually many differences. The adult aphasic is a mature, experienced, and often highly trained individual who has lost only the particular skill of language. The entire approach to therapy must, therefore, be adult although many of the techniques used in teaching children may be helpful. The personalities of patient and therapist sometimes determine the types of therapy best suited to their individualities. The young aphasic who loses his language due to a traumatic accident will respond to a type of therapy different from that provided for the mature professional adult who has suffered a cerebral thrombosis. A clinic situation offers an advantage in that the director has a staff of therapists with varied talents, interests and even hobbies, among whom he can schedule and assign patients. Since patients relate differently to men and to women, even this preference must be considered. An individual therapist, on the other hand, must adapt his own personality and techniques to the patient and rely upon as many resources as possible to meet the problem at hand.

A recognition of varying language defects present in the patient provides the key to the approach most appropriate for the therapy. For example, a patient with severe auditory verbal agnosia will have difficulty understanding spoken language and therefore he should be approached through the visual rather than through the auditory. The patient who no longer has intact reading comprehension should be approached through the auditory rather than through the visual. The so-called global aphasic who is virtually cut off from all communication must first be approached by non-language communication such as gesture and facial expression. The therapist must be on the alert to detect the slightest indication from a patient of this type of any comprehension whatever. Any indication of comprehension may be used as an avenue to language therapy. Frequently the area of numbers stemming from the patient's comprehension of coins has proved to be a starting point.

An identical approach, obviously, is not appropriate for the retraining of three patients who, when presented with a sketch of a fish, actually made the following responses:

(The amnesic aphasic)	*(The paraphasic)*	*(The motor aphasic)*
a. I know what it is but I can't tell you. It's in the water, fun to catch—vacation, you know. It's not an animal, but close to it. It's good to eat. It's a crab—no—close to it though—fisk—FISH! that's it.	b. FEESH! It's not the same kind. Oh yes, I know what that is—it's not the same when you go shape, put in here and he sets this way and the first thing, F-sst! it's gone.	c. Mow - no! bow-sie - no! fairy - no, no! fair - jell - no! (Here the therapist showed the patient the f sound with upper teeth on the lower lip.) f - f - fish, fish, yes, fish.

II. USING THE RETRAINING SECTION

For the most part this section of the handbook is printed in two columns, the righthand column containing sample exercises and directly opposite to the left, remarks and suggestions for their use.

A. Select Exercises Best Suited to the Patient's Needs. It is not intended that a patient proceed page by page from the beginning to the end of the handbook. Use the patient's level of performance and understanding as an index to appropriate exercises for him.

B. Retrain in all Areas of Language. Provide daily practice in speaking. reading, writing and arithmetic. Recognize that a patient performs better in some areas and subjects than in others, therefore use exercises of appropriate difficulty or simplicity from each of the several sections. Give him the satisfaction of succeeding in his "best" subjects even though it appears that he needs little or no help in that particular area.

C. Vary Approaches, Techniques and Exercises. A great deal of repetition—all that a patient can tolerate—usually is needed to make the retraining permanent; however, a patient rarely should be required to repeat one exercise until he does it perfectly. Avoid frustration and feelings of failure by accepting lowered standards and goals, by change of approach, and by variety of subject matter.

D. Use Only Appropriate Exercises. It is not intended that this book be used in its entirety. The therapist will find that many of the suggested approaches and exercises should be used repeatedly both as they are printed and with modifications while others will seldom or never be needed.

E. Make the Retraining Personal. Modify the sample exercises by a substitution of names of persons, places and events in order to give them a personal appeal for the patient.

III. APPROACHES, ATTITUDES AND GENERAL TECHINQUES
FOR THERAPY

A. Fatigue. In working with aphasics the therapist must be cognizant of the fatigue factor in the retraining of new areas of speech. The patient usually cannot tolerate drill longer than five or ten minutes at a time. If his attention is diverted for only a second or two, frequently he can take up the work again with surprising success.

B. Variety of Techniques. A variation in presentation of retraining material often makes the necessary repetition more palatable. The same words may be presented in writing, in reading, and in conversation. In clinics where several therapists are working, it is well for the patient to work with all therapists during the day in order to get the benefit of a variety of techniques and approaches from them.

C. Variations in Ability. The aphasic is often at different levels of understanding and accomplishment in the various areas of mathematics and language. For example, some patients who cannot utter a simple sentence can work algebra or even trigonometry. It is a boost to morale to succeed in an advanced area while retraining at lower levels in other areas. A few patients prefer to review at low levels preparatory to undertaking advanced work.

D. Oral Speech. Any language which the patient can use—even profane—should be accepted until he can cultivate a more extensive vocabulary. The refinements of good grammar seldom can be taken into consideration. The experienced therapist learns to "hear between the lines" and to accept every effort as a successful production. If the patient's language is intelligible at all, it may be wise to withhold correction and criticism. As he develops auditory recognition, he will begin to correct himself. The aphasic who can detect his own errors frequently is highly amused at his distorted language in which case the therapist has a good opportunity to join in the humor of the situation as corrections are suggested.

E. Aiding Recall. Often an aphasic can say the word he wants if he can recall the first syllable or can see the pattern of the first sound in the lips of the therapist. Forming the first letter on the lips and thus leading the patient to recall the word himself is more beneficial to him than giving him the entire word. This technique can be used repeatedly throughout the day even after formal therapy sessions have ended.

F. Supplying Answers. Supplying an inappropriate word for a patient frequently leads him to recall the correct one—often the most ridiculous substitution is the most helpful. For example, the question, "How old is the baby, 18 *years*" frequently will elicit the correct response, "No, 18 months." Or, "Is Mary your *husband*," will bring out the reply, "No, my wife." Language therapy in this vein can be carried on at any chance meeting throughout the day much to the patient's advantage.

G. Singing. Well known songs often help bring out spoken words. One patient was known to sing the kindergarten song, "Good morning to you" long before he could *say* "Good morning." Popular songs heard on radio and television frequently contain useful everyday phrases which the patient can recall with the hum of the tune, for example, *Happy Birthday to You,* and *Over There.*

H. Copy Work. Sometimes a patient has trouble doing copy work from the board. If losing the place is his difficulty, write the work on his paper so that he can copy directly beneath it. He may be able to read and to copy printing when he cannot yet read cursive writing or script. Find out what he can best do, and go on from there.

I. Tracing. The patient may
   1) Trace a pattern before him on the board by gross hand and arm movements "in the air."
   2) Trace with his finger ON the chalk or pencil lines.
   3) Trace with his finger letters made of cardboard, sandpaper, plastic, or wood.
   4) Use chalk or pencil to write directly on the pattern.
   5) Write on tissue paper laid over the original sheet beneath.

J. Using Language Substitutes.
   1) Line drawings and stick figures: simple drawings frequently provide that extra stimulation and suggestion which help the language break through.
   2) The patient himself often can make his wants known to the therapist by the use of drawings, gesture and pantomime.
   3) "Initial Communication Chart for Aphasics," by Maurice Sklar and Daphne Nicholson Bennett, published in *The Journal of the Association for Physical and Mental Rehabilitation,* March-April, 1956; and *Silent Spokesman* by Wayland W. Lessing show practical uses made of drawings.

K. Over-size Letters. Large letters have proved to be stimulating for reading recognition both at the blackboard and on paper.

L. Using Labels. The labeling of objects, furniture and parts of the room is often helpful. To print the name DOOR on a card pinned to the door followed by repeated demonstrations of knocking on the door, opening the door, closing the door, and calling attention to it every time one passes through the door furnish the needed repetition to make the word permanent.

M. Learning Verbs. Some patients experience great difficulty in understanding verbs. Presented with a picture of a boy eating a piece of bread, these patients will likely say "bread" or "boy," disregarding the action portrayed in the picture. If shown a picture of a waitress pouring coffee, the patient may reply, "coffee" or "girl." Even when pressed with, "Yes, but *what* are they *doing?*" the patient usually persists with an answer in nouns rather than that the boy is EATING and the waitress is POURING. Many demonstrations with actual action are needed to retrain for verbs: actually *eating* something and *using the word at the same time,* or *pouring* something and *using the word at the same time* help the patient connect the word with the action. Often to ask what the boy is NOT doing, or what the waitress is NOT doing is helpful. This provides the patient with ideas for comparison purposes. Example, "Is the boy running?" "No, eating, the boy is eating."

N. Using Colors.[1] The use of contrasting colors of chalk and pencil often serves to emphasize or to stress some part of the lesson.

> Examples: B AT, C AT, F AT, M AT
> (In each instance, print AT in color)
> re CEIVE,   con CEIVE,   de CEIVE
> (Write CEIVE in color)
> BRACE,   em BRACE,   BRACE let
> (Write BRACE in color)

Colors are helpful in an exercise such as this to point up identical words:

> I like cake; I like coffee; I want a hot dog; I want coffee cake; I like hot coffee; I like cup cakes; I want a cup of hot coffee.
> (Underline "like" in one color "coffee" in another color, "want" in another, and so on with all repeated words.)

O. For Motivation. The poorly motivated patient often needs to be safeguarded from undue preoccupation with his own disability. This type needs easy success. A technique found helpful with such cases consists of first allowing the patient to browse through magazines such as National Geographic or Arizona Highways which contain many colored pictures. Next assign the patient certain pictures, captions, chapter headings, and definite stories to search out. Ask him to copy key words for spelling lessons. For practice in oral formulation ask him to describe a certain interesting picture, or one of his own choice. Examples: Grand Canyon, Yosemite Falls, American Indians.

P. Hobbies and High Interest Material. Making use of a patient's individual interests, his hobbies, occupation, and other special interests has proved to be good for motivation purposes.

Q. Card Games. Card-game lessons are stimulating to some poorly motivated patients. Arithmetic games and language games are listed in Therapists' Materials and Supplies below.

---

1. *Mix n Match Word Game.* Milton Bradley Company, Springfield, Mass, teaches spelling and reading through letters in colored frames.

R. Personalized Notebook. The personalized notebook is valuable in helping a patient establish an individual basic vocabulary. See Sample Personalized Notebook, Chapter 7.

S. Success Exercises. Patients so severely handicapped that their progress is extremely slow need much encouragement. To close each therapy session on a note of success is a psychological boost to such cases. The following suggestions are recommended since they lend themselves readily to flexibility. The therapist can modify the work to the patient's capabilities at the moment.

1. Copy work. 2. Bingo. 3. Match picture with picture. 4. Match picture with word.

T. Self-correction.[2] Encourage and even insist upon self-correction whenever the patient shows any signs of recognition of his own errors and is amenable to being corrected. His ability to self-correct indicates that the retraining processes are beginning to be effective, that auditory recognition is improving, and that the patient's insight is broadening.

IV. THERAPIST'S MATERIALS AND SUPPLIES

Frequently the aphasia patient comes up with a personal problem or interest which is ideal for a lesson. To meet such demands the therapist needs a wide variety of materials. The following assortment lends itself to many types of therapy.

A. Models

1. Food: fruits, vegetables, meat. Actual size and approximate color are available in department and ten-cent stores or from the Cincinnati Doll Company, 311 East 12th, Cincinnati 10, Ohio.
2. Toy tools: available in variety and ten-cent stores.
3. Toy furniture: doll house and furnishings.
4. Family figures (see Children's Section, Chapter 27, Therapy Materials).

B. Picture Files

The therapist will find very useful in many ways a file of colored pictures clipped from magazines and advertisements and mounted on $8\frac{1}{2}$ x 11 and $5\frac{1}{2}$ x $8\frac{1}{2}$ manila or cardboard. Picture files suggested below lend themselves readily to language therapy for aphasics:

1. For practice in naming: body parts, toilet articles, food, clothing, flowers, houses, farm implements, cooking utensils, animals, table service, famous people, vehicles, well-known places, occupations and jobs, family and relatives, sports.

2. Wepman, Joseph M.: Relationship Between Self-correction and Recovery from Aphasia. *Journal of Speech and Hearing Disorders*, Vol. 23, No. 3, August 1958.

2. For recall of action words: action pictures of people swimming, dancing, running, walking; carpenters building a house, someone driving a car, a boat sailing, woman doing the laundry, etc.
3. For oral and written formulation: composite pictures such as a baseball game, street activities, farm scene with tractors, at the service station, building a house, scene at the beach.
4. For telegraphic speech and the relearning of prepositions: picture of a bird ON a branch, a roast IN the oven, a shelf OVER the stove. It is helpful to type sentences on each picture omitting the preposition which is to be filled in by the patient. *Example:* The roast is _____ the oven.
5. Suggested categories:
    a. *Family:* older man, older woman, children, young people.
    b. *Pets:* dogs, cats, birds, gold fish, animals.
    c. *Home:* various rooms, furniture, yard, car.
    d. *Occupations:* carpenter, plumber, teacher, cook, doctor, dentist, farmer, truck driver, taxi driver, factory worker.
    e. *Famous people:* President of US, actors, TV stars, athletes, sports personalities.
    f. *Famous places:* Washington, D.C., Paris, Rome, Disneyland, United Nations, Sphinx, Leaning Tower of Pisa, Matterhorn.

C. Training Kits

Training kits, stored in uniform boxes and appropriately labeled are helpful for patients needing naming practice. Kits are also time-savers in a busy schedule of language therapy. They should contain a group of actual articles usually used together (or in the same category) with a set of 3 x 5 cards naming each article.

1. Toilet Articles: soap, wash cloth, towel, razor, toothbrush, brush, comb.
2. Sewing Kit: thimble, thread, needle, scissors, piece of cloth, tape measure, pins.
3. Table Service: knife, fork, spoon, cup, saucer, plate, napkin, sugar, creamer, salt, pepper.
4. Tools: hammer (toy), saw, nail, screw driver, pliars.
5. Business: writing materials, check book, application blanks.

D. Maps

1. Atlas.
2. Globe.

3. City maps are particularly helpful when a patient wants to point out a place he has in mind but which he cannot name.
4. State maps.
5. World maps.
6. Map of U.S. (puzzle, cut on state lines; world on reverse side) , Milton Bradley Co., Springfield, Mass.

E. Dictionaries

Therapists working in clinics and hospitals frequently are dealing with bilingual patients. Often there is a need to look up foreign words which come to the patient when the English counterparts cannot be recalled. Paperbacks found in drug and department stores are adequate for this need.
1. *Spanish Dictionary,* Carlos Castillo and Otto F. Bond. Pocket Book, Inc. 35¢
2. Dictionaries in French, German, Italian, etc., Language Research, Inc., Washington Square Press, 630 Fifth Avenue, New York 20, N. Y.
3. Spanish Vocabulary Cards (See Section P, 2, K) .

F. Colors
Paint-sample cards, colored pencils and crayons, colored chalk.

G. Alphabet Letters

A large set of both capital and small letters should be in view at all times. Alphabet board which patient uses to spell out words by pointing to the letters.

H. Money
Coins or pictures of coins, paper money, billfold, purse.

I. Magnifying Reading Glass

Patients often forget their glasses. An available reading glass often makes it possible to have therapy even though a problem in eye sight is involved.

J. Felt Pen
Felt pens are available at stationery, drug and department stores.
1. Carter's Marks-A-Lot (in many colors) .
2. Cado Flow Master Pen.
3. Ball point pens.

K. Mirror

Wall or hand mirror for observing mouth placement (especially for motor aphasia) .

L. Blackboard

A portable blackboard with a cut-out slot for a handle is handy for the therapist who goes to the homes for therapy. Often patients can make gross movements with chalk before fine hand movements with a pencil are possible.

M. Word Lists

Drill books containing word lists include:
1. Schoolfield, Lucille: *Better Speech and Better Reading.* Boston Expression Company, Magnolia, Mass.
2. Birmingham, Anna, and Krapp, George P.: *First Lessons in Speech Improvement.* Charles Scribner's Sons, San Francisco, Calif.
3. Fairbanks, Grant: *Voice and Articulation Drillbook.* Harper and Brothers, New York, N. Y.

N. File Box of Consonant Sounds

1. Prepare a file of pictures to illustrate sounds in the initial, medial and final positions. Patients who cannot read are often able to practice vowel and consonant sounds to good advantage from such pictures. The therapist also can sort out the patient's articulation defects from his naming of these pictures. While several sets are made commercially,[3] an inexpensive set can be made by cutting and pasting colored magazine advertisements on 5 x 8 cards to represent all consonant sounds in the initial, medial and final positions. With a felt pen, the corresponding word should be written on the back of each card. The picture side of the card is to be used with non-readers; the reverse side may be used by those who can read. In addition to testing the patient for articulation defects the therapist may list or set aside the cards needing correction and drill. Following are suggested words which are usually pictured in leading magazines.

	Initial	*Medial*	*Final*
B	BATH:BIRD	RABBIT	CRIB:BATHTUB
CH	CHAIR:CHICK	CATCHER:KITCHEN	WITCH:MATCH
D	DOG	CANDY:SADDLE	CLOUD:BIRD:HAND
J	JUICE	FIRE ENGINE	BRIDGE:ORANGE
G (hard)	GIRL:GATE	WAGON:TIGER	EGG:FLAG:FROG
H	HAND:HAT:HORSE	GRASSHOPPER:LIGHTHOUSE	
K	CAT:KITTEN:CLOCK	PICNIC:MONKEY	SINK:MILK
L	LAMP:LADDER	CELERY:VIOLIN	BELL:PENCIL
M	MONKEY	LEMON	ICE CREAM
N	KNIFE	WINDOW	CURTAIN:TRAIN
P	PUPPY	POPCORN	CUP
ING	INGOT	FINGER	RING
R	RABBIT	FORK	CAR

SK	SCHOOL	BASKET	DESK
S	SOUP	ROOSTER	GRAPES
SH	SHEEP	DISHES	FISH
T	TIE	LETTUCE	CARROT
TH (unvoiced)	THREAD:THREE	BIRTHDAY CAKE	TEETH:MOUTH
TH (voiced)		FEATHER:MOTHER	BATHE
V	VOLCANO	SEVEN-UP: 7	STOVE
W	WATER	FLOWER	
WH	WHEEL	WATER WHEEL	
Z	ZEBRA	SCISSORS	ROSE
ZH		TELEVISION	GARAGE

Word lists for this type of exercise may be found as follows:

First Lessons in Speech Improvement. Birmingham & Krapp, Pt. I, page 2.

Voice and Articulation Drill Book. Grant Fairbanks, Chap. IV, page 51.

Better Speech & Better Reading. Lucille Schoolfield, pages 141-144.

See and Say Consonant Game (Grades 1-6) . Milton Bradley Co., (found in department and book stores.)

2. Alphabetical file (for initial sounds) : pictures to help patients recall initial sounds.

Example: "A" file of apple, apricot, etc.

"B" file of bacon, beans, etc.

Continue throughout the alphabet.

O. Times Tables Cards

1	2	3	4	5	6	7	8	9	10	11	12
2	4	6	8	10	12	14	16	18	20	22	24
3	6	9	12	15	18	21	24	27	30	33	36
4	8	12	16	20	24	28	32	36	40	44	48
5	10	15	20	25	30	35	40	45	50	55	60
6	12	18	24	30	36	42	48	54	60	66	72
7	14	21	28	35	42	49	56	63	70	77	84
8	16	24	32	40	48	56	64	72	80	88	96
9	18	27	36	45	54	63	72	81	90	99	108
10	20	30	40	50	60	70	80	90	100	110	120

P. Flash Cards

1. Hand made cards

a. Primary words (use felt pen) : BED WATER PIE COFFEE TV RADIO MAMA WIFE

b. Phrases and short commands: IN THE BATHROOM I WANT COFFEE   BRING ME A DRINK

c. For advanced reading, oral formulation, and revisualization: Who

---

3. Commercial sets of black and white pictures with phonetic alphabet are available at Warnock-Medlin Word Making, P. O. Box 305, Salt Lake City 10, Utah.

is President of the United States; Name four oceans; What is the meaning of Amphibious?

2. Commercial cards

There are a great many flash cards available in ten-cent stores, drug and department stores. These cards cover a wide variety of subject matter on many grade levels, and are variously priced.

a. *Phonetic Word Builder.* Milton Bradley Company, Springfield, Mass.

b. *Flash Words*—Grades 1 and 2 (100 abstract words, one-half of basic word list). Milton Bradley Company.

c. *Parent-Teacher Aids*—*Phonics* (with progress test sheets). The Gelles-Widmer Co., St. Louis 17, Mo.

d. Arithmetic basic processes: multiplication, addition, subtraction and division, Super Speed Card Co., 41111 Berryman Ave., Los Angeles 66, Calif.

e. *Know Your USA Flash Cards.* Rand McNally.

f. *Know Your Stars and Planets Flash Cards.* Rand McNally.

g. *Know Your World.* Rand McNally.

h. *Know Your Flags.* Rand McNally.

i. *Parent Teacher Aids*—*Spanish* (picture cards)
   and
   Parent Teacher Aids—*Spanish Phrase Cards.* Gelles-Widmer Co., St. Louis 17, Mo.

j. *Book of Knowledge Flash Cards and Quiz Games.* Important Events Series, ED-U-Cards Mfg. Corp, Long Island City, N. Y. or Milton Bradley Co., Springfield 2, Mass.

k. *VIS-ED Spanish Vocabulary Cards.* Visual Education Association, Inc., 230 West Fifth St., Dayton 2, O.

Q. Card Games

1. *Word Rummy.* Educational Cards, Inc., 1302 Industrial Bank Bldg., Detroit 26, Mich.

2. *Fun With Numbers.* Exclusive Playing Card Co., Chicago 5, Ill.

3. *Anagrams.*

R. Card Holders

Many commercial card holders are on the market today but an inexpensive holder can be made of a $1\frac{3}{4}$" x $1\frac{3}{4}$" x 12" block with a slanted groove cut across the top in which to place the cards.

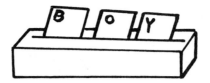

S. Supply Catalogs

1. Milton Bradley Company, Springfield, Mass.
2. Palfrey's School Supply Company, 7715 East Garvey Blvd., South San Gabriel, Calif.
3. Dolch Materials, Expression Company, Magnolia, Mass.
4. Go-Mo Products, Inc., P. O. Box 143, Waterloo, Iowa.

Chapter 6

GROUP THERAPY

I︎N THE RETRAINING of aphasics, the therapeutic value of group interaction cannot be overestimated. The use of group therapy has been well demonstrated in Veterans Administration clinics over a long period of time. Whether patients meet in casual social groups or in structured teaching situations, they obtain important psychological help by being together. Aphasic groups have the denominator of their common problems, the encouragement of one another, identification in successful situations, and many other dynamic factors which cannot exist in individual therapy.

Group situations also have the practical value of providing help for a greater number of patients than otherwise would be practical. The length of therapy periods may be extended since group work is not as intensive as individual. In a group, the patient may learn while relaxing and listening to others without sustaining undue fatigue.

I. GROUP THERAPY IN LANGUAGE SITUATIONS[1]

An example of the use of group therapy is seen in an elementary reading group. Each member has a text, perhaps one of the Readers' Digest Skill Builders Series. The group begins by taking turns reading aloud. Each individual receives auditory training as he listens while another reads. Then the group reads part of the story silently for comprehension and discusses the meaning of the story. The therapist provides a vocabulary drill by writing on the board troublesome words suggested by the members. The story now familiar to the entire group, becomes a basis of many types of language drills.

Oral formulation adapts itself well to group drill. Talking with members of a group is a stimulating process. Topics which often serve as good implementation are discussions of a personal nature such as the accident causing the speech loss. The therapist may serve as moderator allowing the discussion to circulate well in the group. While the patients frequently help each other, the therapist may find it necessary to assist individuals who are having difficulty. Many times such a discussion will reach such a peak of interest that it is difficult to terminate it at the end of the period.

Group therapy may be effectively extended to every type of language retraining.[2] A typical daily schedule, which follows this section, suggests how full a patient's program may be when group therapy is employed.

---

1. See Lesson Plan: Group Therapy for Auditory Recognition, Chapter 9, Section V.
2. Corbin, M. L.: Group speech therapy for motor aphasia and dysarthria. *Journal of Speech and Hearing Disorders*, Vol. 6, No. 1, March 1951.

Except for a larger space, equipment and materials are much the same as those used in individual therapy. One clinic has a large, pleasant room with comfortable seats equipped with left- or right-arm student chairs. A large blackboard, recording equipment and study helps are provided. One end of the room is equipped with large mirrors for the motor speech group. A large bulletin board at the other end of the room displays a series of pictures used in current instruction. Over the board are the alphabet, numbers, and names of persons needed daily. The room serves the dual purpose of a group meeting place plus an excellent study retreat.

II. PSYCHOTHERAPY[3]

Psychotherapy groups meet specifically to resolve common emotional problems. Many of these problems arise from the speech loss and hemiplegia or are accentuated by their presence. These problems may center around family adjustments, inability to pursue former occupations, relationship with members of the opposite sex, in fact, increased difficulties in any daily situation. A remarkable acting out of emotional situations is often observed. The use of figures, maps, diagrams, simple drawings, and similar techniques may supplant verbal responses until spoken language is adequate. A patient who does not choose to participate overtly still undergoes emotional identification and group participation. The frustrations which relate to the language problems and to the hemiplegia may often be alleviated in these groups.

A good therapy program would most certainly include a compatible program of individual and group therapy. An aphasia patient, by himself, is often despaired beyond help. With other patients who have similar difficulties, the aphasic finds reassurance and understanding which are available from no other source.

III. A DAILY CLINIC SCHEDULE

8:30 a.m.   1. *Arithmetic Group:* Oral: learning numbers, tables, counting.
            Written: basic processes, advanced work.

9:00   2. *Reading Group:* May be individual words and or short sentences from the blackboard, or paragraphs and advanced work from books.
            3. *Intermission* of five or ten minutes.

9:45   4. *Writing Group:* In beginning work the writing lesson may well be the same work from the blackboard which has been used for the reading lesson. In *intermediate* work it may be dictation or spelling from the reading lesson. In *advanced* work it may be original formulation, composition, spelling, personal letters.

10:30   5. *Coffee Break:* Medication. Singing.

---

3. Aronson, M., Shatin, Leo, and Cook, J. C.: Socio-psychotherapeutic Approach to the Treatment of Aphasia Patients. *Journal of Speech and Hearing Disorders*, Vol. 21, No. 3, September 1956. Bloom, Lois M.: A rationale for group treatment of aphasic patients. *Journal of Speech and Hearing Disorders*, Vol. 27, No. 1, February 1962.

10:45	6. *Oral Speech Group:* Oral work may be in the form of naming items of clothing, naming from Training Kits, pictures, body parts, furniture; it may be cultivating telegraphic speech, or eliminating telegraphic speech by learning prepositions, adverbs, connectives; it may be group therapy where troubles are aired. The main thing is to talk spontaneously. LUNCH
1:00 p.m.	7. *Individual Therapy:* May be a personal problem, individual motor pattern practice on troublesome consonants, spelling, reading, or whatever the patient particularly needs at the moment.
2:00	8. *Physical Exercise:* Gymnasium, swimming pool, physical and corrective therapy.
2:30	9. *Occupational Therapy:*
4:00-10:00	10. *Recreation:* T. V., movies, games, cards.

IV. REFERENCES

Agranowitz, Aleen; Boone, Daniel; Ruff, Marion; Seacat, Gloria; and Terr, Arthur: Group therapy as a method of retraining aphasics. *Quarterly Journal of Speech,* Vol. 40, No. 2, April 1954.

Corbin, M. L.: Group speech therapy for motor aphasia and dysarthria. *Journal of Speech and Hearing Disorders,* Vol. 6, No. 1, March 1951.

Inskip, Wilma M., and Burris, Grace: A coordinated treatment program for the patient with language disability. *American Archives of Rehabilitation Therapy,* Vol. 7, No. 1, March 1959.

Travis and others: *Handbook of Speech Pathology.* Group Therapy, page 476; Psychotherapy, page 474.

Chapter 7

PERSONALIZED NOTEBOOK

I. INTRODUCTION

T HE PATIENT's Personalized Notebook offers many varied possibilities for retraining therapy. The information—usually secured from family members and from medical records—can be expanded to suit the background and experience of each patient.

This notebook provides the therapist with lesson and discussion material which captures the interest of the patient because it is about *him* and the people and places he knows best. It also provides each patient with his own personal basic vocabulary and may serve as a personal reference sheet to which he can point when he cannot talk.

The notebook furnishes reading and writing material for the early stages of retraining such as the patient's name, the names of his wife, his children and so on:

My name is Bob.   Kate is my wife.   John is my son.   Bob is my husband.
From the personalized information, exercises meaningful to the patient replace a random choice of words and sentences.

A basic vocabulary for the aphasic need not necessarily be made up of one-syllable words. This patient, through personal interest, may recognize the word "Presbyterian" more readily than he will recognize simpler one-syllable words which may be useless and meaningless to him.

Personal-interest material is particularly useful in advanced oral and written formulation as the patient progresses, and his own accounts furnish high interest material for arithmetic.

II. A SAMPLE PATIENT'S PERSONALIZED NOTEBOOK

NAME:	Robert J. Conely (Bob)	Suggestions for Woman's Notebook or for Patient in private hospital.
ADDRESS:	117-15th St., Long Beach, Calif.	
PHONE:	SKyline 7-6540	
	IDENTIFICATION	
HEIGHT	5' 8"	Private hospital _____
WEIGHT	152 lbs.	_____
COMPLEXION:	Fair skin, dark hair, brown eyes.	Address:
AGE:	37	Phone:
HOSPITAL WARD:	N-14 (Aphasia)	Doctor's name:
	PERSONAL HISTORY	Address:
BIRTHPLACE:	Pittsburgh, Pennsylvania	Phone:
BIRTHDATE:	June 3, 1919	Physical Therapist:
NATIONAL BACKGROUND:	Scotch-Irish	Address:
RELIGION:	Presbyterian	Phone:

	FAMILY & FRIENDS	Speech Therapist: _____
WIFE:	Kathryn (Kate) Austin Conley	_____
CHILDREN:	John, 9 years old. Clara, 12 years old—Lincoln School.	Address:
		Phone:
MOTHER:	Ann M. Conley (works at a candy shop)	
FATHER	Walter Conley (works as a cattle buyer and builder)	
BROTHER:	Albert Vincent (2 years younger; farmer)	
FRIENDS:	Pete Smith (San Diego) ; lawyer	
NEIGHBORS:	The Carter family. The Chadwick family.	
HOME:	1. 6 rooms: 3 bedrooms, kitchen, dinette, living room, bath, service porch, attached double garage.	
	2. Lot: 65 x 135	
	3. We are buying the house. $75.00 monthly payments.	
CAR:	Chevrolet 1962, 4-door sedan, black and red.	
THE BUDGET:	House payments $75.00	
	Food _____	
	Insurance _____	
	Car _____	
	Clothing _____	
MY BANK:	First National, Long Beach, California	
INSURANCE:	New York Life; Interstate Indemnity, Los Angeles	
PETS:	Two green parakeets, Poodle dog—Sambeau	

SCHOOL RECORD

HIGH SCHOOL:	Central High School, San Diego, California
COLLEGE:	Oceanside Junior College, Oceanside, California
	Major: Business Course
	Interests: Sports
	Glee Club

WORK RECORD

MAIN OCCUPATION: (or recent)	Real Estate Office, 206 W. Main St., Del Mar, California	
PAST JOBS:	Real Estate Salesman in San Fernando Valley (1 yr.)	OCCUPATION: _____
FUTURE GOALS:	Open a real estate office.	(secretary, beauty operator, housewife, etc.)

SERVICE RECORD

BRANCH:	Air Corps
RANK:	Cpl. (Sgt.—highest held)
LENGTH OF SERVICE:	3 yrs. 7 mos.
SPECIALTY:	Personnel work
STATION:	Nellis Air Corps Hospital, Las Vegas, Nevada

HOBBIES & RECREATION

TV: Sports, Drama, Travel, News

GAMES: Chess, Samba

GAMES: _____
(bridge, playing the piano, golf)

MISC: Appraising Houses. Looking for Real Estate Listings

CLUBS: (Woman's Club, sorority, church guilds)

SPORTS: Baseball, Horse Races, Dog Shows

BOOKS: Household magazines, interior decorating

MUSIC: Popular and semi-classical

CLUBS & ORGANIZATIONS: Elks, Lions Club, Realtors Ass'n.

BOOKS: Murder stories (Ellery Queen) Real Estate Journals

PRESENT DISABILITY

DATE OF OCCURRENCE: May 20, 1954

DIAGNOSIS: Brain contusion, frontal

HOSPITALIZATION: Admitted Nellis AFB Hospital, transferred to Travis AFB Hospital, Letterman, then LBVAH 10-1-54.

RESIDUALS: Rt. Hemiparesis, motor aphasia.

DESCRIPTION OF ACCIDENT: "I was riding on Highway 91 from Las Vegas to Nellis AFB, Nevada, May 20, 1954 when the driver apparently lost control of car. Car skidded and overturned at 10:42 p.m. I was thrown from the car about 39 feet, and was unconscious. I was taken to Nellis AFB Hospital. As a result of the accident I lost my speech and was paralyzed on the right side. I could understand what people said to me and could read and spell out words on my alphabet board, but I could not talk."

AMOUNT OF PENSION: $181.00

SHOPPING INFORMATION

CLOTHES: Shirts: 15-32, sportshirts, white dress shirts; Socks: 10½; Shoes: 8; Pants: 34. Favorite Colors: green, gray

Blouses, dresses 16
Hose 9½
Shoes 7½A

BRANDS: Cigarettes: Camels; Electric razor: Rollectric

FOODS: Roast beef, beef bacon, hot breads, gelatin salads, popcorn, pie, French fries

MEMORABLE INCIDENTS IN LIFE

WEDDING: Presbyterian Church, Long Beach, California, June 6, 1942

TROPHY AWARDS: Award—high school basketball
Award—making the most real estate sales in one year

SERVICE: First parachute jump

MISCELLANEOUS

III. LESSON PLAN TO USE WITH PERSONALIZED NOTEBOOK

A. Writing and Spelling (group or individual therapy)

Either printing or cursive writing may be used but cursive writing usually comes along rather easily and naturally even though the patient may have resorted to block printing in the first stages of his retraining. The patient may show an interest in relearning the alphabet, but it certainly is not necessary to master the entire twenty-six letters before undertaking written words. Almost all patients are interested in writing their own names. The ability to sign checks, credit cards, legal documents, etc., in recognizable script is important to the patient and to his family.

1. Individual Words

a. Names. With clear penmanship and heavy pencil or felt pen, make a sample copy of the patient's name (printing or cursive according to the patient's needs) at the top of the page. Show him that he is to copy his name. After he begins to relearn the spelling, cover the sample so that he learns to spell rather than to continue copying. Slip the cover over each copy he makes, or provide a new sheet, so that he cannot copy. This may take many weeks.

b. Family names. In cases of marked aphasia, it may take a great deal of demonstration and pantomiming to teach the patient whose name he is writing. The names of wife, husband and children usually interest a patient. Some patients can say these names and even recognize them in print, but cannot spell them. Often the ability to write the name of a family member turns out to be a very practical and useful skill to one bereft of oral language.

c. Other individual words for practice include the patient's birth place (provided he knows what he is trying to write), the make of his car, his bank, his church, his occupation.

2. Fill the Blanks

With the spelling of a few words from the notebook mastered, the aphasic who has some reading ability is ready to try his skill at filling blanks. He should copy the entire sentence then fill the blank from memory. At first it will be helpful to have the names he needs for the blanks available to him either in a list below the sentences, or visible in his own Personalized Notebook.

Examples: My name is _____.
I live in _____.
My wife's name is _____.
I am a _____ (occupation).
My son's name is _____.

3. Dictation

Use the same material for dictation first using the words like a spelling lesson, then dictating them in pairs as:

Mary—wife
Sambeau—dog
Car—Buick

Next dictate the same material in short sentences, varying them somewhat from Example A2 above.

Examples: Kate is my wife.
My name is Bob.
We live in Long Beach.
John is my son.

B. Practice with Numbers

The Personalized Notebook contains many numbers. A patient may need some practice in copying and in writing numbers in series. Often aphasics can deal with numbers, can add, subtract and even make change, but cannot name or write a number called for in isolation. In answer to such questions as the following, the patient begins to relearn numbers:

How old are you?   How much do you weigh?
When is your birthday?   How tall are you?
How many rooms are in your house?   What size shoes do you wear?
What size shirt do you wear?   How old is John?

The patient with auditory-verbal agnosia (one who does not understand the language he hears) often will profit from a combination of visual and auditory stimulation by filling blanks in exercises to be read aloud and written for him like the following:

I am _____ years old.   My birthday is _____.
I weigh _____ pounds.   I wear size _____ shoes.
I am _____ tall.   We have _____ rooms in our house.

C. For the Amnesic Aphasic

(The patient who has difficulty speaking because he cannot recall names and words, does not know prepositions, connectives, and word order).

1. Begin to work up a basic personal vocabulary by providing opportunity for the patient to recall *and say*, again and again, words, phrases and sentences through drill such as the following:

Therapist: Tell me your name.   *Patient:* Bob Conley.
Therapist: Is your name John?   *Patient:* No, Bob.
Therapist: What is your last
name?   *Patient:* Conley.
Therapist: Let us practice introducing ourselves. My name is Mrs. Brown. (Patient is helped to say, "My name is Bob Conley").

Therapist: Is your father's name Bob?	*Patient:* No, Walter.
Therapist: Is your son's name Walter?	*Patient:* No, John.
2. *Therapist:* Where do you live, Bob?	*Patient:* Long Beach.
Therapist: Is Long Beach in Oregon?	*Patient:* No, in California.
Therapist: Do your children go to school in Los Angeles?	*Patient:* No, in Long Beach.
3. *Therapist:* How much do you weigh?	*Patient:* 152.
Therapist: How tall are you?	*Patient:* 5 feet 8 inches.
4. *Therapist:* Do you do your banking in Santa Ana?	*Patient:* No.
Therapist: Where do you bank?	*Patient:* In Long Beach.
Therapist: What is the name of your bank?	*Patient:* First National.
5. *Therapist:* What make of car have you?	*Patient:* Chevy.
Therapist: What color is your car, green?	*Patient:* No, black and red.
Therapist: Is your car a coupe?	*Patient:* No, a four-door.
Therapist: You have a black Chevy four-door?	*Patient:* Yes, I have a black Chevy four-door.

D. Reading Lessons

1. Recovery of reading often begins with recognition of individual words.
The patient may be able to recognize that the words, Bob Conley, are his name but may not be able to read them aloud. Write his name for him; ask him to read it aloud. It may help him to write the name "in the air;" also show him the B position of the lips. Amnesic aphasics often can go ahead after they get a clue for the beginning of a word such as the lip position for the B in Bob. Let the patient watch the pencil or chalk movement as the word is written for him. Ask him to trace the word in large movements using his first two fingers.

2. Write several names in a list and ask the patient to point out his own name.

John Smith
Henry Brown
Bob Conley
Arthur Adams

Use other names such as those of his wife, a child, or a favorite family pet. Make two rows for matching such as the following. Ask the patient to connect matching pairs with a line.

Bob	church
Sambeau	wife
Kate	dog
John	me
Presbyterian	son

Note: This is an exercise that can go on for many months. The main point is to use and re-use the same basic personal vocabulary over and over again.

    3. Use short sentences for both oral reading and reading comprehension.

My name is Bob.	My wife's name is Kate.
My dog's name is Sambeau.	I am Bob Conley. .
Sambeau is my dog.	John is my son.

E. For the Motor Aphasic[1] (the patient who cannot speak because he no longer knows how to place his lips and tongue to form the sounds).

    1. It is best to select names and words with beginning sounds easily seen on the lips, for example, the name Bob. Sit before the mirror with the patient. Show him the mouth position for the B sound. The name, Bob, actually involves very little more than closing, opening and closing the mouth. If the patient has difficulty moving his lips because of an apraxia,[2] with the thumb and forefinger gently push his lower lip to meet the upper lip then draw it down again to form the bah sound, then close the lips again for the final B sound (Bah-B, Bob).

---

1. An attempt to use names and words from the Personalized Notebook which begin with "hidden" sounds (those produced far back in the throat) such as k, g, and r would be very discouraging to the patient when a search through the material certainly would reveal easier beginning practice words. For example: army, baseball, Sambeau (the dog), TV, wife, Ford. Names of endearment such as Honey, Dearie, Dad, Sonny, or nicknames may be substituted for difficult family names.

2. See: Terms, Appendix.

    Presentation of Consonant Sounds, Chapter 11, Section III.

Chapter 8

VISUAL AND AUDITORY AIDS
(Recorders and Other Equipment)

I. INTRODUCTION[1]

ATTENTIVE LISTENING to all types of recorded language including radio, television, disc and tape recordings and the movies is invaluable for aphasics. Television and movies have the advantage of providing both visual and auditory stimulation simultaneously. Early emphasis on auditory perception and recognition establishes and re-enforces language patterns. But occasionally an aphasic patient no longer shows an interest in the radio, in television or in the movies, and friends and relatives are perplexed by the change in him. Very often this is because the patient has an auditory-verbal agnosia and cannot understand spoken language sufficiently to follow the news, a plot, or conversation at any length. Sometimes he also has developed double vision, or a hemianopia[2] or a quadrantanopia, which affects his vision to the extent that sustained viewing is annoying.

Although an aphasic may comprehend short sentences spoken at intervals, often he cannot maintain extended listening. He becomes fatigued and confused and loses out entirely. If the patient has been a sports enthusiast, he may still be interested in watching ball games on TV. This is good therapy because he knows essentially what the announcer should say in his description of the play and is therefore apt to recognize the language.

Use of a tape recorder, and particularly the Language Master, is one means of encouraging self-help and self-correction. If the patient can be encouraged and motivated to use recorded material, he can become more self-reliant and thus lessen his dependence on the therapist or family members by "practicing" alone with the recorder at many intervals during the day. Short practice sessions several times a day are less fatiguing and more productive than a long session.

II. THE TAPE RECORDER (Auditory Aid)

In the early stages of retraining, tape on which the therapist and the patient record the particular material suited to the patient's immediate needs is especially helpful.

---

1. *Note:* Although the market today offers many mechanical and commercial aids to speech therapy, their potential seldom supplants the support of a trained speech therapist, resourceful school teacher or home member who, with pad, pencil, magazine and scissors can devise many effective therapy materials.
2. See Terms: Appendix.

The tape recorder provides a good medium for auditory training, for denoting the patient's progress, for diagnoses, criticism and lesson planning, and for demonstration purposes and permanent records. Recordings of repetitious drill material, naming exercises and motor-pattern practice serve to economize the time and effort of the busy therapist or home member.

Recordings by the patient provide him with "tailor-made" material for self appraisal and criticism. When he can operate the recorder himself or with the help of a family member, he can benefit from additional practice between therapy sessions and during the absence of the therapist. The motor aphasic will find the tape recorder more amenable to his retraining than will the amnesic aphasic who sometimes becomes frustrated at his inability to recall language he thinks worthy of a recording. Listening to himself, and becoming aware of his paraphasia and correcting it is one of the best techniques a paraphasic patient can use. Of course, the recorder should never be used if it is traumatizing to a patient.

Since it is almost impossible to write down from memory or from shorthand notes the jumble of language resulting from paraphasia and jargon, recordings are almost the only means by which evidence of these aphasia defects can be studied or preserved.

III. TECHNIQUES WITH THE TAPE RECORDER[3]

Making Recordings. Recordings for the exercises suggested in this section can easily be made in the clinic or home. Daily lessons and practice material used for only one session can be erased by recording new material on the same tape later on. Other recordings of commands, interviews, paraphasic language, and the like may be filed for reference. After an oral command, ample time should be allowed for the patient to carry out the order uninterrupted by the next command.

REMARKS	EXERCISES
A. Identifying sounds develops the patient's auditory perception and provides recall and drill in naming the sounds. It is not sufficient to ask the patient if he recognizes these sounds. His reply of yes or no is not a true indication of recognition. Require him to demonstrate by imitation, or	**A. Naming Sounds** Ask the patient to identify by imitating or naming. *Example:* A laugh, the ring of the telephone, a cough, car horn, whistle, a clap of the hands, footsteps on the floor or pavement, sound of a hammer, water running from the faucet, the vac-

---

3. Pocket-size tape recorders now on the market for less than $25 serve very well for speech therapy when larger and more expensive recorders are not practical.

actually to tell what is going on in the recordings.

B. This exercise provides stimulation for oral formulation. The patient might be able to relate that someone walked across the room, went out the door, got into the car and drove away; or he may indicate his understanding of the recording by means of a combination of gesture and telegraphic speech.

C. Carrying out commands provides retraining in the understanding of spoken language. If a patient is in a wheelchair or is right hemiplegic, of course he should not be given such commands as Stand up, or Raise your right hand. When making this recording, allow time after each command for the patient to carry it out.

D. These commands provide orientation of body scheme and laterality.

E. This technique helps re-establish speech patterns. If the therapist says, "On Sunday I go to ch____" and then hesitates, the

uum cleaner, alarm clock, clatter of dishes, lawn mower.

B. Oral Formulation
The patient is to tell what is taking place in the recording.
Example:
1. Sounds recorded in some sort of sequence such as footsteps, a slamming door, the sound of a car starter and the shift of gears.
2. Recording of a birthday party.
3. Christmas Dinner; New Year's Eve.

C. Auditory Training
The patient is to carry out such commands as:
1. Hold up your hand.
2. Stand up.
3. Shake hands.
4. Sit down.
5. Point to the *window*.
6. Pick up the *pencil*.
7. Open the *door*.
8. Show me the *book*.

D. Use of Body Scheme and Laterality
The patient is to carry out such commands as:
1. Point to your *nose*. (Allow time)
2. Show me your *left hand*.
3. Point to your *left knee*.
4. Show me your *right eye*.
5. Brush your *hair*.

E. Practice of Phonetic Sounds
Example: Record the "ch" sound repeated several times. (See Motor Speech Section, for

force of automatic speech often leads the patient to add the word "church."

Better Speech and Better Reading by Lucille Schoolfield contains good material for recordings of this type.

Write the sentences so that the patient can see and hear them at the same time. Encourage him to read the sentences aloud with the voice on the recording.

the ch sound.) Use the ch sound in a sentence as *I go to church.* Extend the exercise with such questions as: "Where do you go on Sunday?"

Answer: "I go to church on Sunday."

Question: "Who takes you to church?"

Answer: "My wife takes me to church."

Reenforce the ch sound by use of additional ch words:

chick	chin	chop
child	check	chew
chum	chain	

F. A recording of his reading of prose and poetry allows the patient to appraise his own voice, diction and enunciation. With simultaneous auditory and visual stimulation, retraining in reading comprehension is provided when the patient silently reads the text as he hears it spoken on the recording. Play back the recordings as often as needed. Make corrections; drill on difficult sound combinations.

F. Auditory and Visual Stimulation

Record the patient's own productions. Sources of reading material:

1. Newspaper headlines and short articles.

2. Literary Digest Skill Builders.

3. Jingles, nursery rhymes and short poems.

4. Memorized prose and poems.

G. The interview serves as a test in many areas of language:

1. Comprehension of spoken language.

2. Motor speech patterns.

3. Oral language formulation.

4. Arithmetic and concept of numbers.

5. Naming of objects, places and people.

6. Reading recognition.

G. Recording a Conversation

The therapist first records the necessary identifying information such as, "Following is a conversation with (name) on (date). Sample interview questions:

1. What is your name? Reply _____.

2. Where do you live? Reply _____.

3. Can you say Methodist Episcopal?

7. Orientation of body scheme and laterality.

Tape should be reserved at the close of this recording so that a second recording may be added later. It is often interesting to use the same questions much later when the patient has improved. This provides excellent material for comparison purposes. The entire recording is an accurate permanent record.

4. Can you say Massachusetts?

5. What direction is Massachusetts from California?

6. What kind of work do you do?

7. Show me your left hand.

8. Point to your right knee. Therapist replies in the affirmative if the patient complies.

9. What do you like for breakfast?

10. How far can you count?

11. Tell me the days of the week.

12. What month is this?

13. How much is 4 x 5; 4 plus 9; 36 divided by 4; 6 minus 2.

14. Can you write CAT? (Therapist describes in the recording the patient's success at writing.)

15. Write the name of this article. (Therapist names it correctly *after* patient has given his answer.)

16. Will you read what I have written on the board? (If patient does not read correctly, the therapist follows with a correct reading of it.)

17. Name these coins. (Therapist places coins before the patient one at a time and records his success at identifying them.)

18. What color is the American flag?

19. Who is President of the United States?

20. How many states are there in the U.S.?

21. Close with some appropriate friendly conversation.

H. Retelling Stories

Provide recorded short stories and anecdotes to which the patient is to listen then retell in his own words. The therapist may record this material or encourage "advanced" readers from therapy classes to do so. Commercial records for this type of exercise are listed in Section V below. Refer to the treatment of paraphasia by means of recordings, Chapter 14, Section II, A.

IV. RECORD PLAYER AND RECORDINGS (Auditory Aid)

A. Comprehension

Discs for long periods of listening and for language comprehension and literary appreciation are available for record players. Dealers and public libraries stock albums including the Bible, poems, short stories and excerpts from famous authors. These records are narrated by well-known present-day personalities.

Send for catalog:

Literature for Listening—Audio Book Co., St. Joseph, Mich.

Discs for the record player:

Holy Bible—(Protestant and Catholic editions).

Red Badge of Courage—Stephen Crane, read by Robert Ryan or Edmund O'Brien.

Great Tales and Poems of Edgar Allan Poe—Read by Marvin Miller.

Dr. Jekyl and Mr. Hyde—Robert Louis Stevenson, read by Gene Lockhart.

The Best of Mark Twain—Marvin Miller.

The Wizard of Oz—Marvin Miller.

Abraham Lincoln—Raymond Massey.

Plato (Trial of Socrates and Two Dialogues)—Thomas Mitchell.

New Testament—Voice of Scripture, 944 So. Prairie Ave., Hawthorne, Calif.

Psalms—Judith Anderson.

In the Beginning—Charlton Heston.

Old Testament Readings—Charles Laughton.

Leaves of Grass—Dan O'Herlihy.

Book of David—Judith Anderson.

Diego Rivera—in Spanish.

Psalms—Maurice Carnowsky.

See Children's Section for additional listings, Chapter 27, Section V.

B. Music

Aphasics fond of music may enjoy singing along with records of favorite songs. While words may come rather easily with the association of the tune, this type of therapy is diversional rather than therapy for the recall of *spoken* words. The skill of singing the words does not necessarily transfer to the speech area. Songs with repetitive refrains are listed in Chapter 11, Section XII, f.

V. THE LANGUAGE MASTER (Visual and Auditory Aid)[4]

A. The Language Master

A portable electronics device somewhat resembling a tape recorder, this is designed for vocabulary building, diction training and language stimulation. It is operated by the insertion of a $3\frac{1}{2}$ x 9-inch card on which is mounted a strip of sound tape. As the card makes contact, a voice pronounces the words printed on the card together with their phonetic counterpart and picture or definition. The price of the Language Master is comparable to that of the best tape recorder. Cards are priced (1962) at $35 per set of 200. The library of cards consists of six series: The Vocabulary Builder Series, Word Learning Picture Series, Language Stimulation Series, English Development Series, Basic English Phonetics, The Phonics Series.

B. Lesson Plan Using Series II, Set I—Everyday Things

Set I consists of 100 cards each containing a word, a picture and the recorded pronunciation in the following categories: clothing, people, foods, parts and furnishings of a house, colors, personal items and possessions.

First, teach the patient to operate the machine by running several cards through, pronouncing the words with the voice on the recorded tape, which is a part of the card. Encourage the patient to take charge, showing him how to set apart in a separate stack the words he cannot say. He may find it necessary to pronounce the words *with* and *after* the voice for many sessions.

Next, let the patient read the word orally *before* he puts the card into the machine, using the voice to verify or to check his own pronunciation of it.

Test for carryover by assembling a set of pictures of the same items cut and mounted from magazine advertisements or sketched on cards. On the backs of the cards print or write the accompanying words. Test the patient by running through both the pictured side for naming and the printed side

---

4. *Language Master*—Bell and Howell Company, 7100 McCormick Road, Chicago 45, Ill. Schuell, Hildred: *How the Language Master Helps Us to Treat Aphasics.* (Text-Film News, Vol 5, No. 2, March 1957, McGraw-Hill Book Company, 330 West 42 St., New York, N. Y.)

for oral reading. Set aside the cards not well learned so that the patient can sort out the electronic counterparts for review and drill.

VI. THE 35 MM PROJECTOR (Visual Aid)

The 35mm projector has many uses particularly if the patient has been a color slide enthusiast and has a library of slides which are of special interest to him. Commercial slides are available in many camera shops, in drug and department stores. These are usually of local and regional interest. Listings of color slides may be secured from:

a. Color Classics, Arizona Highways, Phoenix, Ariz.
b. Panorama Colorslide Travel Program (with recorded narrative), 111 Fifth Avenue, New York 3, N. Y.
c. Artco Color Slides, Box 455, Van Nuys, Calif.
d. Reeves Visual Education, Box 3164 Hillcrest Station, San Diego, Calif.
e. Wolfe Worldwide Slides in HiFi Color, 1657 Sawtelle Blvd. Box 25903, Los Angeles 25, Calif.
f. Atkins Travel Slides, Inc., 2036 Balboa St., San Francisco 21, Calif.
g. Colonial Color Productions, 611 Magill Road, Box 247, Swarthmore, Pa.
h. Blackhawk Films, Davenport, Iowa.

Viewmaster sets such as Sawyers View-Master Stereo Picture Sets are available for viewing through a binocular-type viewer, or by projection through an electric toy projector. These inexpensive sets of transparencies offer almost as many possibilities as expensive 35 mm equipment.

Sometimes a showing of slides can be used for diversional purposes—a quiet viewing allowing comments to come, or not to come, as they may. On the other hand, interesting and instructive lessons can be built around slides. Such a lesson for advanced oral formulation is outlined in Chapter 13, Section III. This lesson, modified somewhat, is effective for visual recognition.

VII. THE OPAQUE PROJECTOR (Visual Aid)

An opaque projector such as the Vu-Lyte (Charles Beseler Company, East Orange, New Jersey) occasionally is useful in a large clinic with group therapy and for demonstrations before large audiences. This device projects opaque material such as pages from a book, maps, an individual's written work, drawings, diagrams, etc.

Several small opaque projectors 12" x 8" x $4\frac{1}{2}$" with various trade names such as Magnajector, Microscope Projector, etc., are now on the market for less than $10 which will project 3½-inch illustrations to four feet in size. Such a device has possibilities for the therapist whose practice necessitates small, portable equipment.

VIII. MISCELLANEOUS VISUAL AIDS

1. Blackboard (almost indispensable in any situation).
2. Stereoptican.
3. Magic Slate (available in variety, drug and department stores; inexpensive; light weight; easily replaced; unbreakable).
4. Flannel Boards.

Chapter 9

AUDITORY RECOGNITION
(Auditory-Verbal Agnosia) [1]

I. INTRODUCTION

APHASIA PATIENTS with auditory-verbal agnosia no longer can understand spoken language. Family members and friends tend to speak louder to these patients thinking they do not understand because they can't hear.[2] While audiometric tests often are administered in order to rule out a hearing loss, a loud voice adds nothing toward helping an aphasic patient interpret what he hears. He may hear and recognize correctly such non-language sounds as the ringing of a bell or a knock at the door but this is no indication that he can interpret words. The speech of this type of patient is often paraphasic.[3] Since auditory stimulation and perception are imperative in almost all learning situations, recovery from auditory-verbal agnosia is important to the restoration of all other language functions. Fortunately this defect is often among the earliest to recover.

Retraining for auditory-verbal agnosia stresses mainly the use of auditory stimulation; nevertheless visual clues also play an important part. Throughout the day the patient hears a barrage of spoken language which reenforces auditory recognition: requests, directions, conversation, radio, television, and movies.

II. TECHNIQUES

REMARKS

A. Since many aphasics are confused in body scheme,[4] they will receive dual training from this exercise, relearning the names of body parts and gaining auditory recognition of the names.

EXERCISES

A. Using Oral Commands

Give the patient oral commands to be carried out.

Examples:

1. Point to your nose; point to your ear, to your eye, etc.

---

1. Nielsen, J. M.: *A Textbook of Clinical Neurology,* Third Edition. Paul B. Hoeber, Inc. New York, N. Y., page 250.
   Reinhold, Margaret: A case of auditory agnosia. *Brain Journal,* Vol. 73, page 203, 1950.
2. Street, Barbara S.: Hearing loss in aphasia. *Journal of Speech and Hearing Disorders,* Vol. 22, No. 1, March 1957.
3. See Paraphasia—Terms, Appendix.
4. MacDonald, Joanne C.: An investigation of body scheme in adults with cerebral vascular accidents. *American Journal of Occupational Therapy,* Vol. XIV, No. 2, March-April 1960.

This type of exercise can be used for many months and should be increasingly more complex as the patient improves.

2. Point to the door, to the window, etc.

3. Hand me a book from the table.

B. Using Pictures of Single Objects

Show the patient a group of pictures of single items (with no printing or names visible). Pronounce aloud the name of each article pictured and ask the patient to point out the corresponding picture.
Examples:

1. Toilet articles: soap, towel, razor, comb.

2. Clothing: shoes, pants, tie, shirt, shorts, coat, socks.

3. Animals: dog, cat, cow, horse.

C. An interesting technique consists of assembling table service such as a plate, knife, fork, and spoon, cup and saucer, pitcher, sugar bowl, salt and pepper, coffee pot, and napkin. Carry out a lesson as suggested at the right.

Other suggested properties: cigarettes, matchbook, ash tray, lighter; razor, towel, comb, brush, toothbrush.

C. Using a Practical Situation

Enter into a make-believe lunch with such questions and commands as:

1. Please pour me some coffee.
2. May I have the sugar and cream?
3. May I pour you some coffee?
4. Do you use sugar? Help yourself.
5. Pour your coffee on the floor. (This is such a surprise command that the patient can hardly believe his ears!)

D. If the patient also has alexia, he will not be able to do this exercise until his reading problem has, at least, been partially resolved.

D. Using Individual Words for Auditory Recognition

Write the word list on the board. As the therapist pronounces the words, the patient is to show auditory recognition by pointing to each one as it is read (not in order).

1. Body parts: head, hand, eye, ear, nose, mouth, knee, elbow, chin, foot, chest, waist, back, wrist, etc.
2. Objects in the room: window, flowers, curtain, chair, table, picture, door.

III. USING READING MATERIALS

A. Silent reading materials
  1. newspapers
  2. current magazines

A. Following Silent Reading
Direct the patient to follow an article silently while the therapist reads the article aloud. The therapist then tests the patient's ability to identify the printed word with the oral one by stopping at various points and asking the patient to read the next word.

B. Group reading materials:
  1. daily newspaper
  2. current magazines

B. Using Group Reading
A group practice which is entertaining consists of having each member read aloud from a selection; whenever one stops suddenly, the next member is to continue.

IV. USING NUMBERS

A. A list of arithmetic texts may be found at the close of the Arithmetic Section, Chapter 17.

A. Arithmetic Problems
Read aloud simple arithmetic problems which the patient is to solve from hearing them.
Examples:
  1. Multiplication: $6 \times 7 =?$
                   $8 \times 4 =?$
  2. One pencil costs six cents; how much will five pencils cost?

B. Numbers in Series
Give the patient oral numbers in series for completion.

Examples:
1. 2-4-6-8-10-?-?-?
2. 5-10-15-20-25-30-?-?-? etc.

V. LESSON PLAN: GROUP THERAPY FOR AUDITORY-VERBAL RECOGNITION

Seat the group around a table. Assemble on the table a group of articles such as:

1. pen, pencil, paper, book, eraser
2. soap, wash cloth, razor, comb, clothes brush, toothbrush, towel
3. a set of pictures of a house, a barn, a car, a bus, a lawnmower, a taxi
4. package of cigarettes or pipe, lighter or matches, coffee pot, coffee cup, creamer, sugar.
5. thimble, scissors, thread, tape measure, scrap of goods.

A. Practice for Auditory Recognition of the Articles by Name

1. Have the patients (by turns) touch the articles as the therapist names them. (Use gesture and demonstration to help the most severely handicapped patients get the idea of what is wanted.) Repeat the name of the article as often as is needed.
2. Let the patients take their turn at asking one another for the various articles.

B. Increase the Complexity of the Commands

1. Ask one patient to give an article to another patient calling the patient by name. Example: John, pick up the pencil. Now give the pencil to Ed; Ed, lay the pencil down.
2. Use more than one article in the command. Example: Ed, pick up the pencil and the book. Give the book to Bill and the pencil to John.

C. Introduce Prepositions (This may be many months later.)

Example: Bill, put the pencil *under* the book.
John, put the pen *in* your pocket.
Ed, fold the paper and put it *under* the table.

D. Combine Objects with Boby Scheme

Example: Bill, put the pencil *over* your ear.
Ed, put the book *under* your arm.
John, put the pen *over* Ed's ear

E. Use Group Participation

Very likely a group working on auditory recognition as described above, will also profit from the reenforcement of oral work during the exercises. Let a patient (instead of the therapist) give the commands as described above. Then let another patient tell what the command was. Often the execution of the command will not be accurate. Encourage patients to detect errors and to help make the corrections.

> *Example: JOHN:* Ed, pick up the comb. (Ed complies.)
>
> *JOHN:* Ed, give the comb to Bill. (Ed complies.)
>
> *JOHN:* Bill, put the comb in your pocket. (Let us assume that Bill combs his hair instead of placing the comb in his pocket. Some of the patients likely will notice the error and will make the correction.)

VI. REFERENCES

Longerich, Mary C.: *Manual for the Aphasia Patient.* The Macmillan Company, New York, N. Y., Part III, Drills for Receptive Aphasia.

Travis, L. E.: *Handbook of Speech Pathology.* Appleton-Century-Crofts, Inc., New York, N. Y., page 492.

Also refer to techniques suggested in Visual and Auditory Aids, Chapter 8.

Chapter 10

NAMING AND RECALL
(Anomia and Amnesic Aphasia) [1]

I. INTRODUCTION

Some aphasic patients have an inability to recall names of objects, people and places. This is called anomia. When this defect is severe, patients are not able to recall the names of the most common objects. Aphasics with this type of defect frequently make such statements as, "I know what it is, but I can't tell you—it's nice to look at—on the wall—pretty." (picture). They talk *around* the subject as they mentally search for its name. Even though the anomic patient cannot readily say the word he is searching for, he usually can recognize it when he hears someone else say it. He will reject any number of wrong words read from a list, then readily accept the correct one.

Anomia is not the result of involvement of the tongue and lips; it is a loss of recall. Of course, some patients have both a motor defect *and* anomia. In this case, a patient may distort the pronunciation of a word even after he recalls it or has it supplied for him.

Conversely, some anomic patients, once they have recalled a word, cannot keep from repeating it over and over. This is called perseveration.[2] The patient cannot shift and uses the perseverating word or phrase to fill in for other words he cannot express. Perseveration may take the form of a word or even a jargon phrase such as One-o-one, one-o-one.

The amnesic aphasic, besides having difficulty recalling nouns, may also have difficulty recalling verbs, adjectives, adverbs, and prepositions. However, after he has found the naming word, he may recall other words more readily through association.

II. TECHNIQUES

REMARKS	EXERCISES
A. Words for naming practice are presented with many associations. Actual objects should be shown. For example, training kits containing	**A. Naming Objects** 1. Basic Technique a. Show the object to be named, then write the word on

---

1. Nielsen, J. M.: *Memory and Amnesia.* San Lucas Press, Los Angeles, Calif., 1958, page 175.
    ———: *Textbook of Clinical Neurology*, page 280.

2. See **Lesson Plan on Perseveration**, Chapter 10, Section IV; also Samples of Patients' Work, Chapter 19.

toilet articles, items of clothing, table service, tools, fruits, flowers, study materials, woman's workbasket of needles, thread, scissors, thimble, etc., can easily be assembled. Miniature articles and toys are good substitutes.

b. Review is necessary day after day. At the close of each therapy session, it is well to run through the items studied for the day with the simple question, "What is this—and this—and this.....?"

2. Since the patient is usually learning to read at the same time that he is relearning names, use short meaningful sentences written on the board. The patient may attempt to read the whole sentence, or simply may supply the naming word to complete the sentence read by the therapist.

3. When actual objects or pictures are not available, stick figures or simple outline sketches on the blackboard are effective.

the board and pronounce it. Next, direct the patient to write the word and to pronounce it. Give the object to the patient to handle. Let him outline a line drawing or picture of the article with his finger. Ask him to repeat the naming word several times.

b. After some intervening conversation, the therapist again asks the patient for a recall of the new words.

2. Supplying the naming word
Sample sentences:

    a. I see the *picture*.
    b. I go to the *gym*.
    c. I read my *book*.
    d. I write a *letter*.
    e. I want *paper* and *pencil*.

3. Using line drawings
Use the same technique as above with the addition of line drawings.

The man wears a *hat*.
The *cat* is black.

4. Association and recall are

4. Recall from memory

further heightened by suggesting a familiar situation. Here the patient must recall names without seeing the item or a picture of it.

Example:
Therapist: Today we are going to visit the canteen. What could you buy at the canteen?
1st Patient: toothpaste, toothbrush.
2nd Patient: shaving cream.
3rd Patient: ice cream, soda, cigarettes.

5. The use of pictures greatly increases the scope of subjects which can be touched upon in naming practice. The therapist can be sure he has provided consistent repetition when he presents the same picture file for review after appropriate lapses of time. Pictures cut from colored advertisements in magazines and mounted on tag board are space saving and economical. This type of material can be kept fresh and up-to-date.

5. Using Pictures
   Use pictures in the same way as actual items are used. Present them, one at a time, to a group or to an individual. Often a good deal of side conversation arises from this technique.
A suggested file of pictures: animals, cars, clothing, farm, birds, fish, flags, famous places, flowers, food, fruit, holidays, house-home, money, music instruments, well-known people, athletics-sports, travel, toilet articles, vehicles, utensils-tools, occupations-jobs, action pictures for verbs, weather.

6. Using Recordings (Refer to Visual and Auditory Aids, Chapter 8). A stimulating technique consists of playing a tape recording on which have been recorded associated sounds such as a baby crying, a bell ringing, a dog barking, etc. The patient is to listen to them then tell the names of the sounds he hears. The same exercise can be carried out when it is convenient to listen to the radio and T.V.

B. Suggested Categories of Words Useful for Naming Exercises
   1. Hospital Vocabulary: nurse, doctor, bed, pills, water, latrine, O. T., P. T., gym., canteen, bank, mess hall, clothes, ward, visitors, mail—letter, book, pencil, shop, show, pass, telephone.
   2. Home Vocabulary: wife (Mary), car, dog, water (drink), door, toilet, bedroom, kitchen, living room, bathroom, children (Betty, Bob), garage, TV, hall, porch.
   3. Clothes Vocabulary: shirt, shoes, undershirt, pants, slippers, shorts, socks, tie, sweater, pajamas, coat, hat, blouse, dress.
   4. Food and Drink Vocabulary: Use the patient's favorite foods and

drinks. It is often helpful to have the patient use other senses such as touching, smelling, tasting, and hearing when identifying objects. This technique is helpful with items of food using taste and smell; and with T. V., radio, and records or tape recordings for the hearing sense.

C. Suggested Units
1. Types of Travel: car, plane, bus, boat, train.
2. Machines: tractor, plow, combine, disc, sewing machine, washer and dryer.
3. Seasons, days, months, holidays.
4. Colors.
5. Town Facilities: stores, garage, cleaners, bank, hotel, railway station, post office, service station, beauty parlor.
6. Body Parts: ear, chin, arm, face, leg, elbow, head, knee, thumb, neck, chest, foot, back, mouth (It is quite common for aphasics to have lost the ability to name body parts.)
7. Toilet Articles: toothbrush, soap, razor, comb, towel.
8. Occupations: barber, chef, teacher, carpenter, doctor, stenographer, clerk.
9. From the Personalized Notebook: family names, hobbies and interests, places and types of work, friends, military service. (See Personalized Notebook, Chapter 7.)

D. Patients who have motor aphasia as well as anomia may be able at first to say only words which are very easy to imitate and to pronounce. See Chapter 11 on Motor Speech Patterns, Section VII, Reading for Motor Aphasics.

D. Naming Exercises for the Motor Aphasic
Select naming words plainly visible on the lips. The word pipe is a better choice for the motor aphasic than "pajama;" "eye" and "arm" are easier to pronounce than "shoulder." Sit before the mirror when working with this type of patient so that he can take advantage of visual *and* auditory clues.

III LESSON PLAN FOR NAMING
This lesson is based on a common useful object, a hammer.
1. Show the actual article. Ask what it is. The patient may or may not be able to name it.
2. Show pictures of different types of hammers: claw, ball peen.
3. Ask the patient to handle the hammer.
4. Ask the patient to demonstrate its use.

5. Demonstrate pounding sounds.

6. Ask the patient to say the word "hammer." If he has difficulty, demonstrate the initial consonant h—like a sigh. He may recognize the first syllable "ham" from previous lessons. Ask him to use this as the first syllable of the word "hammer" and lead him into saying the entire word.

7. Say the word "hammer" aloud on each presentation.

8. Write the word "hammer" on the board. Let the patient write the word.

9. Associate the word in sentence context: the carpenter uses a *hammer*.

10. Pair the word with such words as *nail* and *saw*.

Other words to use for such a drill include pencil, book, shoes, sandwich, popcorn, coffee, necktie.

IV. LESSON PLAN ON PERSEVERATION

1. In either written or oral work a patient may repeat the same word, syllable or letters many times. For example, in writing the word *man*, the patient may make six or seven "humps" on the final n, thus: mannnnnn; in writing the word *wash*, he may write washshshshshsh. In speaking he may consecutively name every part of the body "knee," or may name all the foods on the table "pie," "pie."

To help the patient correct this, interject a verbal interruption to break the perseveration in oral language; in written work provide strips of paper too narrow for repetition of the letters, or stay the pencil stroke at the proper place. In any event the patient should be interrupted to prevent his establishing an incorrect pattern of perseveration.

2. Word List: bow, bean, beat, bare, bite, bail, bake, bay.

In reading the above list of words, suppose the patient is successful with the first three: bow, bean, beat, then suppose he perseverates on the word *bare* and is not able to go to the word *bite*. First, it may be helpful to try some association for the word *bite* such as, Watch out, that dog might _____! If the patient still perseverates on the word *bare*, began at the beginning of the list, omit the word bare, and go on to the next word, bite. Do this several times. Then try again to get through the list including the word *bare*.

3. Some motor cases find it almost impossible to repeat a word several times in succession. This is almost like perseveration in reverse in that the word refuses to come again and again. Allow rest periods of a few seconds, then try again for a repetition of the word.

V. REFERENCES

Dolch, E. W.: *Dolch Cards.* The Hart Vance Company, St. Louis 3, Mo.

Longerich, Mary C.: *Longerich Aphasia Therapy Sets.* 2007 Wilshire Blvd., Los Angeles 57, Calif.

McCausland, Margaret, Miller, Marie B., and Okie, Isabel: *Speech Through Pictures.* Expression Company, Magnolia, Mass.

Oftedal, Laura, and Jacob, Nina: *My First Dictionary.* Grosset and Dunlap, New York, N. Y.

Taylor, Martha L., and Marks, Morton: *Aphasia Rehabilitation Manual and Therapy Kit.* Saxon Press, 207 East 37th Street, New York 16, N. Y.

Utley, Jean: *What's Its Name.* University of Illinois Press, Urbana, Ill.

Walpole, Ellen Wales: *The Golden Dictionary.* Simon and Schuster, New York, N. Y.

Watters, Garnette, and Courtis, S. A.: *The Picture Dictionary for Children.* Grosset and Dunlap, New York, N. Y.

Wright, Wendell W.: *The Rainbow Dictionary.* World Publishing Company, New York, N. Y.

The Language Master—Chapter 8, Section V.

＊　＊　＊　＊　＊

Nielsen, J. M.: *Memory and Amnesia.* San Lucas Press, Los Angeles, 1958, Recall, page 17, 28, Amnesic Aphasia, page 175.

———: *Textbook of Clinical Neurology,* Third Edition. Paul B. Hoeber, Inc., New York 16, N. Y., 1951, Anomia, page 281; Amnesic Aphasia, pages 281, 461.

Travis, L. E.: *Handbook of Speech Pathology.* Appleton-Century-Crofts, Inc., New York, N. Y., pages 492, 499.

Wepman, Joseph M., *et al.:* Psycholinguistic study of aphasia; revision of the concept of anomia. *Journal of Speech and Hearing Disorders,* Vol. 21, No. 4, Dec. 1956.

Note: See Chapter 11, Section XII for Lesson Plan for Correlating Speech Drill, Reading, Writing, Singing.

MOTOR SPEECH PATTERNS
(Motor Aphasia or Apraxia of Speech) [1]

I. INTRODUCTION

A PATIENT WITH a motor speech defect no longer can execute the movements for spoken words because of an inability to recall the motor patterns of speech. This defect, known as motor aphasia or apraxia of speech results in difficulty in combining speech sounds into syllables and words. Although his ability to *recall* words remains intact, the patient has lost the memory of the movements for producing words. However, he can still use the speech organs for chewing, swallowing, clearing his throat and pursing his lips. This defect ranges from a complete inability to produce intelligible sounds to a telegraphic-type speech which is characterized by the omission of prepositions, connectives and modifiers.

Exercises for the motor aphasic are also helpful for the dysarthric. The dysarthric who has no accompanying aphasia defects knows the sounds he should make, but poor muscular control results in distorted words.

A distinction must be made between an apraxia of speech and an apraxia of the mouth. An apraxia of the mouth is an inability *on command* to protrude the tongue, purse the lips, show the teeth, although the patient can make these same movements spontaneously when they are not related to language.

II. EXERCISES FOR APRAXIA OF THE MOUTH

In the early stages of language retraining for the motor aphasic, the patient is usually dependent on imitation of the therapist directly or in a mirror, or upon manipulation of the patient's speech musculature.[2] A large mirror should be available in the working area, preferably hanging above a work table or desk.

---

1. Nielsen, J. M.: *A Textbook of Clinical Neurology.* Paul B. Hoeber, Inc., New York, N. Y., pp. 268, 284.

   ————: Motor aphasia with recovery, *Bulletin of the Los Angeles Neurological Society,* Vol. 22, No. 3, September 1957.

   Travis, L. E.: *Handbook of Speech Pathology.* Appleton-Century-Crofts, New York, N. Y., pp. 494, 495.

2. The Edna Hill Young Moto-Kinesthetic method is effective where actual manipulation is indicated and when a therapist especially trained in the method is available. (Text listed in bibliography.) Also see Section IX, this Chapter.

REMARKS

A. If the patient has difficulty following directions, use the following techniques:

1. Imitation of the therapist.
2. Manipulation of speech organs.
3. Diagrams of speech musculature.[3]

Exercises in this entire section are helpful for dysarthria. (See Terms, Appendix).

EXERCISES

A. Controlling the Speech Musculature

Ask the patient to do the following either by direct command or in imitation of the therapist:

1. Protrude the tongue.
2. Place the tongue at either corner of the mouth.
3. Touch the inner cheek with the tongue (as the therapist touches the outer cheek).
4. Touch the back teeth and extend the tongue to the roof of the mouth.
5. Whistle or purse the lips as in a kiss.
6. Blow out a match or blow tissue strips.

III. PRESENTATION OF CONSONANT SOUNDS

Note: The use of symbols of the phonetic alphabet with aphasics usually is not practical since to do so only adds new complicated symbols to be learned. However, an understanding of phonetics is helpful to the therapist.

Although the therapist usually selects sounds which can be easily observed on the lips as a starting point, the patient's own ability to make certain sounds will help set the order of presentation. If the patient can make *any* sounds at the outset of retraining, these should be used in order to promote a feeling of success at once. The combination of an initial consonant with an accompanying vowel sound is much more effective than the use of the consonant alone.

A. Show the alphabet letter (not the phonetic symbol) as each new sound is practiced in order to correlate the visual, the auditory and the motor.

As new consonant sounds are mastered, they should be incorporated

A. The Consonant Sounds

1. m— Place the lips lightly together and hum. If patient cannot do this voluntarily, get him to hum a tune, then demonstrate that this is the sound of m.

2. p—Place the lips together, then open them with a soft expul-

---

3. Nemoy, Elizabeth and Davis, Serena: *Correction of Defective Consonant Sounds.* Expression Company, Magnolia, Mass.

into one-syllable words and drilled upon before further consonants are taken up.

3. While it is often expedient to present both voiced and unvoiced counterparts consecutively, it is sometimes difficult for the patient to realize the difference between them. Helpful demonstrations are:

    a. Exaggerating the difference between a loud voiced sound and a soft unvoiced sound;

    b. Using the "hush" gesture to indicate the unvoiced sounds;

    c. Blowing to indicate an airstream for unvoiced sounds.

4. Sample words combining initial consonants with vowels:

may	me	my	mow	moo
pay	pea	pie	Poe	pooh!
bay	bee	by	bow	boo!
Fay	fee	fie	foe	———
———	V	vie	———	———
say	see	sigh	sow	sue
———	———	———	———	zoo
———	tea	tie	toe	two
day	D	die	doe	do
———	———	———	———	chew
jay	———	———	Joe	jew
ray	———	rye	row	rue
lay	lea	lie	low	lieu
nay	knee	nigh	no	new
hay	he	high	hoe	who
K	key	———	———	coo
gay	———	guy	go	———
shay	she	shy	show	shoe
they	thee	thy	though	———

Since almost all sounds can be made with variations in the position of

sion of air. Sometimes this can also be elicited by puffing the smoke of a cigarette or by puffing out a match.

3. **b**—(the voiced counterpart of p) After the p has been formed successfully, it is often possible to elicit its voiced counterpart, b, by asking the patient to put sound to the same pattern.

4. **f**—Bring the lower lip up against the upper teeth and blow. If patient cannot do this, press the underlip with a tongue depressor to help him get the correct position for the sound.

5. **v**—(the voiced counterpart of f) Place the lower lip against the upper teeth, blow and add sound.

6. **s**—Place the teeth nearly together and blow a thin stream of air down the midline of the tongue. Blowing a tissue or a lighted match may be used to elicit the idea of the air stream.

7. **z**—(the voiced counterpart of s) Make s and put a hum or voice to it.

8. **t**—Place the tongue directly behind the upper front teeth to intercept the breath stream, then release the air stream with a downward movement of the tongue.

9. **d**—(the voiced counterpart of t) Make a t with sound added.

10. **ch**—Place the tongue in position for the t sound, then make the sh sound (number 20).

11. **j**—(the voiced counterpart of ch) Make the ch sound and add voice.

12. **r**—(often one of the more diffi-

the tongue, teeth and lips, the suggestions for mouth positions can be flexible.

cult sound for the aphasic) Cough Turn a wide tip of the tongue toward the roof of the mouth and add sound. Sometimes a tongue depressor is useful in helping the patient get the feel of tipping the tongue up.

13. l—Touch the roof of the mouth just behind the upper dental ridge with the tip of the tongue and add sound. It is often helpful to start with the r position then raise the tongue to touch the roof of the mouth.

14. n—Place the tongue against the upper dental ridge and emit sound by a humming sound. The lips remain slightly apart.

15. h—Open the mouth and blow out air like a sigh.

16. c—(k) (often the most difficult sound for the aphasic) cough voluntarily. Allow the patient to feel the therapist's throat while he makes the K sound. Press upward on the patient's throat.

17. g—(the voiced counterpart of k) Make the K sound and add voice. Suggest the frog sound.

18. th—(unvoiced) Place the tongue between the teeth and blow.

19. th—(voiced) Place the tongue between the teeth and add sound.

20. sh—Nearly close the teeth, purse the lips somewhat and blow out a broad stream of air. The concept may be obtained by imitating the "hush" sound.

21. zh—(the voiced counterpart of sh) Make the sh sound and add voice or sound.

B. Vocal Exercises

As a patient becomes proficient in the knowledge of sound movements, he may vary his practice of these sound positions in conjunction with vowel sounds: ma, pa, ta, fa, sa, ka, cha, sha, ba, da, va, za, la, ga, ja, zha.

IV. PRESENTATION OF VOWEL SOUNDS AND DIPHTHONGS[4]

Introduce vowels early, or even first if they are easy for the patient. In the early stages of consonant drill, vowels can be combined to make short words: mow, no, toe, so. Patients often have the memory of the vowel sequence as presented in elementary school: may, me, my, mow, moo.

A. The position of these four vowel sounds can easily be observed as they are formed by the therapist. Continue to work before the mirror as long as necessary.

A. Vowel Sounds Visible on the Lips
Examples:
1. o—as in open
2. e—as in eat
3. { o—as in shop
     a—as in army
4. oo—as in moon

B. The positions of these vowel sounds are more difficult to observe. The vowels can sometimes be elicited by showing the patient the approximate position of the mouth or by repeating the sounds many times.

B. Sounds Requiring Keener Auditory Discrimination
1. i—as in ill, pill
2. e—as in end, men
3. a—as in hat, at
4. u—as in cup
5. oo—as in book
6. a—as in ball
7. u—as in burn

Vowel sounds which require acute auditory discrimination must often be disregarded in retraining an aphasic. Example: a as in *at* contrasted with a as in *ask*.[5]

---

4. Birmingham, Anna, and Krapp, George: *First Lessons in Speech Improvement*. Scribner's Sons, New York, N. Y.
   Fairbanks, Grant: *Voice and Articulation Drill Book*. Harper and Bros. New York, N. Y., Chapters II & III.
   Schoolfield, Lucille D.: *Better Speech and Better Reading*. Expression Company, Magnolia, Mass.
5. See Cultivating Vowel-Sound Discrimination, Chapter 16, Section VI, E.

C. Diphthongs and Vowel Combinations. Diphthongs constitute a combination of vowel sounds.

List of words for practice in vowel combinations:

	(o-oo)	(ah-oo)	(ay-ee)	(ah-ee)	(oi)	(e-oo)
	oak	ouch	ache	eyes	oil	unite
Initial	oat	out	apron	iron	oily	use
	old	owl	ate	ivory	ointment	usual
	————	————	————	————	————	————
	go	cow	day	pie	boy	beauty
Final	hello	plow	pay	sky	enjoy	fuel
	show	brow	clay	fly	toy	cure
	————	————	————	————	————	————
	boat	about	baby	like	boil	acute
Medial	home	down	cake	night	point	Hugh
	pony	house	lace	cried	voice	huge

V. SOUND DRILLS

A. Early sound drills should be limited to an initial consonant plus a single vowel but as soon as practicable should be increased in difficulty by adding a final consonant sound.

A. Examples of Extended Drills Containing Final Consonants.

1. *(may)* *(me)* *(my)* *(mow)* *(moo)*

made	mead	mice	mode	mood
make	meal	Mike	mole	moon
male	meek	mile	moan	moot
mame	mean	mine	mope	
main	meat	might	mower	
maze			moat	
mate			mows	

2.

(pay)	*(pea)*
paid	peach
pale	peak
pace	peal
pave	peep
pain	peas
	Pete
	peeve

3.

(ma)	*(pa)*
mom	pop
mob	pod
mock	par
mop	park

mar
mark

B. Sound drills recommended in III. Presentation of Consonant Sounds above consist of consonants followed by the long sound of the vowels. As soon as practicable add variations of vowel sounds and pair them with the long vowel sounds.

1.
bat	bait	bet	beet	bit	bite	bott	boat	but	boot
fat	fate		feet	fit	fight				
hat	hate		heat	hit	height	hot		hut	hoot
cat	Kate			kit	kite	cot	coat	cut	
pat	pate	pet	Pete	pit		pot		putt	poot
mat	mate	met	meet	mitt	might		moat	mutt	moot
rat	rate			Rit	right	rot	rote	rut	root
sat	sate	set	seat	sit	sight	sot			suit

2.
Kate	cat	caught	cot	coat	kit	kite	cut	cute
bait	bat	bought	bott	boat	bit	bite	but	butte
pain	pan	pawn			pin	pine	pun	
fain	fan	fawn		phone	fin	fine	fun	

C. Increase the length of words.

C. Two-syllable words

1.

maybe	meter
maiden	motor
mainly	mitre
money	

D. Use of Numbers

Ask the patient to give the answers to simple oral-arithmetic combinations for practical drill in using relearned placement of speech musculature.
1. For initial consonants:

The F sound

Therapist:

2 plus 2	....	Patient: four
3 plus 1	....	four
3 plus 2	....	five
4 plus 1	....	five
2 times 7	....	fourteen
3 times 5	....	fifteen
4 times 10	....	forty
5 times 10	....	fifty

The T sound

        1 plus 1   ....two

        4 minus 2   ....two

The TW sound

        10 plus 2   ....twelve

        10 plus 10 ....twenty

        12 plus 12 ....twenty-four

        5 times 5   ....twenty-five

The TH sound

        2 plus 1   ....three

        10 plus 3   ....thirteen

        6 times 5   ....thirty

        7 times 5   ....thirty-five

The N sound

        8 plus 1   ....nine

        3 times 3   ....nine

        10 plus 9   ....nineteen

        10 times 9 ....ninety

The S sound

        5 plus 1   ....six

        10 plus 6   ....sixteen

        10 plus 7   ....seventeen

        6 times 10 ....sixty

        10 times 7 ....seventy

The W sound

        0 plus 1   ....one

        5 minus 4   ....one

        1 times 1   ....one

2. For vowel sounds:

The E sound

        10 plus 1   ....eleven

        6 plus 5   ....eleven

The long A sound

        7 plus 1   ....eight

        2 times 4   ....eight

        10 times 8 ....eighty

        10 plus 8   ....eighteen

VI. BLENDS

Patients with a motor aphasia or dysarthria usually have difficulty with consonant blends. In working out the correct pronunciation of the sample words in the list at the left, help the patient drill several times on the word in column 1, then in column 2 until he can produce them quite fluently before adding column 3, showing the pronunciation.

Sample Words	Column 1	Column 2	Column 3
bread	bed, bed	red, red, red	b-red
bring	bing, bing	ring, ring, ring	b-ring
bright	bite, bite	right, right, right	b-right
black	back, back	lack, lack, lack	b-lack
break	bake, bake	rake, rake, rake	b-rake
brow	bow, bow	row, row, row	b-row
broom	boom, boom	room, room, room	b-room
blow	bow, beau	low, low, low	b-low
clap	cap, cap	lap, lap, lap	c-lap
clean	keen	lean	k-lean
creep	keep	reap	k-reap
drum	dumb	rum	d-rum
drug	dug	rug	d-rug
dry	die	rye	d-rye
dwell	dell	well	d-well
Fred	fed	red	f-red
fright	fight	right	f-right
flea	fee	lea	f-lea
flow	foe	low	f-low
flag	fag	lag	f-lag
free	fee	ree	f-ree
glass	gas	lass	g-lass
glide	guide	lied	g-lied
glow	go	low	g-low
grow	go	row	g-row
gray	gay	ray	g-ray
grain	gain	rain	g-rain
great	gate	rate	g-rate
plump	pump	lump	p-lump
play	pay	lay	p-lay
pray	pay	ray	p-ray
prize	pies	rise	p-rise
spin	sin	pin	s-pin
spill	sill	pill	s-pill
small	Saul	mall	s-mall
smack	sack	Mack	s-mack
skin	sin	kin	s-kin
slow	sew	low	s-low
scold	sold	cold	s-cold
scream	scheme	ream	sk-ream
store	sore	tore	s-tore
snow	sew	no	s-no

Sample Words	Column 1	Column 2	Column 3
snap	sap	nap	s-nap
sled	said	led	s-led
sleep	seep	leap	s-leap
stop	sop	top	s-top
string	sting	ring	st-ring
sweep	seep	weep	s-weep
steel	seal	teal	s-teal
scat	sat	cat	s-cat
try	tie	rye	t-rye
tree	tea	ree	t-ree

VII. READING FOR MOTOR APHASICS

Reading for the motor aphasic actually begins with the inception of speech retraining since sounds or words are seldom presented without their written counterparts. Since the motor aphasic may *understand* the meaning of the words but has primary difficulty in making the correct sounds, the most helpful reading practice is oral reading—an extension of the motor pattern practice.

The consonant and vowel sounds already known to the patient should be predominant in the exercises. Often the choice of words may not necessarily be the most useful, but rather, the most possible phonetically. Flash cards, flannel board, pad and pencil, or blackboard presentations can be used interchangeably to vary the drills. The therapist should discern whether to use printing or cursive writing. Cursive writing is always preferred to printing if the patient can interpret it.

A. Individual words usually constitute beginning reading drills.

A. **Individual Words for Reading Drill from Pad or Blackboard**
   1. pen, paper, pay, penny, puppy

B. Sentences are not often possible until a number of consonants and vowel combinations have been achieved. Sentences should be constructed emphasizing the particular sound being studied.

B. **Sentences Emphasizing the letter p.** Sample sentences:
   1. I want a *pen* and *paper.*
   2. I *pay* a *penny* for the *paper.*
   3. *Put* the *puppy* on the *paper.*

C. As the patient advances, sentences with a modicum of meaning and within phonetic reach of the motor aphasic should be composed. It is always advisable to use all possible clues, such as the visual, by see-

C. **Words for Sentences:** pass, barber, window, home, butter, no money.
Sample sentences:
   1. I want a pass.
   2. I went home.

ing the sentence and also watching mouth movements in the mirror.

3. I have no money.
4. I want to eat.
5. Open the window.
6. Pass the butter.
7. I want the barber.

D. A few familiar phrases are adaptable to the motor aphasic. Familiarity appears to have an added impetus.

D. Familiar Phrases
1. Hello.
2. How are you?
3. Fine.
4. Hi!
5. Bye (Good bye)
6. No.
7. Yes. (sometimes difficult)

E. Some rote items may be within reach of the aphasic. Three and six are often difficult.

E. Rote Items
1. 1-2-3-4-5-6-7-8-9-10
2. Monday, Tuesday, Wednesday, Thursday, Friday, Saturday, Sunday.
3. January, February, March, April, May, etc.

F. More extensive material may be used with motor aphasics if they can be encouraged to skip words which are not phonetically possible, and to read the remainder of the sentence. (The therapist should supply the difficult words.)

F. Use of More Extensive Material
1. I want to go home on (therapist will supply the day such as Thanksgiving, Easter, Christmas, etc.)
2. I want a piece of (therapist will supply such words as pumpkin, peach, mince) pie.

G. Items from the Personalized Notebook, Chapter 7, are sometimes feasible for motor aphasics. The motivation of working on familiar items is often helpful.

G. Personal Information
1. My name is *Bob*.
2. I live in *Long Beach*.
3. My brother's name is *Al*.
4. I was in the *Air Corps*.

H. High interest subjects such as sports often can be used to good advantage.

H. High Interest Subjects
Baseball: Draw a sketch of the baseball diamond, labeling the bases for the reading lesson.

Others:
1. First base
2. Second base
3. Home plate
4. Mound
5. Out field
6. A hit
7. Home run
8. Batter up!
9. Safe!
10. Out!

I. Changing Medial Sounds Into Initial Sounds

Sometimes a patient can make a sound in the middle of a word, but cannot initiate the same sound at the beginning of a word. For example, suppose a patient cannot say any words beginning with the "k" sound such as "coat" and "kite," but he can say "pumpkin." A helpful technique is to lead him into saying:

> pump-kin, kin, kin
> pump-king, king, king
> pump-cat, cat, cat
> pump-coat, coat, coat

Next ask him to *think* pump (but not to *say* it) then say *kin*
— *think* pump (but not to *say* it) then say *king*
— *think* pump (but not to *say* it) then say *cat*
— *think* pump (but not to *say* it) then say *coat*

Now try the list: kin, king, cat, coat, omitting "pump" altogether.

J. As improvement continues, motor aphasics should read with other reading groups. (See Reading Recognition and Comprehension, Chapter 15.)

K. Word Formulation

A *word* formulation defect is a motor defect while a *sentence* formulation defect is an amnesic defect. A patient with a word formulation defect knows the word. For example, he would not say cow for horse, but he might say "corse." He garbles the word, not the sentence.

1. Suppose a patient says, "I forgot my axles" meaning that he forgot his glasses. Sometimes he can detect the error when he hears someone else make the same error, as: "You forgot your *axles*? What are *axles*?" In attempting to make himself clear he probably will point to his eyes or to the glasses someone else is wearing. Take him to the blackboard and write the word *glasses* on the board. Let the patient write it and say it several times. Ask him again what he forgot so that he can recall the word, glasses. Let him say several times, "I forgot my glasses." In some cases it would be well to compare the words, axel and glasses, but it is usually best to concentrate on the correct word needed.

2. One patient in the clinic actually said, "Do you like cucumburgers?" In this case the therapist, who had a plastic model of a cucumber and a plaster-of-Paris hamburger, presented both to the patient to see which one he was referring to. Both words were written out, identified, and drilled on for pronunciation. Such sentences as I like cucumbers, Cucumbers are green, I like hamburgers, and I like hamburgers and cucumbers, were practiced.

VIII. REFERENCE CHART FOR TEACHING CONSONANT SOUNDS

Consonant	Placement of Tongue, Teeth and Lips	Special Techniques for Eliciting Sounds	Word Drills
m	Place lips together lightly and hum	Hum familiar tune with patient	may, me, my, mow, ma, moo.
p	Place lips together, puff out air	Puff out match—puff smoke of cigarette	pay, pea, pie, pa, Poe
b	Place lips together puff out sound	"Baa" of lamb	bay, bee, by, bow, boo
f	Place upper teeth on lower lip and blow	"F-f-f"—cat fight	fay, fee, fie, foe "fee, fie, fo, fum"
v	Place upper teeth on lower lip and blow out sound	Hum with upper teeth on lower lip	vee, vie, vow
s	Place teeth together and blow thin stream of air down mid line of tongue	"Snake" sound—blow thin air stream on patient's hand. Blow tissue or match	say, see, sigh, sow, sue
z	Place teeth together, blow and add voice	"Buzz" of a bee	zee, zoe, zoo
t	Place tongue on gums behind upper teeth and push out air	With the tip of the tongue touch upper gum in rapid succession	tea, tie, toe, too
d	Place tongue on gums behind upper teeth and push out sound	Try saying "dah, dah dah."	day, dee, die, dough, do
r	Turn the tip of the tongue toward the roof of the mouth and add sound	Turn tip of tongue back with tongue blade. Drop tongue from roof of mouth. Mimic the rooster crow	ray, rye, row, rue
l	Touch the roof of the mouth with tongue and add sound	Start with "r" position, raise tongue. Try saying "lah, lah"	lay, lee, lie, low, loo
n	Place tongue against upper dental ridge and hum	Start with the pointed tongue in the l position then widen and flatten the tip	nay, knee, nigh, no, knew
k c (hard)	Make a "cough" sound	Cough voluntarily—feel own or therapist's throat	kay, key, cow, coo
g	Add sound to the "K"	Frog sound "garumph"	gay, guy, go
h	Open mouth and blow out air	Sigh	hay, he, hi, hoe, ha, who
th (unvoiced)	Place tongue between teeth and blow		thigh, thumb, theme
th (voiced)	Place tongue between teeth and blow out sound		they, thee, thy, though
sh	Nearly close teeth, purse lips, blow broad stream of air	Imitate "hush" sound	shay, she, shy, show, shoe
zh	Make the "sh" sound and add voice		a-zure pleasure, leisure
ch	Place tongue in position for t and make a sh sound	Make the "choo-choo" sound of the train	chum, chew
j	Make ch and add sound		jay, joe

IX. THE MOTO-KINESTHETIC METHOD FOR MOTOR APHASIA

The Moto-kinesthetic method as described by Edna Hill Young in the text, *Moto-Kinesthetic Speech Training*[6] sets forth complete modalities for a manipulative approach for motor-speech production. Chapters 3, 4 and 5 are especially helpful for the voiceless consonants, vowels and voiced consonants. There are sixteen pages of photographs illustrating positions of tongue, teeth and lip movement helpful to the individual who has not had the opportunity to study directly from Mrs. Young. Mrs. Young has taught graduate classes in conjunction with the University of Southern California at Los Angeles. Several other universities, notably Denver University, offer this course under the direction of students of Mrs. Young.

X. DYSARTHRIA

Dysarthria is an inability to pronounce or articulate accurately because of a lack of muscular control. Dysarthria differs from motor aphasia in that the motor aphasic fails to recall the memory patterns of how sounds are made, while the dysarthric recalls the motor speech patterns for the sounds, but cannot execute them because of lack of control of the musculature. The motor aphasic can use his tongue, lips and throat for eating, chewing and swallowing, while he cannot use them effectively for speaking, but the dysarthric often drools, chokes on food and has difficulty swallowing.

Exercises for the motor aphasic are also helpful for the dysarthric. It is not uncommon for a patient to have both motor aphasia and dysarthria.

XI. DYSPROSODY[7]

Another speech defect related to motor speech patterns is dysprosody which is a disturbance of intonation, tone quality or modulation. This type of monotonous voice occurs in cases of paralysis agitans and in Parkinsonism when muscles are rigid; and it has been found also in stroke and accident cases. Often the patient with dysprosody can correct the defect *if* he gives it his direct attention and concentrates on the inflection of his voice. But, since it is difficult for him to concentrate on both his voice and his thoughts, he does not make the self-correction.

XII. LESSON PLAN FOR CORRELATING SPEECH DRILL, READING, WRITING, SINGING

A. Salutations

1. As the patient enters the work area the therapist has a good opportunity to introduce basic sounds in greeting him.

---

6. Hawk, Sara S., and Young, Edna Hill: *Moto-Kinesthetic Speech Training.* Stanford University Press, Palo Alto, Calif., 1955.
7. Nielsen, J. M., and McKeown, Milfred: Dysprosody, A report of two cases. *Bulletin of the Los Angeles Neurological Society,* Vol. 26, No. 3, September 1961.

Example: "Hi!" "How are you?" "Fine." "Hello!" etc.

2. It should go without saying that the next thing to do is to establish a feeling of warm acceptance, permissiveness, and personal interest in the patient. This is the time to foster enthusiasm for serious work on the *language* problem. (There should be opportunity at another time for the patient to air his troubles and complaints so that he need not be burdened with them during the language lesson.)

B. Speech

1. Practice the sounds selected for study and review. For example: m s o r

2. Make these sounds into simple one-syllable words which can be used as the answers to the therapist's questions. This gives the patient success at participating in a conversation. Support him with written clues if needed.

Example: *Therapist:* When your grass needs mowing, what do you do?

(Demonstrate the act of pushing a lawn mower.)

Patient:　　Mow. (He may need to see the initial sound on the lips of the therapist or see the word on the blackboard.)

Therapist: How do you plant grass in your yard?

(Demonstrate the act of sowing seed.)

Patient:　　Sow.

Therapist: Suppose we are in a boat. How can we get to the shore?

(Demonstrate the act of rowing a boat.)

Patient:　　Row.

3. Show pictures which will elicit the words being studied. Ask the patient to tell what each one is doing.

(Picture of a man running a lawn mower) —Mow.

(Picture of a farmer sowing seed) —Sow.

(Picture of a man rowing a boat) —Row.

C. Singing

1. Sing "Row, Row, Row Your Boat."

a. Sometimes all the patient can contribute is "row, row, row." In that case, the therapist should continue alone, cueing the patient in on the words that he CAN sing.

b. Patients who do not like to sing should not be coerced to do so. Those who do enjoy it get much satisfaction out of being able to sing several words in succession since they have been deprived of speaking more than a syllable at a time.

c. Sometimes "Row, row, row your boat" can be paraphrased by using such lines as "Mow, mow, mow the lawn" with appropriate conclusions to the jingle.

INTERMISSION— (Frequent rest periods are imperative in working with aphasics due to the extreme fatigue factor.) Erase the board so that the next reading lesson will be fresh.

D. Reading

1. Write the words mow, sow, row on the board to use as a reading lesson on individual words.

2. Let the patient trace over the letters with his fingers for kinesthetic clues if he has demonstrated that this method is helpful to him.

3. Use flash cards for reading individual words. A three-inch letter often is more stimulating than small print or handwriting. The Flo-master felt pen produces excellent permanent flash cards.

E. Writing

1. Let the patient copy the words several times.

2. Use the following technique for learning to write and to spell the word:

a. As the patient watches, the therapist writes the word on the board, sounding it out and pronouncing it as he finishes writing it. Erase the board.

b. This process is repeated three times.

c. The patient then is to attempt to write the word on a sheet of paper.

d. The therapist then checks the patient's work.

e. If the patient has written the word correctly, he is to destroy that sheet and write the word again on a second sheet. (This method insures that the patient is not doing copy work only.)

f. The patient should repeat the writing of the word once to a sheet of paper until he has learned to write it correctly.

3. The patient is to add the missing letter, then say the words over many times.

s_w;   r_w;   m_w;   mo_;   ro_;   so_

4. Fill the blanks. (The therapist may need to read the sentences to the patient in order to lead him to fill in the proper missing words.)

a. I can m_____ the grass.

b. Get in the boat and r____ across the river.

c. Help me s____ the seed.

d. "_____, _____, _____ your boat."

F. Songs and Jingles

Songs and jingles with repetitious phrases and refrains are listed herewith. It should be borne in mind that singing the words will not necessarily have

any carryover in speaking the same words, although singing the words provides a satisfying experience.[8]

My Bonnie (Bring back, bring back, etc.)
Go Tell Aunt Rhody
Battle Hymn of the Republic (Glory, glory, hallelujah)
Good Night, Ladies
Old Black Joe (I'm coming, I'm coming)
For He's a Jolly Good Fellow
Jimmy Cracked Corn
The More We get Together
Happy Birthday to You
Style All the While

New popular songs with repetitive phrases come into favor every year, many
of them in keeping with events current at the time. For example: 1917—Over
There; Oh, Johnny, Oh, Johnny; Johnny Get Your Gun.

REFERENCES FOR SONGS

1. *The New Golden Song Book*—Norman Lloyd, Golden Press, New York, N. Y., Words and
music for 74 favorite songs and singing games.
2. *Twice 55 Plus, Community Songs*—C. C. Birchard & Co., Boston, Mass.
3. *Men's Get-Together Songs*—Lorenz Publishing Co., 501 East Third, Dayton 1, O.

XIII REFERENCES

Arnold, Genevieve: *Sound and Articulation Game.* Expression Company, Boston, Mass.
Birmingham, Anna I., and Krapp, George P.: *First Lessons in Speech Improvement.*
Charles Scribner's Sons, New York, N. Y.
Corbin, M. L.: Group speech therapy for motor aphasia and dysarthria. *Journal of Speech
and Hearing Disorders,* Vol. 16, No. 1, March 1951.
Fairbanks, Grant: *Voice and Articulation Drillbook,* Second Edition. Harper and Brothers,
New York, N. Y.
Nemoy, Elizabeth M., and Davis, Serena F.: *Correction of Defective Consonant Sounds.*
Expression Company, Boston, Mass.
Penn, Erta V.: *Handbook for the Remedial Speech and Phonics Program; A Teaching
Aid for the Classroom Teacher.* Reef—Sunset Schools, Avenal, Calif., 1957.
Richards, I. A., and Gibson, Christine: *Words on Paper.* English Language Research, Inc.,
13 Kirkland St., Cambridge 38, Mass.
Schoolfield, Lucille D.: *Better Speech and Better Reading.* Expression Company, Magnolia,
Mass., Articulation Test, pp. 137–145.
Phonics Flash Cards—Parent Teacher Aids. Gelles-Widmer Co., St. Louis 17, Mo.

---

8. Longerich, Mary, and Bordeaux, Jean: *Aphasia Therapeutics.* Macmillan Company, New
York, 1954, page 40.
Page, Irvine H., *et al.: Stokes.* E. P. Dutton & Company, Inc., New York 10, N. Y. 1961, page 212.

Chapter 12

ORAL FORMULATION—INTERMEDIATE
(Amnesic Aphasia)[1]

I. INTRODUCTION

As the aphasic patient gains in his skill at naming, he should begin to apply his newly found vocabulary by conveying his wants in practical situations. He is now ready to learn basic sentence patterns which will facilitate his use of more nearly complete sentences. All patients with anomia do not necessarily have a formulation loss. A formulation loss often results from auditory-verbal agnosia (not understanding oral language) and from amnesic defects.

It should be stressed that accuracy and grammatical correctness are certainly not goals at this point—and may never be if they were formerly not an important factor to the patient.

II. TECHNIQUES

REMARKS

A. The development of salutations and conversational phrases is often psychologically one of the most important facets of speech. At the beginning of therapy sessions stress salutations incidentally. Conversational phrases often lend themselves to imaginary and play-acting situations between patient and therapist.

2. This is an excellent opportunity for group practice with personal names.

3. Take care that the card has been removed from the patient's

EXERCISES

A. Basic Techniques
1. Developing salutations and conversational phrases
Therapist: "Hello"
Patient: "Hello"
Therapist: "How are you?"
Patient: "Fine."
Therapist may interpose, "Now you ask me."
Patient: "How are you?"
Therapist: "Fine, what have you been doing?"

2. Learning names
    Hello, *John.*
    How are you, *Mary?*

3. Using flash cards.
    a. Print greetings on flash

1. Nielsen, J. M.: *Memory and Amnesia.* San Lucas Press, Los Angeles, Calif., 1958, page 175.
————: *A Textbook of Clinical Neurology* Third Edition. Paul B. Hoeber, Inc., New York, N. Y., page 281.

view as he first tries to formulate each phrase or word; he should be formulating, not reading.

b. (How do you feel today?)

FINE	SICK	TIRED

(What did you have for breakfast?)

HAM AND EGGS
CEREAL AND JUICE
COFFEE

B. The need arises at this time to add other useful words such as descriptive or limiting words and action verbs. Action verbs often appear to be almost as easy to acquire as nouns. These may be evolved from simple pictures (such as a person singing, a child running, a man swimming, a team playing baseball) depicting actions, or by actual demonstration.

2. Some of these words express complete thoughts in themselves.

C. The use of action verbs stimulates associations which can be coupled readily with nouns. This is often the beginning of oral sentence formulation for many patients. Some patients may require visual clues. When needed, put the lists on the board. After some drill, erase the right hand column, then both columns and drill again with only auditory clues.

D. Adjectives and adverbs are not only as useful as nouns and verbs,

cards. If the patient hesitates to respond to a greeting, flash the appropriate response before him for a visual clue.

Hello; goodbye; good morning; good night.

b. Ask questions to which one of the flash cards is the answer or make up a situation which requires one of the flash cards as the appropriate response. If the patient hesitates, give him the visual clue on the card.

B. Learning Action Words

1. Use pantomime or pictures to help the patient recall such words as the following:

eat	run	stop
sleep	sit down	close
read	stand up	cut
write	open	draw
go	watch	work
see	talk	sing
walk	drink	talk

2. Run! Hurry! Stop! Sing!

C. Using Simple Associations

The Therapist says:	*The Patient responds with:*
read	book
write	letter
eat	supper
watch	television
open	door
close	window

D. Using Descriptive Words

Present pictures which depict com-

but appear relatively easy for aphasics to acquire because of their frequent use or because of their emotional content.

Example: Picture of children playing.

Therapist: Are the children sad?

Patient: No, happy.

Therapist: The children are ____?

Patient: Happy. The children are happy.

Continue using other adjectives the picture portrays.

E. Among the descriptive words are colors. These may be learned from color charts, colored crayons and chalk, and by identifying colors in the surroundings and from magazine pictures. (Paint stores usually can supply colored squares.)

2. Pictures or actual objects provide the basis for this practice. Often the patient quite naturally combines colors with the objects which he can name. Sometimes he transposes the color, putting it after the noun. Help him correct this error before it becomes an established pattern.

4. It is helpful to associate colors with familiar objects. Note:

mon descriptive words. Elicit from the patient adjectives which describe the pictures.

hungry	big	fat
tall	rich	short
tired	little	high
happy	old	sad
pretty	new	clean

E. Learning Colors

1. Use colored squares, colored chalk or crayons.

Red	White	Blue	Black
Yellow	Orange	Green	Purple

2. Combine colors with objects.

white shirt
red tie
blue suit
yellow socks
black shoes

3. Lead the patient into an oral sentence completion exercise such as the following:

Therapist: You are wearing a (color) (item).
Around your neck is a (color) (item).
On your feet you wear (color) (item).

4. Associate colors with familiar objects. Show the patient pictures

In the above exercises the color precedes the noun. Also teach the patient to use the color word following the verb as a predicate adjective.

The <u>cat</u> is black.

F. Personal pronouns are usually difficult for aphasics. They confuse genders using the masculine for the feminine. Demonstrative pronouns such as *that* and *them* are used frequently by aphasics, particularly those with amnesic defects.

of objects and ask him to name the appropriate colors.

Examples:

Therapist: The colors of the American Flag are ____, ____, ____.

The top and bottom stripes are

_____.

The stars are _____.

There are six _____ stripes and seven _____ stripes.

The field is _____.

An apple is _____.

I like a _____ apple.

Do you want a _____ _____?

The grass is _____.

We sat on the _____ _____.

G_____ _____ is cool.

The cat is _____.

This is a _____ cat.

A _____ cat is bad luck.

A witch and a _____ _____ remind me of Hallowe'en.

F. Learning Personal Pronouns

1. It is often helpful to present pronouns in connection with stick figures to help association.

Drill on such sentences as: John is going; HE is going. I see John; HE is here. Who is John: HE is my brother.

HE SHE THEY IT

2. Pronouns and linking verbs which often form the basis of common conversational sentences appear to be difficult for aphasics. Nevertheless, constant repetition of such sentences as these leads to correct use.

2. Using pronouns and linking verbs. The patient is to supply such endings as those underlined in the following examples:

He is: a friend; John; a patient.

She is: my teacher; Mary; my wife.

They are: patients; my teachers.

It is: my book; the chair; a pencil.

G. Complete sentences are not a goal at this time; any intelligible speech should be accepted. Example: "Go show?" in place of "Shall we go to the show?"

G. Completing Sentences
By describing pictures or actual demonstrations, lead the patient to develop sentences.

In both written and oral formulation he may be ready to complete sentences if supplied with a question to answer:

Therapist:
1. Is he running?
2. Is she reading?
3. Are they singing?

6. (What are the children doing?)

Patient:
1. He is running.
2. She is reading.
3. They are singing.
4. She reads a _____. (book)
5. He opens the _____. (door)
6. (They) (are) (singing)

_____ _____ _____

H. Unscrambling sentences helps develop sentence recognition.

These may be increased in complexity by the addition of colors, adjectives, and adverbs.

H. Working for Correct Word Order
1. Write groups of words on the blackboard for rearrangement in proper order.
Examples:
a. window man the opens the

2. It is good practice to copy the sentences, to *read* them orally, then to *say* them from memory.

Next, dictate these same sentences exactly as they are; then begin to make slight changes such as adding adjectives, and changing them to the negative.

b. man paper the reads the old

c. wooden on green desk plant the put the

2. Hand the patient a group of 3 x 5 cards on which individual words are printed or written. The patient is to arrange the cards in the proper order to make intelligible sentences. Begin with two- and/or three-word sentences, gradually building up to longer sentences.

Examples:

I. Extend this exercise by providing each patient with two or three articles which must be named in the exchange process.

Give me your _____ and _____.

I want your _____ and _____.

I. Exchange Items

Give each one in the group an article such as an ash tray, a cigarette, a match, a pencil. One patient is to ask another for his item. The second patient is to ask the first for the item which he has as they exchange items. It may be helpful to write on the board such sentence beginnings as:

Give me your _____.

I want your _____.

J. Both oral and written procedures are useful with this exercise.

As an oral exercise, the therapist should speak the first part, then hesitate long enough to give the patient time orally to fill the blank.

As a written exercise, the patient is to select the proper word from a list or fill the blanks from memory.

J. Use of Cliches and Familiar Sayings to Facilitate Recall
Examples:
1. Light as a ____ (feather).
2. Blind as a ____ (bat).
3. Wise as an ____ (owl).
4. Cool as a ____ (cucumber).
5. Bright as a ____ (dollar).
6. Hot as a ____ (firecracker).
7. Green as ____ (grass).
8. Old as ____ (Methuselah).
9. Dumb as an ____ (ox).
10. Heavy as ____ (lead).

K. Motor and amnesic aphasic patients often have been without connected speech, (particularly propositional speech) for such a long time that they may be out of the habit of saying more than a word or two at a time. The force of automatic speech resulting from memory work stored up from childhood may provide these patients with profitable connected-speech practice. Reference: The New Golden Song Book: 74 Favorite Songs and Singing Games arranged by Norman Lloyd, 1955.

K. Use of Jingles, Rhymes, Rounds
Give the patient a start on each line, allowing him to recall—when he can—the remainder. Encourage him to repeat the verses often.
Examples:
1. One, two, buckle my shoe . . .
2. Row, row, row your boat . . .
3. Mary had a little lamb . . . . . .
4. Hickory, Dickory, dock . . . . .
5. Jack be nimble, Jack be quick . . . . . .
6. Little Jack Horner sat in the corner . . . . . .
7. Jack and Jill went up the hill . . . . . .

L. This technique is helpful in promoting connected sentences so that eventually a paragraph will result. Other situations might be:

A day at the beach (what did you do?)

A day as Knott's Berry Farm (what did you see?)

How I spent my vacation (where did you go?)

How to serve a luncheon

L. Sentence Building
Begin by putting the patient "in the situation" or by "setting the stage" with such a statement as, "Let us suppose we are going to town to do the marketing. We'll take turns in naming what we are going to buy."
Example:
I am going to buy a package of cigarettes.

I am going to buy some gum.

Getting a permanent at the beauty parlor

I am going to buy shaving cream.

Extend the exercise by combining two and then three items:

I am going to buy a package of cigarettes and a package of gum.

I am going to buy a package of cigarettes, a package of gum and some shaving cream.

M. Emphasizing Memory

1. On the board, write a short sentence which the patient can read aloud, such as I RING THE BELL. Have the patient read it several times, then say it looking away from the board.
2. Erase the last word: I RING THE _____. Have the patient read it supplying the last word from memory.
3. Erase another word: I _____ THE _____. Have the patient supply the missing words from memory.
4. Erase all the words, leaving only the blanks: __ _____ ____ _____. Instruct the patient to *do* what the sentence says and to say it at the same time.
5. Let others ring the bell and instruct the patient to tell what they are doing: I RING THE BELL; YOU RING THE BELL; JOHN RING (S) THE BELL.

III. LESSON PLAN FOR INTERMEDIATE ORAL FORMULATION

Assemble such items as a coffee pot, cup and saucer, spoon, sugar and creamer.

1. Ask a patient to pick up the coffee pot and (pretend to) pour a cup of coffee. Emphasize the phrase POUR A CUP OF COFFEE as he pours. Ask him to repeat the phrase as he pours.
2. Ask him to pick up the cup and (pretend to) drink the coffee. Repeat the phrase DRINK IT and have the patient say it several times as he tips the (empty) cup to his lips.
3. In group situations, let one patient instruct another to POUR A CUP OF COFFEE and to DRINK IT.
4. Expand the situation by using cream and sugar, and by stirring the coffee. Add appropriate commands such as STIR YOUR COFFEE. Ask the patient to tell what he is doing. Accept any appropriate formulation such as I STIR, STIR COFFEE, STIRRING, etc.
5. Continue to review, coaxing the patient to formulate orally both when he carries out the acts and when he sees others carry them out.

6. Formulation expected from this exercise includes:

I pour a cup of coffee.	John likes sugar.
I pour a cup of coffee and drink it.	John stirs his coffee.
John pours a cup of coffee.	I want coffee black.
You drink coffee.	John drinks coffee with cream.
I like cream.	The coffee is hot.
I stir my coffee.	The coffee is cold.
I pour cream in my coffee.	Do you want coffee?
I want a spoon.	I don't like coffee.
I don't use sugar.	John likes sugar.

7. Vary the exercise with such materials as:[2]

a milk bottle and a glass

tea pot, lemon, cream, sugar, spoon

bread, butter, jelly, knife

IV. REFERENCES

Gregory, Frederick K.: *Timothy Gee's Tiny Textbooks.* Alpha Book, People, Objects, Farm, 1516 N. Gardner, Hollywood 46, Calif.

McCausland, Margaret, Miller, Marie B., and Okie, Isabel: *Speech Through Pictures.* Expression Company, Magnolia, Mass.

Neiman, Irving Gaynor: *Linguapix.* Simon and Schuster, New York, N. Y.

Oftedal, Laura, and Jacob, Nina: *My First Dictionary.* Grosset & Dunlap, New York, N. Y.

Richards, I. A., and Gibson, C. M.: *English Through Pictures.* Pocket Books, Inc., New York, N. Y.

Walpole, Ellen W.: *The Golden Dictionary.* Simon and Schuster, New York, N. Y.

Watters, Garnette, and Courtis, S. A.: *The Picture Dictionary for Children.* Grosset & Dunlap, New York, N. Y.

Werner, Jane: *The Golden Book of Words.* Simon and Schuster, New York, N. Y.

Wright, Wendell W.: *The Rainbow Dictionary.* World Publishing Company, Cleveland, O., and New York, N. Y.

Utley, Jean: *What's Its Name?* University of Illinois Press, Urbana, Ill.

---

2. Food models for this type of drill may be purchased at the Cincinnati Doll Company, 311 East Twelfth St., Cincinnati 10, O.

Chapter 13

ORAL FORMULATION—ADVANCED
(Amnesic Aphasia)

I. INTRODUCTION

WHILE MANY APHASIC patients never achieve more than a basic vocabulary —the ability to name objects and people and to use a few verbs and descriptive words, others are capable of cultivating a high degree of fluency. Such patients are now ready for formulation[1] of their own thoughts in complete sentences with phrases, modifiers, and connectives.

II. TECHNIQUES

REMARKS

A. This technique frequently is employed by aphasia therapists in actual situations where aphasics severely limited in oral language need to make their wants known. A sentence beginning often will call forth the remainder.

EXERCISES

A. Sentence Completion

Ask the patient to complete such sentences as the following. The therapist orally initiates the first part of each:

    1. Your wife went to _____.
    2. The doctor said, "_____."
    3. For dinner we had _____.
    4. The TV program was about a _____.

B. Some patients have been 35 mm. color-slide enthusiasts and will welcome the opportunity to talk about their pictures.

    The stereoptican is surprisingly effective for this type of exercise. Patients appear to enjoy the old-style apparel and the antiquated customs of a half century ago as much as they do up-to-date material.

    See Lesson Plan: Using 35 mm. Slides, Section III.

B. Thirty-five mm. Slides and Stereoptican Views

Write on the blackboard the beginning phrases of sentences to be used over and over for sentence completion as each scene is viewed.

Examples:

    1. This is a picture of _____.
    2. I see a _____.
    3. Look at the _____.

---

1. Nielsen, J. M.: *A Textbook of Clinical Neurology,* Third Edition. Paul B. Hoeber, Inc., New York, N. Y., page 280.

C. Other sentence suggestions:
   1. I have a car.
   2. I like to wear sport clothes.
   3. My house is made of _____.
      It is small. It has 5 rooms.

D. Many amnesic aphasic patients read silently with good comprehension but need practice retelling what they have read.

   If reading comprehension is extremely limited, the therapist may read aloud to the patient or permit him to make use of recorded material.

E. Let the patient talk in his own way. Withhold corrections in grammar or sentence construction until he completes his description. Seldom can an aphasic exceed his premorbid level of speech; consequently, one who was limited in the refinements of language before he had aphasia cannot be expected now to speak without grammatical errors.

F. It is often helpful to let the patient tell how to do something, or to make something *at the same time* that he is doing it.

C. Additions to Basic Sentences

Ask the patient to add the color, the number, the quality, kind, etc. to such basic sentences as the following:
   1. I have a dress. (Patient is to add the color, the number, etc.)
   2. I have a blue dress.
   3. I have two blue dresses.
   4. I have an old blue dress.
   5. I have a new blue dress.

D. Retelling Stories

Use the Reader's Digest, daily papers, or comparable publications for brief articles, anecdotes and short stories.

   Ask the patient to read a story, then retell it in his own words.

E. Description of Pictures

Present a picture (magazine ads are acceptable). For example, this picture may be a man fixing a tire on his car. Ask the patient to describe the picture and to tell what is going on.

F. Giving Directions

Ask the patient to tell
   1. how to get to the drug store.
   2. how to get to the garage, to the bath, to the porch, to bed.
   3. how to make a bed.
   4. how to make some article done in his former work or as a hobby.

G. Personal History. Use the Personalized Notebook, Chapter 7. Ask the patient to describe in more detail certain sections of the notebook.

H. Word Definitions.[2] Ask the patient to tell what certain words mean to him. Examples: home, book, wheelchair, car, grocery store, cane, television, electric stove, sewing machine.

I. News Accounts. Ask the patient to retell current news accounts which he has read about or heard on the TV or radio. *Examples:* sports, politics, celebrities visiting in the area, fashions in clothes.

J. Personal Experiences. Ask the patient to relate some current or past experience. *Examples:* his stay in the hospital; war stories; his children's antics; taking care of the fish, the dog, or cat; Christmas Day at home.

K. Personal pronouns are difficult for aphasics to learn; however, they almost invariably use demonstrative pronouns such as this, that, them as substitutes for nouns.

    See: Writing Opposites, Chapter 16, Section V, F.

Examples:

K. Review of Personal Pronouns

    1. Ask the patient to supply the appropriate pronouns in place of stick figures placed in the blanks.

1. _____ is my sister.

2. _____ are following the boy.

3. _____ is following the dog.

4. _____ are man and wife.

L. The oral speech of many aphasics is described as "telegraphic" partly because they cannot use prepositions and phrases.

L. Prepositional Phrases

    1. On the blackboard write a subject with an appropriate predicate, leaving a space *after* the subject in which the patient may supply

---

2. See Lesson Plan: Reading Recognition and Comprehension. Chapter 15, Section V.

Pictures may be selected which will suggest the sentences to be worked out with prepositional phrases as modifiers of the subject, or of the verb, and later of other parts of a sentence such as the object.

1. Example of subject modifier. The boy *on the horse* is John.
2. Example of verb modifier. The boy is sitting *on the horse*.
3. Example of object modifier. The boy rode the horse *with the black mane*.

(either orally or in writing) a prepositional phrase in answer to the question, "Which one."

    a. The man (———) is my father. The therapist interposes the question, "WHICH man?" (Answer: with a cane . . . . . .) The man *with a cane* is my father.

    b. The child (———) is my daughter. The child (WHICH child?) in the red dress . . . . . . The child *in the red dress*. . . .

    c. The dog (———) is a Dalmatian. (WHICH dog?) The dog *with the black spots*. . . . . .

2. In the same manner, select subjects and predicates, leaving space for prepositional phrases after the verb as modifiers of the verb. Use the word "Where?"

    a. My son ran ———— (ran WHERE?) into the house. My son ran *into the house*.

    b. The man sat ———— (sat WHERE?) on the porch. The man sat *on the porch*.

M. It is almost impossible to separate oral and written practice in the retraining of aphasics. Many techniques described in the Writing Section will prove useful for retraining in oral formulation.

III. LESSON PLAN USING 35 MM SLIDE[3]

This lesson plan is designed to follow techniques outlined under II B above. Let us assume that the patient has practiced saying "This is a picture of (*the ocean*, for example), "I see a (*boat*)" etc. as suggested. Now it is time to expand the exercise by such techniques as the following:

A. Project a slide on the screen, say a marine scene which includes a sail boat with people in the boat, blue sky with white clouds, the ocean, and perhaps some shore line. Begin with questions which will elicit the same replies used previously such as:

---

3. See Chapter 8 for commercial slides.

QUESTIONS BY THERAPIST	SAMPLE ANSWERS EXPECTED FROM THE PATIENT
1. What is this a picture of?	1. This is a picture of a boat. or This is a picture of the ocean. or This is a picture of some people in a boat.
2. What do you see here?	2. I see a boat, or the ocean, or people in a boat, or a blue sky with white clouds.
3. What color is the ocean?	3. Sometimes gray, blue or green.
4. Is this a motor boat?	4. No—a sail boat.
5. How many people are in the boat?	5. Father and two children.
6. What is that triangular white cloth over the boat?	6. Catches the wind—makes the boat go; a sail.
7. Do you see any land? Tell me about it.	7. Palm trees, sandy shore, etc.

Proceed in this manner leaving the slide in full view. Encourage the patient to talk about it as he chooses, bringing in everything he can pertaining to the picture.

B. At a later session, withdraw all visual clues and start talking about the picture from memory. Support the patient's efforts by leading questions if he begins to block.

C. Reenforce the vocabulary and formulation by showing 35 mm. slides somewhat similar to the first scene which will call forth parallel formulation and vocabulary as the patient attempts to describe the slide. Such scenes might be a large ship such as an ocean liner, or a navy ship, or a canoe on a lake, or a motorboat.

D. The patient's personal slides are particularly good for a lesson of this type because of the added interest of using names of his own family or friends, using his own address perhaps, and providing the opportunity for him to talk about places of special interest to him.

IV. LESSON PLANS ON FORMULATION USING PREPOSITIONS

A. This lesson plan is designed to follow techniques outlined in II-L above. Assemble such items as pencil, knife, fork, scissors, spoon, bar of soap, razor, and cane.

1. Write on the board such sentences as:
   a. I write with a pencil.
   b. I cut with a knife.
   c. I stir with a spoon.
   d. I wash with soap.
   e. I shave with a razor.
   f. I eat with a fork.
   g. I cut with the scissors.
   h. I walk with a cane.

Read these sentences with the patient. Let him read them aloud several times.

2. Erase the last word, encouraging the patient to supply it:
   a. I write with a _____. (Show a pencil if necessary).
   b. I cut with a _____. Etc.
3. Erase the verb in each sentence, leaving the last word for a clue:
   a. I _____ with a pencil.
   b. I _____ with a knife.
4. If the patient is having some difficulty, practice pairing the verbs and nouns, then the nouns and verbs. Ask:
   a. What goes with pencil? (write)
   b. What goes with scissors? (cut) Etc.

Now switch the order. Ask:
   a. What goes with write? (pencil)
   b. What goes with shave? (razor) Etc.

5. Erase the preposition:
   a. I write _____ a pencil.
   b. I cut _____ a knife.
6. Hold up each item in turn asking the patient to tell what he does with it.
   a. (pencil) I write with a pencil.
   b. (knife) I cut with a knife.

B. Lesson Plan for Additional Help with Prepositions[4]

Select some small item which can be easily handled. Place this item in various places asking the patient where it is. *Example:* Use a handkerchief. Place it ON the patient's shoulder. Ask him *where* it is. Emphasize the word ON. Let him say, "ON my shoulder." Place the handkerchief ON various other places so that the patient has the opportunity to use the word ON

---

4. Richards, I. A. and Gibson, Christine M.: *English Through Pictures.* Pocket Books, Inc., New York, N. Y.

several times; ON the table, ON a book, ON the floor, ON his knee. Ask him to place the handkerchief ON several other places as he states what he is doing.

In the same way, place the handkerchief:

1. IN the patient's pocket; IN the drawer
2. UNDER the chair; UNDER a book; UNDER his arm
3. BETWEEN his knees; BETWEEN two books

Invent other demonstrations for use with such prepositions as from, to, back of, behind.

V. REFERENCES

Decker, Frieda: *Progressive Lessons for Language Retraining.* Harper Bros., New York, N. Y. 1960.

> Book I — The Days at Home
> Book II — Mr. and Mrs. Day Go Shopping
> Book III — The Days Take a Trip
> Book IV — The Days Buy a House

Elmo, Horace: *Golden Picture Book of Questions and Answers.* Simon & Schuster, New York, N. Y.

Hobbs, Valine: *Our World Neighbors.* Steck Company, Austin, Texas.

Hobbs, Valine: *Our Community.* Steck Company, Austin, Texas.

Chapter 14

JARGON, AND GARBLED ORAL AND WRITTEN LANGUAGE
(Paraphasia and Paragraphia) [1]

I. INTRODUCTION

W HEN AN APHASIA PATIENT uses many inappropriate and garbled words, rambles while talking, and cannot explain his point clearly, he is said to have paraphasia. In extreme cases his language may be a jargon. The untrained inner language is making errors. One of the characteristics of the paraphasic is unawareness of his inappropriate language (due to auditory-verbal agnosia), so that he often speaks with much expression and many gestures, believing he is making his point clear. The ideas of this patient remain intact but he recalls the wrong words to express them. An oral expression results in paraphasia, and a written expression results in paragraphia. Retraining the paraphasic to recognize his errors and substitute correct language constitutes one of the most difficult problems of therapy.

II. TECHNIQUES

REMARKS

A. The paraphasic patient needs to learn to recognize his own errors. Since other language defects may be present, modalities of retraining must be selected according to the language abilities present. Since paraphasia is often the result of auditory-verbal agnosia, retraining procedures suggested in the section on auditory recognition are appropriate.[2] The patient may recognize his own errors when he hears his speech on a recorder, or as it is repeated by the therapist.

EXERCISES

A. Auditory Training With Tape Recordings

1. Record the patient's speech as he talks, then play back portions of it asking him to point out the errors. In a second recording, direct the conversation to include corrections made previously.

2. If a recorder is not available, simply repeat portions of the patient's speech, asking him to listen for errors. For example, the patient may say, "I to the want to the you know, tonight." On hearing this repeated, he may be able to substitute

---

1. Nielsen, J. M.: *A Textbook of Clinical Neurology,* Third Edition. Paul B. Hoeber, Inc., New York, N. Y., page 285.

————: *Memory and Amnesia.* San Lucas Press, Los Angeles, Calif., 1958, page 176.

2. See Chapter 9.

more appropriate words such as, "you know it's the show I want to." The therapist should help him complete the idea by supplying, "I want to go to the show tonight." The patient should repeat this a number of times, especially following some intervening conversation.

B. It is often helpful for the patient to see his own expressions in writing.

B. Visual Recognition

1. Write or type the patient's expressions as he says them.

2. Help him point out and evaluate his errors.

3. Assist him in correcting his statement. The corrected statement should now be used for practice as in the example, "I want to go to the show tonight."

C. One of the most useful approaches, especially with severe paraphasia (jargon) is the employment of phonetics. As the patient learns to recognize the sounds he wants to use, he is supplied with the tools for forming his own speech. Many of the exercises in the section on motor aphasia are applicable.[3]

c. The paraphasic patient will often be able to complete a word correctly if he is provided with the initial sound. Since he does not have to learn how to make sounds (as is necessary for the motor aphasic), more complicated words may be selected.

C. Phonetic Approach

1. Presentation of initial consonant sounds.

   a. Present an initial sound for drill such as *m*.

   b. Ask the patient to make the sound (or demonstrate it to him). Show him the symbol *m* and ask him to write it.

   c. Present a list of words with the initial sound *m*. Use objects and pictures to help the patient identify the words. Such a list might include:
   man   mailman   meat   money
   moon   monkey   magazine   mop

   d. As the patient attempts to say the words in the list, continually remind him of the initial sound *m* and ask him to produce it even though he cannot.

---

3. See Motor Speech Patterns, Chapter 11.

get the rest of the word without help. Ask the patient to repeat the words many times for accuracy.

    e. Combine oral exercises with written practice frequently.

2. Texts containing helpful word lists include:

Voice and Articulation Drill Book —Grant Fairbanks, Chapter 4.

Speech Through Pictures—McCausland, Miller and Okie.

First Lessons in Speech Improvement—Birmingham and Krapp, Part I.

2. Phonetic drills based on medial and final consonants should be added.

CONSONANT	MEDIAL	FINAL
M	animal	blossom
P	apple	cape
B	rabbit	knob
K	basket	book

D. Familiar phrases such as greetings can sometimes be memorized by the patient with paraphasia. These are helpful in social situations and provide the patient with substitutions for his inappropriate language. Some of the practices suggested in "Oral Formulation," are also helpful. Chapter 12.

D. Use of Familiar Phrases

1. Use common phrases in an attempt to make them automatic.

How are you?	No!
Hello!	Yes!
Good-bye!	Fine!
Thank you!	OK!

It may be necessary to supply the pattern many times before the patient can initiate it by himself.

2. Provide conversational situations so that the patient may use the phrases correctly.

3. Extend the practice to include simple sentences useful in everyday life:

I want coffee.
I am tired.
How much it it?
I want a paper.
Let's go to the show.

E. The paraphasic patient usually has the same difficulties in writing as he has in oral speech. Since the association of written patterns in

E. Written Formulation

1. Combine writing practice simultaneously or as a related drill following oral practice.

formulation is often helpful in the relearning of oral speech, writing constitutes an important aspect of retraining the paraphasic.

2. As the patient improves ask him to formulate his ideas in writing as well as in oral speech.

F. Sample Case of Paraphasia

A patient said, "You are always carrying those buttons," as he looked at the strand of beads the therapist wore frequently. The therapist wrote his sentence on the board. Directly beneath, she wrote, *You are always wearing those beads.* The difference between *carry* and *wear* was pointed out, and the words, *buttons* and *beads,* were compared. Actual buttons and beads were handled and talked about. The acts of carrying buttons and wearing beads were demonstrated. The patient was encouraged to say which statement he had intended to say.

Many times the therapist cannot interpret the paraphasia in such a sentence as, "We got it all be nightie curly better." In such cases there is little point in pursuing it any further. Later on the patient may be able to say what he had in mind in a more intelligible manner.

Chapter 15

READING RECOGNITION AND COMPREHENSION
(Alexia) [1]

I. INTRODUCTION

T HE MAJORITY OF aphasics experience some defect in understanding written and printed language. Occasionally amnesic and motor aphasics can understand essentially what they read even though they cannot talk; some patients with semantic alexia can read aloud but do not comprehend the reading content. Since the need for retraining varies with each patient, this chapter contains exercises for retraining in the recognition and comprehension of written and printed language from the use of simple words to the development of reading comprehension at intermediate and advanced levels.

II. TECHNIQUES FOR RECOGNITION OF INDIVIDUAL WORDS

REMARKS	EXERCISES
A. *Matching Articles, Pictures and Words.*	**A. Using Articles, Pictures and Word Cards for Word Recognition**
Word recognition is a first step in reading. In teaching word recognition it is helpful to use pictures with their corresponding items. For many aphasics the actual item and the picture of it are not the same; therefore, the use of both is often helpful.	1. Make up a kit of familiar items, pictures of these items, and corresponding word cards.
	2. Ask the patient to group together the item, the picture of it, and the matching word card. (In making up the word card, it may be helpful to *write* the word on one side and to *print* it on the other.)
Over-size letters are more stimulating than standard size. Encourage tracing with the finger.	3. As soon as the patient can identify the word card, withdraw the item and the picture of it.
A few suggested items:	

---

1. Nielsen, J. M.: *A Textbook of Clinical Neurology,* Third Edition. Paul B. Hoeber, Inc., New York, N. Y., pp. 245, 285.
———: *Memory and Amnesia.* San Lucas Press, Los Angeles, Calif., 1958, page 35.

1. Coffee advertisement—coffee can.

2. Various soap advertisements —bars of soap.

3. Cigarette advertisement— pack of cigarettes.

4. Hand lotion advertisement— the bottle of lotion.

5. Shampoo advertisement—the tube or bottle of shampoo.

Magazine advertisements are most helpful, particularly the colored ads which match the actual items.

B. *Pictures for Word Recognition.*[2] Using pictures and words together is one of the most common practices used to develop recognition of words.

Re-test frequently by asking the patient to read the word cards only. Example:

B. Using Pictures for Word Recognition

1. Present several pictures with accompanying identifying word cards. Ask the patient to match and to read the name of each item pictured.

2. The second time around, present the word cards only, asking the patient to read them. Refer to the picture as often as is necessary.

3. When picture dictionaries are used, test word recognition and comprehension either by covering the picture or by requiring identification of the study words listed on the board or on paper.

3. Some patients object if easy material has the appearance of being too juvenile. In that case, custom-made materials are more acceptable than picture dictionaries.

SOURCE MATERIAL:

a. *Golden Dictionary*—Ellen W. Walpole

b. *My First Dictionary*—Laura Oftedal & Nina Jacob

c. *What's Its Name*—Jean Utley

d. *Speech Through Pictures*— Margaret McCausland, Marie B. Miller, and Isabel Okie

---

2. Taylor, Martha L., and Marks, Morton M.: *Aphasia Rehabilitation Manual and Therapy Kit.* Saxon Press, 207 East 37th St., New York 16, N. Y., $7.50.

C. Traffic Signs: Road Sign Charts (Form DL-37, in colors, may be secured from the Department of Motor Vehicles—Division of Drivers' Licenses, in your own state.) If the therapist draws these signs, it is helpful to use colors identical with the actual signs.

D. An exercise such as this should be made up to fit the patient's particular environment. A home member will need an entirely different set of words such as his own name (on his mail box), his house number, signs on near-by store windows, etc.

E. It is possible for a patient to *recognize* a word without *comprehending* its meaning: each function should be evaluated. Tests and appropriate retraining for both recognition and comprehension should be carried out in a manner similar to these exercises.

C. Using Traffic Signs

1. Present the patient with miniature copies of traffic signs. Ask him to show or tell what each sign means.

2. Signs:
STOP GO SLOW CURVE DANGER SCHOOL HOSPITAL LEFT RIGHT etc.

D. Using Single-word Answers

1. On the board, write a list of words including those which are often seen in the immediate environment. Ask the patient to point out the correct words in answer to the therapist's questions.

> List: canteen
> nurse
> men
> secretary

Oral questions:

1. Which word is on the toilet door? (Men)

2. Where do you go to get a cup of coffee? (Canteen)

3. Who wears a white uniform? (Nurse)

4. Who types your pass on Fridays? (Secretary)

E. Distinguishing between Recognition and Comprehension

1. Make up a list of words such as MAN CAT APPLE.

2. For word RECOGNITION ask the patient to circle the word *man:* then *cat;* then *apple.*

3. For word COMPREHENSION ask the patient to circle the word which means something to eat

(apple) ; an animal (cat) ; you (man) .

F. Using colors is a good way in which to introduce the study of adjectives later on.

Assemble the items including with them a few which are not listed on the board.

G. Some patients may need auditory stimulation to bring out the association. Occasionally spelling the words aloud may help. The patient may also get additional help from tracing the word with his finger.

F. Learning with Colors

1. Ask the patient to point out the items listed on the board.
Sample list:

    a. A red book
    b. A yellow pencil
    c. A black book
    d. A large book (not the same color as above)
    e. A blue pen

2. Flash cards

Supply the patient with a stack of color cards or 3 x 5 cards on which a square of water color has been painted. Flash a word card before the patient, asking him to match it with the appropriate color card.

G. Matching (nouns or names) with Action Words

Ask the patient to put the words together in pairs so as to make good sense. (The words may be printed on separate cards or simply pointed out on the blackboard.)
Sample list:

DOGS	SHINES
BABY	BARK
SUN	CRIES
MARY (family member)	SINGS

H. Pantomiming Daily Activities

1. The therapist pantomimes these activities and asks the patient to pair up the words which describe the action. (Brush hair; open door; erase board; sweep floor; close window)

Make up two lists of words:

VERBS	NOUNS
open	hair
close	door
brush	window
erase	board
sweep	floor

2. Along with the language loss, many aphasia patients have also lost the ability to gesture and pantomime.

2. Ask the patient to carry out in pantomime sentences written on the board such as the following:

    a. open the window; close the window

    b. open the door; close the door

    c. shave

    d. sing

    e. brush your hair

    f. erase the board

    g. sweep the floor

I. *Sorting cards.*

While making word cards, it may be well to print the word on one side and to write it on the other.

Later on, the patient may be successful with abstract words such as love, hate, January, December, Tuesday, swift, misery, fast, etc.

I. Sorting Words into Categories
Make a set of cards, each card containing the name of a concrete article. Shuffle the cards then ask the patient to sort them into stacks such as animals, food, furniture, etc.
Word cards:

    cat, table, peas, dog, chair, bed, orange, horse, lettuce

Proper sorting would be:

cat	table	peas
dog	bed	orange
horse	chair	lettuce

J. Many exercises in Writing, Chapter 16, are also helpful in reading recognition and comprehension.

III. COMPREHENSION OF SENTENCES

A. Many weeks of drill may be necessary before aphasics of some types can read sentences. Some may read the commands orally and still

A. Reading Commands for Sentence Comprehension

Ask the patient to read each command then carry it out. (He

not be able to execute them because they do not comprehend their meaning. This is semantic alexia.

may read orally or silently.)
Example:

1. Hand me the key (present several items from which to select the key).
2. Close the door.
3. Comb your hair.
4. Clean your glasses.
5. Stand up.
6. Erase the board.
7. Point to your toe.

B. Material suggested by the patients is the most meaningful and the most flexible. Such material can range from the simplest to the difficult.

B. Reading Material Suggested by the Patients

Ask the patient to make a statement about something he is interested in. Write it on the board for a reading lesson.
Example:

1. My wife is coming to visit today. (Read it as it is written then test comprehension by substituting *son* for *wife* to see if the patient notices the change.)
2. We had fish for dinner; I don't like fish. (Later test comprehension by substituting *ham* for *fish* to see if patient notices the change.)

C. Maps of the United States or North America (on the wall or in the hands of the patient) are needed for this exercise. Many service people have been all over the world and can recall much geography. The exercise may be carried out further with maps of individual states and cities.

C. Using Maps

Write the following directions to be read and carried out by referring to the map.

1. Point to California.
2. Point to the Mississippi River.
3. Point to your home state.
4. Draw Kansas.
5. What country is north of the United States.

D. **Identifying Objects and People**

On the board, write a short description of some object or person in plain view. Ask the patient to read the description silently then to name what (or who) has been described.

Example:

1. This object is made of wood; it has a square flat top and four legs. (Table)

2. He is a young man; he has blue eyes, dark hair and writes right handed. (A member of the group)

E. Other confusing pairs are:

must-most	will-well
lamb-lamp	shin-chin
tall-tell	check-cheek
home-horse-house	
quiet-quite	
ever-every-very	
think-thank	
though-thought-through	
walk-work	

F. This exercise is also helpful in relearning the alphabet.

G. Reading arithmetic problems here is for comprehending the problem and applying the proper reasoning, not necessarily to arrive at the correct answer.

H. The preparation of this material is excellent practice for advanced students. The technique gives slow readers plenty of time to read and also frees the therapist to give individual help where it is needed.

E. **Selecting the Correct Word for Sentence Comprehension**

Ask the patient to select the correct word within the parentheses.

1. I (went want) to the canteen.
2. I (want went) a candy bar.
3. I (saw was) a good TV program.
4. I found a (shell shall) on the beach.

F. **Using the Index**

Ask the patient to find certain topics in the index of a suitable book.

G. **Comprehending Arithmetic Problems**

Ask the patient to read and to solve arithmetic problems which are within his grasp.

H. **Paragraph Reading**

Select complete paragraphs from such a source as Reader's Digest. These paragraphs should be only ten or eleven lines in length. Make up five or six fill-in or multiple-choice questions to be typed on 3 x 5 cards. On another card type the correct answers to these questions.

Ask the patient to read the story, then to answer the questions from the Question Card. After he finishes, he can check his answers with the Answer Card which he secures from the card file or from the therapist.

Sample QUESTION CARD and ANSWER CARD (Used in connection with a story *My Sad Life as a Southpaw* by James Collier, *Reader's Digest*, May 1961).

MY SAD LIFE AS A SOUTHPAW

James Collier

(*Reader's Digest*—May 1961)

1. (10%) (35%) of all the world is _____ handed.
2. Southpaw means (a father from Georgia) (a left-handed person) (an animal living near the South Pole).
3. The author should have played ball best (at first base) (at left field) (as catcher).
4. The author did not become a musician or learn to play golf because (his father could not afford it) (instruments are designed for right handers).
5. The author never found it difficult to use (the phone in the booth) (the tin snippers) (a mirror).

ANSWER CARD

(My Sad Life as a Southpaw)

1. 10%   *left*
2. a left-handed person
3. at first base
4. the instruments are designed for righthanders
5. a mirror

I. Sample Paragraph for Detailed Reading:

I bought two dozen egg and a

I. Detailed Reading

Write out for the patient a set of instructions, such as suggested be-

pound of butter. Just as I started home it began to rain so I ran as fast as I could to keep from getting wet. As I reached my cabin, I slipped on a wet leaf, fell down and broke all twenty-four eggs.

low, to be carried out in the paragraph of reading matter at the left.

1. Add "s" to the fifth word.

2. Draw a circle around the third "as" in the paragraph.

3. Underline the name of the living quarters.

4. Underline the word which means the same as two-dozen.

J. *The Wordy Game* is available at many book and game counters. It consists of seven "dice" with words printed on the six sides of each cube. The player throws the dice from a shaker and attempts to form a sentence with the seven words.

IV. SAMPLE WORD-STUDY UNIT

(This can be carried out best when the patient is reading orally; it will strengthen and enlarge his reading vocabulary.)

1. List errors as the patient reads, jot down on 3 x 5 cards each word he mispronounces, distorts, or appears not to understand. At the close of the session, flash these cards before him for review.

2. Study derivatives and modifications: whenever a word is a derivative itself, or has derivatives, study all of them in order to strengthen comprehension in general.

Example: disobedient: obey, obediently, disobey, disobedience, obedience

preparation: prepare, prepared, preparing, unprepared, preparedness

3. Synonyms and Homonyms: suppose the patient encounters UNDAUNTED in his reading and he fails to get the meaning. Tell him the meaning, then ask him to give a word with the *same* meaning and another with the *opposite* meaning.

Example: UNDAUNTED is the *same* as brave, unafraid, fearless

UNDAUNTED is the *opposite* of timid, fearful, afraid

V. LESSON PLAN FOR RECALL AND ORAL EXPRESSION

A. A great deal of the language used in retraining, of necessity, is on a very elementary level. Even though many adult aphasics are still in possession of a great many facts and may possess technical and professional skills, they seldom have an opportunity to use them because of their limited language. If a therapist has some technical, artistic or specialized skills, he certainly should contrive to use this ability in the patient's behalf to draw him out, to cause him to think and to express himself as best he can. Most rewarding lessons can come from a knowledge of good music, the symphonies, noted composers and artists, from discussions on art, history, electronics, geography, sports, the stock market, the trades and even medicine.

Miscellaneous information questions and even brain twisters have proved most entertaining and effective through the use of flash-card lessons. Of course the patient must have reading comprehension to play the game. One-word answers, a show of numbers on the fingers, or sometimes a nod of the head or a facial expression will allow a speechless patient to participate in an advanced group if he has reading comprehension.

Following is a partial list to suggest the type of questions which can be written with felt pen on 5" x 12" cards for repeated use with advanced patients:

Name three great arts.

Name eight states of the U. S. which begin with M.

Who was Diego Rivera?

What words rhyme with cat?

What is the difference between health and wealth?

What do mind, body, and soul belong to?

What great thing took place at Promontory, Utah in 1869?

Smooth is to rough and soft is to _____.

Arm is to elbow and leg is to ____.

Tailor is to clothes and baker is to _____.

What are the three elements of a triode and what are their uses?

What is a dead man's pedal?

How long does it take light from the sun to reach the earth?

How is the Beethoven Ninth Symphony different from other symphonies?

What is the difference between a tune in the major and one in the minor?

What state has these cities: Ogden, Moab, Salt Lake City?

What type of current does a transformer pass?

What is surrealism?

Who is Picasso?

What is moire?

What is Germantown?

B. References Helpful for Making Flash Cards:

Elmo, Horace: *Golden Picture Book of Questions and Answers*. Simon & Schuster, New York, N. Y.

The Lookies: The lively question marks of the Look-It-Up Club. *World Book Encyclopedia*. Field Enterprises Educational Corporation, Merchandise Mart Plaza, Chicago 54, Ill., 1960.

Through the Year with the World Book: Field Enterprizes Educational Corporation, Merchandise Mart Plaza, Chicago 54, Ill.

Carlisle, Norman, Romney, Arnold, and Mott-Smith, Geoffrey: *Modern Wonderbook of Knowledge.* Winston Company, 1949.

Information Please: Los Angeles Evening Herald and Express, The Macmillan Co., New York, N. Y.

World Almanac and Book of Facts: New York World Telegram, 125 Barclay Street, New York 15, N. Y.

VI. READING MATERIAL WITH TESTS

Material of adult interest but with simple vocabulary is listed below. Tests for reading comprehension are most essential, especially if the reading has been done silently. Good testing material is supplied with each of the following texts. Consult "High Interest, Low Vocabulary" booklists such as that published by Boston University's Educational Clinic, Boston University School of Education, 332 Bay State Road, Boston 15, Mass.

1. *SRA Better Reading:* Books I, II, III by Simpson, Elizabeth. Science Research Associates, Inc. 57 West Grand Ave., Chicago 10, Ill.
2. *SRA Reading Laboratory,* Elementary Edition: Science Research Associates, Inc., 57 West Grand Ave., Chicago 10, Ill., 1958. Kit contains: 150 cards (15 at 10 different grade levels, each grade is designated by a color);
    key cards
    40 answer booklets
    student record book
    teacher handbook
    colored checking pencils
3. *Reader's Digest Reading Skill Builder:* Books 1, 2, 3, 4, 5. Reader's Digest Educational Service, Inc., Pleasantville, N. Y.
4. *Reader's Digest Adult Education Reader:* Levels A, B, C, Reader's Digest Educational Service, Inc., Pleasantville, N. Y.
5. Leavell, Ullin W. and Davis, Betty: *New Adventures in Reading.* Steck Company, Austin, Tex., 1953.
6. Brueckner, Leo J., and Lewis, William Dodge: *Diagnostic Tests and Remedial Exercises in Reading.* John C. Winston Company, Philadelphia, Pa.

VII. LOW LEVEL READING MATERIAL OF ADULT INTEREST

1. *Elementary Education for Adults*—Owens, Albert A. and Sharlip, William. John C. Winston Company, Philadelphia, Pa.
2. *Beginning Lessons in English*—Fisher, Isobel Yealy and Dixson, Robert J. Regents Publishing Company, New York, N. Y.
3. *Illustrated Minute Biographies*—Nisenson, Samuel and DeWitt, William A. Grosset & Dunlap, New York, N. Y.

4. *Magic Teacher Puzzle Plans,* Reading Set R1, R2. Follett Publishing Company, 1255 S. Wabash Ave., Chicago, Ill.

5. *E. W. Dolch Reading Games and Cards.* The Hart Vance Company, St. Louis 3, Mo.
    —Look
    —The Sentence Game
    —Popper Words
    —Match, Set 1, Set 2

6. *Educational Cards,* 1302 Industrial Bank Bldg., Detroit 26, Mich.

7. *Let's Read About Russia*—Shapovalov, Michael and Walsh, Warren B. Fideler Co., Grand Rapids, Mich.

8. *Let's Read About Alaska*—Timpkins, Stuart R. Fideler Co., Grand Rapids, Mich.

9. *Let's Read About Canada*—Harris, Leila and Kilroy. Fideler Co., Grand Rapids, Mich.

10. *Let's Read About South America*—Goetz, Delia. Fideler Co., Grand Rapids, Mich.

11. *World Atlas,* Rand McNally, New York, N. Y.

12. *I Want to Read and Write*—Smith, Harley A. and King, Ida Lee. The Steck Co., Austin, Tex.

13. *The Story of Noah's Ark*—Palazzo, Tony. Garden City Books, Garden City, N. Y.

14. *How to Read Better*—Smith, Harley A. and King, Ida Lee. Steck Co., Austin, Tex.

15. *Our Community*—Hobbs, Valine. Steck Company, Austin, Tex.

16. *Our World Neighbors*—Hobbs, Valine. Steck Company, Austin, Tex.

17. *Words on Paper*—First Steps in Reading—I. A. Richards and Christine Gibson. English Language Research, Inc., 13 Kirkland St., Cambridge 38, Mass.

18. *Story of America*—Fisher, Margaret and Fowler, Mary J. Fideler Company, Grand Rapids, Mich., 1960. Five books: Great Explorers, Colonial America, Pioneer Days, Transportation, Great Americans

19. *Golden Home and High School Encyclopedia*—Golden Press, North Road, Poughkeepsie, N. Y., Twenty volumes. Available in supermarkets, drug and department stores.

20. *Golden Book Encyclopedia*—Golden Press, Rockefeller Center, New York, N. Y., 16 volumes.

21. *Golden Book Picture Atlas of the World,* Golden Press, Rockefeller Center, New York, N. Y., (6 volumes)

22. Webster Classroom Science Library: Ware, Kay; Sutherland, Leo J., and

Lewis, Wm. Dodge. Webster Publishing Co., Pasadena, Calif. Twelve paper-back booklets:

Let's Read About Insects

Let's Read About Birds

Let's Read About Fishes

Let's Read About Stars

Let's Read About Rocks & Minerals

Let's Read About Trees

Let's Read About Sea Shells

Let's Read About Prehistoric Animals

Let's Read About Butterflies

Let's Read About Reptiles & Amphibians

Let's Read About Flowers

Let's Read About Mountains and Volcanoes

23. *Junior Airman's Book of Airplanes* (1958) ; *The Book of Missiles* (1959); *Messages from Space* (1961) —Davis, Clive E., Dodd, Mead & Co., New York, N. Y.

For the Therapist:

1. Russell, David and Karp, Etta E.: *Reading Aids Through the Grades.* Bureau of Publications, Teachers College, Columbia University, New York, N. Y.

2. Travis, E. L.: *Handbook of Speech Pathology.* Appleton-Century-Crofts, New York, N. Y., page 489.

3. Waldman, John: *Reading Made Simple,* Junior Series. Doubleday and Co., Inc., Garden City, N. Y.

4. Americanization material prepared by local schools for adult classes for the foreign born.

5. See: Chapter 33, Section IV.

Chapter 16

WRITING
(Agraphia) [1]

I. INTRODUCTION

T HE ACT OF writing is a combination of motor and mental processes so complicated that the loss of it—called agraphia—is the most difficult of all the aphasias to analyze.

 There are two types of agraphia. Apractic or motor agraphia applies to the patient who cannot write because he no longer knows how to form the letters although he may or may not be able to spell orally. Agnostic or amnesic agraphia is a spelling loss. The patient can form the letters, but he does not know what to write.

Paragraphia is a term used when the patient fails to recall the correct words and consequently writes the wrong words. This is comparable to paraphasia. An example of paragraphia taken from clinic files: The carriee the mail the morote an letter.

Handedness[2]

The question is often asked whether or not an aphasic who still has the use of his major hand should change handedness. The act of changing handedness simply creates a new motor writing center in the other hemisphere. Some patients appear to be more ambidextrous than others and can readily change handedness. Occasionally there are psychological involvements wherein the patient does not want to change handedness, in which case it is not wise to force the issue. A safe guide is to let the patient decide for himself which hand he prefers to use. In the case of hemiplegics, of course, there is no choice —they must change handedness.

Writing is usually considered a most helpful medium in a learning situ-

1. Nielsen, J. M.: *A Textbook of Clinical Neurology,* Third Edition. Paul B. Hoeber, Inc., New York, N. Y., pp. 267, 268, 279, 285, 286.

    ————: *Memory and Amnesia.* San Lucas Press, Los Angeles, Calif., 1958, pp. 36, 170, 175.
2. Subirana, Antonio: The relationship between handedness and language function. *Logos,* Vol. 4, No. 2, October 1961.

    Travis, E. L.: *Handbook of Speech Pathology.* Appleton-Century-Crofts, New York, N. Y., pp. 483, 496.

ation—in calculating, in spelling, and in various types of memory work. Consequently many of the writing exercises in this section serve for retraining in areas other than in the writing area alone.

It is not the intention here that a patient should begin with exercise A and proceed chronologically through the section. Usually a patient repeats one type of exercise for many weeks. The chapter contains samples of material from which to pattern other exercises to fit the needs of individual patients.

II. MATERIALS FOR LOWEST-LEVEL AGRAPHIA

The therapist should determine which materials best meet the immediate needs of the patient. He usually works best with pencil and paper since that has been his customary medium. Even though he demonstrates a need for gross movements at first, in all probability he will soon revert to normal-size handwriting.

Materials

1. Portable blackboard about 16 x 22 to be used as a lapboard with chalk.

2. Large sheets of paper to be used with crayon. (This type of beginning work can be filed for future reference.)

3. Block, raised, or grooved letters for use with the kinesthetic method.

4. Ordinary ruled paper $8\frac{1}{2}$ x 11 inches with onion skin paper for tracing; pencil.

III. HANDWRITING

REMARKS

A. Every patient may not need to start here. If one demonstrates that he can do this exercise, go on immediately until his level is ascertained. Determine where he can function, then continue from there. If he demonstrates that he can begin with cursive writing, by all means use it immediately.

EXERCISES

A. Tracing and Copying Lines and Curves

1. "Write" straight lines, circles and curves. Supply smaller copy for the patient as soon as his control warrants it. Help the patient hold the pencil, and guide his hand if he cannot copy or trace.

B. Some patients have an aptitude for drawing, others have not. If such an aptitude is discovered, encourage the patient to make use of it; but if one is not inclined to draw, it is best not to spend time trying to cultivate a new skill at this point.

C. Raised letters, letters cut from sandpaper or pasteboard are helpful for those patients who need to learn by the kinesthetic method. Anagram sets frequently can be used.

Sometimes it is helpful to write the letter in the patient's palm so that he can get tactile clue.

f. Provide the item, or a picture of it, so that the patient can associate the symbol and the item.

D. Patients often are able to begin with cursive writing instead of with printing. Don't do any of this type of exercise just for the sake of good penmanship unless the patient particularly desires it. If the patient can write legibly, concentrate on spelling exercises.

Write words as soon as possible. The patient should know what he is writing. Say the letter, sound, or word as it is being written.

B. Drawing

C. Tracing and Copying Alphabet Letters and Numbers

Incorporate straight lines into printed letters and numbers.

I A M N W E F X Y V H Z
K L T   1 4 7

2. Combining circles with straight lines:

O C Q D G P R S U B
2 3 5 6 8 9   BUS DOG COP

3. Using initials, abbreviations, numbers, words:

     a. Patient's initials
     b. T.V. (television)
     c. Hospital ward designation such as N 14
     d. Patient's age
     e. Patient's weight
     f. One-syllable words: MAN HAT KEY FAN PIPE

D. Introducing Cursive Writing

IV. COPY WORK
(These exercises can easily be placed on the blackboard for group therapy or on tablet paper for therapy with an individual.)

REMARKS

A. The therapist will need to add many words. Stick figures, pictures of items and/or the actual items with accompanying word cards are a necessity.

A patient needs to do this type of work usually for many months. Present the word card and the picture card (or item) for copy work, audibly *name* the item. After a few days' practice, present only the picture cards or items. The patient is to recall and to write the names. Later on, simply pronounce the words as a spelling list.

Materials: (1) Dolch Cards (2) Warnock-Medlin: Word Making Cards (3) I. A. Richards and C. M. Gibson: English Through Pictures.

B. Incorporate words learned above into simple sentences. Later on, substitute a picture or line drawing of the noun in order to give the patient practice in recalling the names. *Examples:*

I like

I see a

EXERCISES

A. Copying the Names of Objects
   Display objects or pictures of objects to be named. (A card file of pictures[3] can be handed to patients for naming.) Sample exercise:

pie   pipe   clock

book   apple   cap

cow   cat   pen

B. Copying Simple Sentences
Examples:
   1. I like pie.
   2. I see a clock.
   3. I want a book.
   4. I like a pipe.
   5. I want a pen.

---

3. See Picture files, Chapter 5, Section IV.

C. Keep this exercise on a *concrete* level, for aphasics have great difficulty with the abstract. The therapist should demonstrate with a few examples how the exercise is to be done.

FOOD   CLOTHING BODY

1 _____ 1. _____   1 _____
2 _____ 2. _____   2 _____
       etc.   etc.   etc.

C. Selecting and Copying Words from a List

Show the patient a list of words either on the board or on paper. Direct him to copy in one column:

1. The words which name something to eat such as *pie*.

2. In a second column, he is to write the words which name something to wear such as a coat.

3. In a third column, he is to write the words which name parts of the body—such as *eye*.

The list: toe, coffee, knee, foot, chest, arm, shirt, hat, head, corn, ear, cap, mouth, bread, socks, nose, oranges, shoes, hand, onions, eye, pie, bacon, ham, leg, tie, coat, pants, shoulder, stomach, sweater.

D. Copying One-Word Answers

Write on the blackboard several questions such as the following. Show the patient one of the items named in each question, then ask him to copy the appropriate word. Examples:

1. Is this a pen or a pencil? pen
2. Is this a glass or a cup? _____
3. Is this a book or a paper? ____
4. Is this a ring or a watch? ____

E. The patient may have learned to spell the days of the week if he has formed the habit of writing the day on his daily practice sheets.

Later on try dictating the entire sentence especially if the patient has demonstrated that he can write the first words without copying.

E. Copying from the Calendar

The patient is to copy the *sentences* from the board, but select the *days* from the calendar.

Fill the blanks:

1. I go to church on _____.
2. I go home on _____.
3. Wash day is on _____.

4. Today is _____.

5. Pay day is _____.

V. SPELLING

A. Using a Remedial Technique

(This successful technique is described in *Remedial Techniques in Basic School Subjects* by Grace M. Fernald.)

Provide the patient with several slips of paper. The therapist writes (on the board) a word once. Patients look at it (they do not write). Patients pronounce the word. ERASE the board. Go through this same process three times. (The patients have written nothing thus far.) Next, the patient attempts to write the word and to pronounce it. (Notice the board is erased.) The therapist checks the patient's copy and if it is correct, destroys it. The patient is now instructed to write the word three times on three separate slips of paper taking care not to copy from the preceding slip. There should be nothing in view from which to copy. Each time, the patient is to *recall* the word, to *write* it and *say* it. The therapist makes corrections where needed.

B. The therapist will find it easy to make flash cards especially with the use of the Flo Master felt pen.

After the patient has written the word, place the flash card in plain sight so that he can check his spelling.

B. Filling Blanks with the Use of Flash Cards

Sample exercise:

1. First practice the words as a spelling lesson, or as a review of words already presented. For example: pie, pipe, pen, I like, I smoke, I want, I see. On the board write sentence beginnings like a, b, c, below, leaving blanks to be filled with appropriate words. The patient is to write the word flashed before him in any of the blanks to make sense. Obviously he is not to write *I eat pipe*.

a. I want a _____.

b. I smoke a _____.

c. I eat _____.

In the same manner, write examples like d, e, f, below with the blanks first and the nouns last. The patient is to fill in, from the flash cards, the appropriate phrases to complete the subject and verb. Obviously he must not write *I smoke pie.*

    d. __ _____ pie.

    e. __ _____ a pipe.

    f. __ _____ a pen.

2. Flash entire simple short sentences for writing practice. Examples:

    a. Come in.

    b. Shut the door.

    c. Play ball.

    d. Dogs bark.

C. Mount colored pictures of fruits, vegetables, meats, clothing, tools, etc. on cards. On each card write the beginning letter or first two or three letters of the item pictured, and also some random letters in order to provide a multiple-choice exercise.

Often a patient can complete a word after he gets the proper start.

D. Select sentences which suggest an automatic completion. Using the Fernald remedial technique described in A above, first practice writing the words to be used in the sentences selected for the lesson. As soon as the patient appears to have the spelling mastered, present the

C. Multiple Choice

The patient is to select the correct beginning letters to name the item pictured, then complete the word. *Examples:*

Pictures	*Letters printed on picture card*	
orange	acw	ora
sandwich	bib	san
tomato	vif	to
bacon	b	c
hammer	rny	ham

D. Initiating Words Automatically

Ask the patient to finish the sentence, thus:

1. "I shine my _____." Patient supplies "shoes" which is the only part of the sentence which is to be written.

sentences (on the board, or on paper) to be completed.

The same sentences may be used for dictation practice later on.

2. "Give me a cup and _____."
   (saucer)
3. "I like ham and _____." (eggs)
4. "Do you use cream and _____?"
   (sugar)
5. "Can you hear the baby _____?"
   (cry)
6. "Dogs _____." (bark)

E. Many aphasics appear to have lost their former resourcefulness. This exercise is the beginning of retraining in the use of the dictionary. In some cases the patient may need the picture beside the word. Stick drawings or small magazine ads are helpful. Use this system over a period of months, composing exercises using the words listed and adding new ones. The exercises should be made up so that the patient has to find the words he needs from his "custom-made" dictionary.

E. Making a Dictionary of Words in Chosen Categories

Prepare a notebook in which patients can add words as they are used. Categories such as food, clothing, toilet articles, family names, and household words are the most useful. List the new words under the proper categories.

F. The therapist *says* the first sentence, and asks the patient to write the part shown in parentheses. In this type of exercise the patient with anomia has the added practice of the recall of names which he greatly needs.

This exercise provides a review of pronouns.

F. Writing Opposites

Example: The therapist says, Bill (patient's name) is not a woman. The patient is to write, "He is a man."

1. Bill does not eat dinner in the morning. (He eats at _____.)
2. Bill's shoes are not on his head. (They are on his _____.)
3. Mary (patient's wife) is not my husband. (She is my _____.)
4. Bill's hands are not dirty. (They are _____.)

G. Patients on this level may not yet be able to think of terms in the abstract; but appropriate words may come through occasionally. Keep

G. Using Automatic Associations

Write the first two words on the board; the patient is to initiate and to spell the second word of the pair.

introducing a few abstract ideas from time to time.

After the exercise is fairly well mastered as it is, switch the word order. Lastly, require the patient to spell the pairs from dictation.

1. black and _____ 9. good and ____
2. uncle and _____ 10. rich and _____
3. coffee and _____ 11. high and ____
4. mother and ___ 12. old and _____
5. ham and _____ 13. sweet and ____
6. brother and ___ 14. cup and _____
7. girl and _____ 15. knife and ____
8. gold and _____

H. Vary the lesson by encouraging a patient to be the performer while others recall and write the appropriate word to describe the action.

H. Playing Elementary Charades
The patient is to write in one word what the therapist does.
1. Therapist *hums.*
   Patient should write HUM.
2. Therapist sings.
   Patient should write SING.
3. Therapist stands.
   Patient should write STAND, RISE.
4. Therapist sits, writes, smokes, whistles, reads, walks, etc.

I. Patients often enjoy this exercise borrowed from the hard-of-hearing.

Let the patient try to spell the words himself. Help him if he needs it.

Use labials as much as possible to enable the patient to SEE the initial sounds.

Later on try complete sentences for lip reading.

I. Lip-Reading Exercise
First put the patient "in the situation" such as *in the grocery store, in the cafe, in the meat market,* etc., then "mouth" short words which he is to "read," then write. Examples:

1. Grocery store:
   potatoes
   bread
   bananas
   tomatoes
   apples
2. Meat Market:
   beef
   bacon
   pork
   lamb

3. Cafe:
   pie
   meat
   ice cream
   pumpkin pie
   salad
4. Furniture Store:
   bed
   chair
   table
   lamp

J. This can also be used as an elementary dictionary exercise. Let the patient copy appropriate words from the dictionary.

It is helpful to have a printed alphabet in plain sight to which the patients may refer, as many no longer know the alphabet in its entirety.

Other word beginnings should be added.

K. Make a strong appeal to the visual image. This is a good place to use colored chalk either on the initial letter or on the last part of the word.

Other "families": -all; -ace; -ell; -ill; -ilk; -ade; -ink; -ase; -ane.

Encourage the patient to run through the entire alphabet seeking appropriate initial letters for these words.

L. It is helpful to put the patient "in the situation" such as:

"Dinner-table" situation

"Breakfast" situation

J. Using Word Beginnings

The patient is to write all the words he can recall beginning with:

1. ba____ 1. ma ___ 1. fa ____ 1. ta ____
2. _____ 2. _____ 2. _____ 2. _____
3. _____ 3. _____ 3. _____ 3. _____
4. _____ 4. _____ 4. _____ 4. _____

K. Using Families of Words or Rhyming Words

The patient is to write all the words he can think of which belong to the same "family" or which rhyme.

-ake	-ack	-ame	-ate
1. bake	1. back	1. dame	1. date
2.	2.	2.	2.
3.	3.	3.	3.
4.	4.	4.	4.

L. Supplying Missing Letters

The patient is to supply the missing letters.

The therapist explains that these items are found on the dinner table:

1. pl--e   5. na-k--
2. kn---   6. g--ss
3. f---   7. c-- and s---r
4. sp---

"For breakfast we often have some of these foods. What are they?"

1. t---t   4. b----
2. j---y   5. h-- c---s
3. --g   6. ce---l

M. The Word Game[4]

1. *The Word Game,* which can be found in many daily papers, is especially good for encouraging use of the dictionary. Patients should look up words

---

4. Permission to use the Word Game was granted by the *Los Angeles Times* and The Bell Syndicate.

they are in doubt about. RULES OF THE GAME: Words must be of four or more letters. Proper names are not used. Only one form of a word is to be used. A three-letter word with s added is not permitted. A letter cannot be used twice in a word unless it occurs twice in the key word.

Can	you	find	24	words	in	the	Key	word	BEGINNER
"	"	"	27	"	"	"	"	"	ENABLED
"	"	"	28	"	"	"	"	"	REFINED
"	"	"	16	"	"	"	"	"	INEXACT
"	"	"	18	"	"	"	"	"	ENDURED
"	"	"	19	"	"	"	"	"	LIVABLE
"	"	"	21	"	"	"	"	"	OUTSIDE
"	"	"	20	"	"	"	"	"	SPANKING
"	"	"	22	"	"	"	"	"	COMMITTEE

2. *Win-a-Throw Game.* This "dice" game is available at many book and game counters. It consists of lettered dice to be thrown from a shaker. The player is to make as many words as possible from the twelve dice thrown face up.

N. The Hangman's Game. The popular Hangman's Game has been a favorite among clinic groups for spelling practice and word recall.

Rules of the Game: Draw the scaffold and the noose.

2. The leader selects a word which he does not reveal to the group. He draws a blank for each letter of the word and which he will fill in as the game progresses.

For example: W A T E R (five letters which necessitates five blanks beside the scaffold as shown above.)

3. Each patient takes his turn at suggesting a letter of the alphabet. If the letter happens to be in the word the leader has chosen, the leader writes it in the proper blank and the same patient guesses again until he "misses."

(The alphabet should be in view. Each time a letter is used, it should be striken out or erased.)

4. The next patient takes his turn at suggesting a letter. Suppose he suggests N, which is not in the word, W A T E R. The leader begins to *hang* the man by drawing a head in the noose. Suppose the next patient suggests S which is not in the word WATER. The leader draws an eye on the head.

5. Every time a patient suggests a letter in the word, the letter is placed on the proper blank. Every time a letter not in the word is suggested, another part of the body is drawn on the scaffold. After the head, add the eyes, the ears, nose, mouth, a straight line for the trunk, then the arms, hands, legs, feet.

6. If the group has not guessed the word by the time a complete man has been drawn on the scaffold, the leader has "hanged" the man and won the game.

VI. WRITTEN FORMULATION
(Words, Phrases, Sentences, Paragraphs)

A. The therapist writes the question leaving the patient to supply the answer from the words in the question itself. He may need a great deal of oral drill on this exercise before he can formulate his own simple answers.

A. Writing Simple Sentences

The patient is to write the answer by selecting the appropriate words from the question.

1. Do you wear a skirt or pants?
   I wear _____.
2. Do you smoke an apple or a cigarette?
   I smoke a _____.
3. Do you read a letter or wash it?
   I _____ a letter.
4. Do you drink coffee or wear it?
   I _____ coffee.
5. Do you eat a book or read it?
   I _____ a book.

B. Show the article or a picture of it. Next ask what color it is, then add the adjective to the noun. As soon as the patient can spell the colors, begin to talk about size, shape, etc. Now ask if the apple is a *big* apple or a *little* apple, if the book is a *big* book or a *little* book, etc. Teach the spelling of these additional adjectives.

1. The patient is to write the color and the names of these articles:

   a. red apple   e. blue ink
   b. red book   f. tan shoes
   c. red chair   g. green pants
   d. red pen   h. green rug

2. Next, use other adjectives:

   a. big apple—little apple
   b. big book—little book
   c. hot water—cold water
   d. long pencil—short pencil
   e. sunny day—cloudy day

3. Next combine the two adjectives before the noun: big red apple, little red book, etc.

C. Often the patient cannot keep the sentence in mind. It is helpful for him to say the sentence aloud several times before he starts to write. Certain types of aphasics can write well from dictation even though they cannot initiate their own sentences.

D. This is an opportune time to drill on plurals with the addition of *s* and *es,* and with the past tense *ed,* and the present participle *ing.*

Have the alphabet in plain sight as many aphasics no longer know the entire alphabet.

Additional suggestions:
1. able
2. ate
3. oat
4. act
5. an-āne
6. in-īne
7. it-īte
8. eet
9. lea
10. ear
11. oil
12. ill

C. Dictation Exercises
1. Hello
2. Come in
3. Sweep the floor
4. Dust the chairs
5. Shut the door
6. Play ball
7. Wash the dishes
8. Make the beds

D. A Modified Phonetic Approach to Writing

Explain that A-R-M has the sound of arm no matter where it is seen. Direct the patient to prefix the three letters with other consonants to form new words.

Use prefixes:	Then try *adding* suffixes:
1. arm	arms
farm	army
harm	armed
charm	armory
alarm	armpit
2. aƷƷ	basset
bass	lassie
lass	lasso
mass	passing
pass	passport
class	password
compass	classic
	classmate
	classy
3. eat	eaten, eater
beat	beaten, beater (egg beater)
heat	heated
neat	neatly
seat	seated
meat	meaty

E. Draw the appropriate number of columns on the blackboard heading each column with a key word containing the vowel (or diphthong) sound to be used in all words in the column. (See key words in column at right.) Dictate a word to be placed in one of the columns leaving it up to the patient to ascertain in which column the word belongs. Next, instruct the patient to think of all other words he can with the same initial and final sounds to be written in the remaining columns.

Many suggestions for other columns may be found in *Voice and Articulation Drill Book,* Grant Fairbanks, Harper & Bros., Chapters II through IV.

F. Other suggestions: These words are often easily confused.

	taken	
	token	
how		down
now	spoken	drown
won	broken	brown
	bought	drown
	brought	drawn
	work	
	waltz	
	walk	

E. Cultivating Vowel-Sound Discrimination
Sample columns for exercise:
Key words: ought, oat, out, **cot, cut.**

(ought)	(oat)	(out)	(cot)	(cut)
1. bought	boat	bout		but
2. caught	coat		cot	cut
3. taught	tote		tot	

When the columns have been completed, read each row from left to right several times. Then read each column from top to bottom.

F. Using Words with Similar Elements
The patient is to use the proper words for filling the blanks. Examples: WAS and SAW
1. The dog _____ black.
2. I _____ the black dog.
WHERE THERE WERE HERE
1. _____ do you live?
2. _____ are 40 patients in the ward.
3. The patients _____ in Ward N-14.
4. I put the book _____ on the table.
5. I do not know _____ you live.
6. Please come _____.
 THOUGH THROUGH THOUGHT
1. The man tossed a bottle _____ the gate.

2. We may escape, _____ I think not.
3. John _____ he heard a shot.
   WHITHER   WHETHER
   WEATHER   WITHER
1. Tell me _____ or not you **are** coming.
2. I do not like warm _____.
3. "_____ goest thou?"
4. The hot _____ makes the flowers _____.

G. Other categories
NOUNS:
   Traveler: tourist, wanderer, rover, passenger, voyager
   Animal: beast, brute, creature
   Boy: lad, youth, youngster
   Boat: ship, craft, vessel
VERBS:
   Look: view, see, observe, peer, watch
   Go: depart, leave, set out, proceed, exit
ADJECTIVES:
   Happy: glad, cheerful, delighted
   Old: aged, elderly, senile
   Cold: chilly, frigid, bleak

G. Using Synonyms
   Write synonyms according to category. Use a thesaurus or dictionary if necessary. Provide the initial and final letters and the correct number of blanks.

HOME[5]	CLOTHING
1. a---e	1. g--b
2. r-------e	2. r----t
3. d------g	3. a----e
4. d-----e	4. a-----l

H.
1. An aphasic usually has to relearn the meaning of a preposition. Demonstrate for him by placing an object such as a pencil, a handkerchief, or a book in various places emphasizing the preposition with the action. Place the pencil IN the drawer, ON the table, UNDER the table, ON your head, etc.
2. Prepositional phrases are very difficult for aphasics. Their lack of

H. Relearning Prepositions
1. Direct the patient to write a prepositional phrase describing where the therapist places the object. Examples:
   a. in the drawer
   b. on the table
   c. on your head
   d. under the table

2. Using Prepositions.
   Show the patient pictures from

5. HOME: abode, residence, dwelling, domicile. CLOTHING: garb, raiment, attire, apparel.

the use of prepositions and connectives results in what is called "telegraphic" speech. Often aphasics can't use the preposition although they can use its object.

magazines which depict something which can be described by prepositional phrases.

Direct him to write appropriate phrases to complete the sentences initiated by the therapist.
Examples:
- a. (Picture: people in a car)
  These people are riding
  _____ __ _____.
- b. (Picture: bird on the fence)
  The bird sits _____ _____
  _____.

I. This type of exercise can be used over and over again. Sentences describing some event of the day in which the patient participated are often more meaningful to him.

I. Word-Order Practice
The patient is to unscramble the words and rearrange them so that they make a meaningful sentence. *Example:*
1. With shave a I razor.
2. Cream drink with and I coffee sugar.
3. You many at can canteen things the buy.

J. Using the Four W's
Head four columns with WHO WHAT WHEN WHERE, then begin sentence formulation by filling in appropriate words under each column.

WHO   WHAT   WHEN   WHERE

1. Talk about the word *who* and lead the patient into suggesting the name of a person present or well-known: John. Write the name in the WHO column .... John
2. Now talk about the word *what* stating that the next thing to be done is to write down what was done or what took place: went

	WHO	WHAT	WHEN	WHERE
swimming	John	went swimming		

3. Next, discuss *when* John went swimming, whether in the morning, afternoon or evening and write it in the next column ....

	WHO	WHAT	WHEN	WHERE
	John	went swimming	in the afternoon	

4. Last, discuss *where* John went swimming, whether in the ocean, in the river, or in the pool and write it in the last column ....

	WHO	WHAT	WHEN	WHERE
	John	went swimming	in the afternoon	in the pool

As the patient progresses switch the order of the columns using WHEN first: In the afternoon John went swimming in the pool.

Later on add the HOW and/or the WHY in order to expand the sentences.

VII. WRITING IN PARAGRAPHS

A. Describing Objects 1. Present some object such as the American flag. Ask the patient to write two or three sentences describing it. If necessary supply a few words at first such as the colors, stripe, field.

2. Describe something not in view.

3. Describe some process or movement such as how to shave; how to dress; how to light a cigarette.

B. Using "Action English" 1. Ask one or two patients to act out some simple situation, then ask the patient to write down what they did.

Suggestions: Borrow a cigarette and a match; carry on a telephone conversation; get a haircut at the barber shop.

2. Orally give a patient some simple act to carry out or duty to perform. After he has carried out the action, ask him to write what he did. Example: Take a book from the desk. Open it to page 176 and read the last three words on the page.

3. Write directions for reaching some local establishment. Example: How do you get to the post office from here? How do you reach the beach from the hospital?

C. Writing a Paragraph Following a Topic Sentence
Examples

1. Pictures improve the appearance of a room.

2. Every Friday we have a choice of fish or hash for dinner.

3. We like a Volkswagen car because . . .

D. Describing Pictures 1. Present the patient with a picture showing some situation such as a car with a flat tire. Ask him to write what happened. Fiction magazines are replete with appropriate pictures for this exercise.

2. Present the patient with a picture with something omitted, or with an anachronism pictured. Ask him to write what is missing or what is unusual about the picture.

Manuals used for psychological testing usually contain a few pictures with parts missing. Line drawings may be used such as a wagon with a wheel missing, a person with a body part left out, or clock with numbers incorrectly placed.

E. Rewriting Paragraphs Read a paragraph to the patient and ask him to write the context in his own words. Later he may be able to do the same with a short story.

F. Letter Writing Let the patient actually write his own personal letters. Incorporate proper heading, salutation and closing. Vary the exercise by composing job applications and business letters,[6] invitations, letters of thanks, etc.

G. Writing an Autobiography Ask the patient to write about some interesting part of his life such as: College Days, In the Service, My First Job, Getting Married.

VIII. TYPEWRITING

Many aphasics are hemiplegics with the resultant impairment of one hand. Typewriting with one hand necessitates a specialized approach unless the patient resorts to the "hunt and peck" system. A specialized one-hand system for aphasics with the hand placed over the F G H J keys as the home-row is described in "Picture Lessons in Typewriting for Aphasics" by Dr. Roy Nyquist and Georgia Crosthwaite. Another text for one-handed typing is "Type with One Hand" by Nina K. Richardson. (See References below.)

IX. REFERENCES

Betts, Emmett A., and Greene, Harry A.: *Daily Drills,* Series One through Eight. Row, Peterson and Company, White Plains, N. Y.

Billington, Lillian E.: *Using Words,* Series One through Eight. Silver Burdett Company, New York, N. Y.

Decker, Frieda: *Progressive Lessons for Language Retraining.* Harper and Brothers, New York, N. Y., 1960.

---

6. See Unit for Advanced Case, Chapter 18.

Gardner, Warren W.: *Left-Hand Writing*. Interstate Press, Danville, Ill., 1945.

Nyquist, Roy, and Crosthwaite, Georgia: Picture lessons in typewriting. *Archives of Physical Medicine and Rehabilitation,* June 1955. Reprints available from Dr. Roy Nyquist, Veterans Administration Hospital, Long Beach 4, Calif.

Richardson, Nina K.: *Type with One Hand*. South-Western Publishing Company, Dallas, Tex.

Robertson, M. S.: *Learning and Writing English*. The Steck Company, Austin, Tex.

Smith, Ellen, and McAnulty, Leona: *Essentials in English-Laboratory Method*. McCormick-Mathers Publishing Company, Wichita, Kans., Books 1, 2, 3, 4.

Smith, Harley A., and King, Ida Lee: *I Want to Learn English*. The Steck Company, Austin, Tex.

Phono-Word Wheels: Set A, Initial Consonants; Set 2, Prefixes; Set 3, Suffixes. The Steck Company, Austin, Tex.

Chapter 17

ARITHMETIC
(Acalculia) [1]

I. INTRODUCTION

Sᴏᴍᴇ ᴘᴀᴛɪᴇɴᴛs ᴡɪᴛʜ a severe speech and reading loss can still comprehend numbers and work basic arithmetic processes. A few can work advanced arithmetic and algebra. Consequently, arithmetic often furnishes an avenue for success when many other areas are severely blocked. Such patients may work independently through a good arithmetic workbook (see list at the close of this section) until they reach the place where they need help. Many, however, have great difficulty with numbers and will need to retrain beginning with the concept of numbers and

counting. The therapist cannot assume that a patient who can count automatically has a clear understanding of numbers. Some cannot name numbers not in sequence even though they may count perfectly. Others may be able to write the correct answer to a problem even though they voice the answer incorrectly, and vice versa.

II. THE CONCEPT OF NUMBERS

REMARKS	EXERCISES

REMARKS

A. A patient must have the concept (understanding) of the numbers. Therefore, it is helpful to have concrete items to count such as marbles, matches, chips, and buttons.

EXERCISES

A. Learning to Count

Drill both orally and in writing:
1, 2, 3, etc.
5, 10, 15, 20, etc.
10, 20, 30, 40, 50, etc.

B. Writing Numbers

At first the patient may need to copy numbers. Dictate them as soon as possible and require that the dictation be read back or identified by pointing to numbers called for.

---

1. Nielsen, J. M.: *A Textbook of Clinical Neurology,* Third Edition. Paul B. Hoeber, Inc., New York, N. Y., page 246.

C. Magazines and comic sections of newspapers often print number pictures. It is well to clip and save these for future use. This exercise is recommended for low-interest cases and for children.

Counting on the fingers is a very acceptable device for aphasics.

C. Checking on Chronological Order

Direct the patient to connect numbers in chronological order to form outlines of figures. These may be put on the blackboard for group work or duplicated on paper for individual work.

Examples:

```
   (star)              (kite)
     4                   2
 1       2       4          3
   3  5
                         5
                         1
                         6
                         7
                          8
                          9
                           10 11 12
```

D. Using Dice

Crap shooting is useful for oral naming of numbers, in adding for the "point," and in strengthening the concept of numbers. It also may hold the interest of a poorly motivated patient.

E. Using Dominoes

A game of dominoes is useful for addition practice.

F. Playing Solitaire

If a patient can play 'Sol," he will retrain himself in putting numbers in chronological order.

G. Aphasics often can deal with money and make change when they can do little else with numbers. Take advantage of this by incorporating money in arithmetic problems.

G. Using Money

Ask the patient to stack up five cents in pennies; $1.00 in dimes; $2.00 in quarters, etc.

H. The patient must know the meaning of the signs PLUS and MINUS.

2. *Numbers We See* by Anita Riess, Maurice L. Hartung and Catharine Mahoney is a good text for this type of exercise.

3. Demonstrate with the actual objects, taking away one apple from the four, and so on.

4. Many patients still retain the value of coins.

   (Explain the "equals" sign)

H. Written Work in Simplest Arithmetic

1. Addition

1 apple	2 matches	2 marbles
+1 apple	+1 match	+2 marbles

1	5	4	**4**
4	2	3	**2**

(Expand to include all the combinations)

2. Using Pictures: Ask such questions as: How many _____ are in this picture?

3. Subtraction: (Be sure patient understands the minus sign.)

4 apples	3 pencils	2 marbles
−1 apple	−1 pencil	−2 marbles

4. Using Coins:

   5 pennies take away 2 pennies =
   _____

   1 nickel take away 1 nickel =
   _____

I. Miscellaneous Suggestions for Strengthening the Concept of Numbers

1. Using the Calendar. Talk about the date each day. Take advantage of special days such as:
   a. When is your birthday? When is Lincoln's birthday? Washington's birthday?
   b. What date is Christmas? New Years? Columbus Day?
   c. What date is pay day?   d. What day does May 4th fall on?
   e. What year is this?   f. How many days in February?
2. Using Personal Data. Ask the patient the following:
   a. How old are you?   c. How much do you weigh?
   b. How tall are you?   d. How many children have you?
   e. How many wives have you? (Levity keeps the lessons from becoming boresome and tiring.)
3. Using Postage. Ask the patient various questions such as:
   a. Which stamp must I put on a letter for regular mail? For airmail? How much will it cost?

4. Telling Time, spending time, counting time. These questions may be repeated every day for many weeks. The Weston Clock (cardboard) with movable hands is useful for demonstrating time. Ask appropriate questions such as:

   a. How many hours do you sleep?
   b. When do you go to breakfast?
   c. When do you go to lunch?
   d. When do you eat dinner?
   e. When do you go to Occupational Therapy?
   f. How much time do you spend in bed?

5. Words: *More* and *Less*

   a. Which glass holds *more* water, which holds *less?*

   b. Which is more, 8 or 6? Which is more, 15 or 51?
   c. Which is less, 14 or 15?

   Some patients can answer orally; others will have to show on their fingers or point to a watch or clock face. Some will be able to write the answers. Since the point here is getting the concept of numbers, accept a correct response in whatever form the patient is able to use.

III. ELEMENTARY ARITHMETIC

A. Seldom can a patient at this level read well enough to attempt a so-called "paragraph" problem. Nevertheless, it is always well to add concrete items to the numbers—such as $23 and $41 more put together make $_____.

Many elementary workbooks written and illustrated for children are rejected by adults. Therefore, problems written on the board are often more acceptable.

A. Addition

1. Adding two and three columns:

$23	16¢	$134	116 marbles
41	12	62	323

2. Addition with "carrying":

$24	63¢	13 marbles
18	29	24
		18

B. Subtraction

1. Subtracting in two and three columns:

$47	36¢	$478	824 apples
−21	−12	−234	−203

(It is always wise to test a patient on material which is suspected to be below his level in order to correct any defects in basic processes.)

C. *Fun With Numbers* (Exclusive Playing Card Company, Chicago, Ill.) is a set of card games composed of twelve decks ranging in difficulty from first to fourth grades, using addition, subtraction, multiplication, and division. Often the use of such games makes the relearning of combinations, times tables, and memory work a little more palatable. These cards are available at drug and department stores.

The recitation of the times tables is a matter of memory rather than an indication of mathematical ability.

At this time workbooks are helpful, especially when the patient can work independently with "seat work," going along at his own speed.

2. Subtraction with borrowing:

521	891	600
−296	−483	−385

C. Multiplication Tables

1. Getting the concept of multiplication appears to be much more difficult for aphasics than addition or subtraction. Demonstrate 2 x 3 pencils by laying 3 pencils out on the table twice, then count them. Lay 2 pencils out on the table three times, then count them, thus showing that both 3 x 2 and 2 x 3 = **6**. Drill orally and in writing on the times tables up through the 5's. Then put them into practice.

43	24	13
x 2	x 2	x 3

2. Multiplication with "carrying": Using single numbers as the multiplier:

44	24
x 4	x 3

3. The following procedure has proved helpful for many aphasics in multiplication of multiple numbers.

Example:

465   First, multiply by 9 and write the numbers thus: (9 x 5)   45
x 69   (9 x 6)   54
-----   (9 x 4)   36
4185   -----
2790   Add 4185

32085

Next, multiply by 6 and write the numbers in the same way   (6 x 5)   30
                                                             (6 x 6)   36
                                                             (6 x 4)   24

                                                             Add 2790

Lastly; copy the two rows under the problem and add as shown above in the example.

D. In division, plan the problems so as to have no remainder until fractions have been studied.

Here again, much demonstration may be needed such as dividing among the group such items as pencils, money, marbles, etc. in order to help the patient get the concept of what is taking place in division.

E. Refer to texts listed at the close of this section.

F. The simple and most obvious fractions are all that an aphasic with acalculia usually can grasp at first.

After these few simple fractions have been mastered, it may be well to let fractions rest a while.

Almost all aphasics can handle money. Using parts of a dollar with a 50-cent piece, the quarter, and dime is helpful.

Make drawings of pies, squares and

D. Short Division

Explain the divide signs: ÷ and
)

1. $2\overline{)\ 4}$　　$3\overline{)\ 33}$　　$2\overline{)\ 8}$

　$2\overline{)\ 24}$　　$3\overline{)\ 9}$

2. $8 \div 2 =$　$12 \div 2 =$　$12 \div 3 =$
$18 \div 6 =$

3. 24 pencils divided among 4 patients = _____ pencils for each patient.

18 marbles divided among 6 boys = _____ marbles for each boy.

E. Introducing Propositions

As soon as possible begin to use written problems and arithmetical situations such as:

buying, making change, selling, measuring.

F. Fractions

1. Sharing to teach the concept of fractions:

   a. Give me half of your pie.

   b. Divide your pack of cigarettes among us. Each man now has $\frac{1}{2}$ or $\frac{1}{4}$ of a pack.

2. Adding fractions: Use simple fractions such as:

one-half dollar
one-third apple
one-fourth pie

1/2 dollar	1/3 apple	1/4 pie
1/2	1/3	1/4
	1/3	1/4
		1/4

cut up apples to put the concept across.

G. Measurements

Ask the patient actually to take these measurements:

1. How long is this desk?
2. How tall are you?
3. How long is our room?
4. How wide is the window?
5. How far is it around this room?
6. How far is it from your chair to the blackboard?

H. Using Patient's Occupation

Find out the patient's occupation. Compose arithmetic problems which will interest him in the light of his former work. Suggestions:

1. Carpenter (measurements)
2. Merchant (sales, discounts, profit, yards, inches)
3. Salesman (commission)
4. Market (weights, dozen, pint, quart)
5. Milk route (pint, quart, gallon, pound)
6. Service Station (gallons, quarts)
7. Banker (interest)
8. Farmer (bushel, acre, ton)
9. Drygoods clerk (yards, inches)
10. Bookkeeper (credits, debits)

IV. INTERMEDIATE ARITHMETIC

A. At this level, the therapist should discover a patient's weaknesses, and work toward eliminating them. A workbook at about a fifth grade level is useful for this type of therapy.

A. Review Basic Processes

Paragraph problems using all processes will be helpful in finding weak spots.

B. Writing Checks

This is practical as many patients will be writing checks and keeping stubs.

C. Multiplication Tables

Drill on the multiplication tables above the five's.

D. To say "five times nothing is still nothing" is much more understandable than to say "zero times 5 is zero." There may be many errors involving the zero in all the basic processes.

D. Using the Zero
Multiply using the zero.

207	1203	1407
x 4	x 26	x 20

E. Long Division
Show the patient how to work a short-division problem with long division, then take up double numbers in long division.

F. Use many paragraph problems involving fractions as the concept is usually difficult for aphasics. Many say they had difficulty with fractions even before they had aphasia.

Cancellation should be included in multiplying fractions.

If the terms *numerator* and *denominator* are too difficult, say "top number" and "bottom number."

F. Fractions and Mixed Numbers
1. Follow a standard workbook. Review addition of simple fractions first. Illustrate with pie, butter, quarters, money. Continue with subtraction, multiplication, and division.
2. Changing mixed numbers to improper fractions.
3. Scale of miles in the map. Example:
   a. How far is it to San Francisco?
   b. If it is $2\frac{1}{4}$ inches on the map from Seattle to Portland, how far is it in miles using the scale shown on the map?

G. Measurements
1. Review length, width, perimeter.
2. Add *area* of rectangles and *volume* of cubes (avoid triangles, circles, prisms, and cones for the present).

H. Arithmetic on a Practical Level

1. Practice writing checks and keeping the stubs; check up an actual check book when possible.
2. Budget the income: house money, rent, car expense, insurance.

3. Prepare order blanks from commercial catalogs including weights, postage, sales tax.

V. ADVANCED ARITHMETIC AND ELEMENTARY ALGEBRA

It is not uncommon to find aphasics who cannot talk but who can recall advanced arithmetic and algebra. It is often a boost to their morale to be successful in some academic field such as this.

Suggested Outline:

A. Review fractions and take up decimals.
B. Percentage: Types 1, 2, and 3; discounts, commissions, interest, selling price.
C. Ratio and proportion.
D. Square root.
E. Circles: circumference; area.
F. Triangles: area, angles.
G. Volume: cubes, prisms, cylinders, cones.
H. Area of trapezoid and other irregular figures.
I. Elementary algebra.

VI. REFERENCES

Alves, H. F., Fertsch, L. M., and Matthys, Fred: *Modern Practice Book in Arithmetic,* Book 3. Steck Co., Austin, Tex.

Karstens, Harry: *Mastering Basic Arithmetic.* Lyons & Carnahan, Pasadena, Calif.

Knight, F. B., Studebaker, J. W., and Tate, Gladys: *Self-Help Arithmetic Workbook.* Scott, Foresman and Company, New York, N. Y.

Riess, Anita, Hartung, Maurice L., and Mahoney, Catharine: *Numbers We See.* Scott, Foresman and Company, New York, N. Y.

Warp's Review Workbooks: *Book I, Arithmetic Around Us; Book II, Going Forward in Arithmetic; Book III, Using Arithmetic in Everyday Life; Book IV, Making Progress in Arithmetic.* Warp Publishing Co., Minden, Nebr., 1957.

* * * * * *

The Chinese Abacus

Fun With Numbers—Card Games in Addition, Subtraction, Multiplication and Division. Exclusive Playing Card Company, Chicago, Ill.

Winston Clock Face—John C. Winston Company, Philadelphia 7, Penn.

Chapter 18

UNIT FOR ADVANCED CASE

W<small>HEN THE SO-CALLED</small> advanced case has recovered sufficient language to meet his daily needs, it is sometimes difficult to interest him in continued retraining. A review of something in line with individual interests or in an actual practical situation often serves as a means to keep him motivated.

I. GETTING A JOB

A. The Application Blank (Spelling, reading and writing practice).

The time comes when some aphasics become interested in returning to work. Some become bewildered at an employment office window when they are confronted with an application blank to be filled out.

1. Make up a list of the more difficult words and phrases usually found in an application blank. Use this list for spelling, reading recognition and writing practice.

address	examination	former	education
marital status	residence	employment	college
citizen	registration	physical handicap	trade school
birthplace	nationality	misconduct	skill
supervisor	salary	training	dependents
military service	post office	promotion	occupation
		references	

2. Direct the patient to prepare the answers to questions which are customarily asked in application blanks. If the patient has prepared and studied his Personalized Notebook (Chapter 7) he will have this information ready to use.

Example:

name _____ (husband's name _____

date of birth _____ (wife's name _____

birthplace _____ former position _____

type of work applied for _____ dates of military service _____

B. The Interview (Oral speech)

Sometimes patients talk themselves out of a job by alluding frequently to their disabilities and by referring to the skills they have lost rather than by stressing their remaining assets.

Prepare appropriate questions for an interview with the patient. This training has practical value for the patient when he actually goes job hunting. Stress the actual facts needed rather than grammar and vocabulary.

C. Investigating Jobs (Reading Comprehension and Oral Formulation)

1. Use want ads, civil service announcements, and other employment bulletins for oral and silent reading. A discussion of this interesting and practical high-interest material offers a good opportunity for oral formulation.

2. Read job qualifications with the patient. Often the pamphlets and magazines which describe jobs and give necessary qualifications for them open up new avenues leading patients into work situations suited to their disabilities. (See references).

D. Writing an Application (Spelling and Written Formulation)

At best, a letter of application is difficult to write. Nevertheless, an attempt to do so is good practice for aphasics who show an interest in it. With corrections, rewriting and recopying, the patient may produce a letter suitable for actual use. (See references at close of the chapter.)

II. SUGGESTIONS FOR OTHER UNITS

DRIVING LICENSE:	Secure actual tests from the Motor-Vehicle Department.
HOUSEHOLD UNIT:	Schedule of daily duties, meal planning, shopping, budgeting.
GARDENING UNIT:	Plot the ground, selection of plants, cost, fertilizing.
CHILD CARE UNIT:	Proper food, play activities, behavior problems.
HOBBY UNIT:	Stamps, handwork, plastics, tropical fish, parakeets, leathercraft.
MUSIC UNIT:	Records, favorite performers, radio, T.V.
VACATION UNIT:	Plan a trip, map study, mileage, cost.
NEWSPAPER READING:	Workbook available from Gary D. Lawson, Route 2, Box 2804, Elk Grove, Calif.

III. REFERENCES

Lawson, Gary D.: *Everyday Business.* Workbook in banking, buying, budgeting, Federal Income Tax, insurance, Rt. 2, Box 2804, Elk Grove, Calif.

Liveright, L. L.: *Job Letters.* B'nai B'rith Vocational Service Bureau, 1003 K Street, N. W., Washington, D. C.

Swartz, Marcel M.: *How to Write Successful Business Letters.* Grossett & Dunlap, New York, N. Y.

The Occupational Outlook Handbook: U. S. Department of Labor, Bureau of Statistics, Superintendent of Documents, Government Printing Office, Washington, D. C. $4.25; found in employment offices, counseling centers and in school and college libraries.

Brochures of many types of work are available at state employment offices and from nationally known companies.

Chapter 19

SAMPLE OF PATIENTS' WORK

SAMPLES OF ADULT aphasics' work are shown below. By comparison, the beginning therapist or family member may be able to categorize the language problem of his patient and arrive at a plan for therapy. The progress shown in some of these samples may lend encouragement to the patient and to the therapist, and at the same time give them a better understanding of the problems to be met.

A. Seventy-year-old former printer. Sample of paragraphia.
Assignment: Tell about your former job.

Job Printer Conmity. Ptsinct Satict puntree Press Telegram. Secoate Printing. Chaplain at Vatersian Secant 3, March 27th 1957.

B. A Motor Aphasic's attempts to name a group of Fruits and Vegetables: (taken from tape recording)

pomato—tomandy (tomato)   enijuns (onions)
chippy—chelry (celery)   topato—potta (potato)
sherapist (radish)   poneapple—penapply (pineapple)
graprite (grapefruit)   opal (apple)
                    bannies (bananas)

C. Twenty-eight-year-old right handed navy cook; spastic paralysis. Switching to left-handedness.

Attempt to write F G H of the alphabet, January 1954.

Copy work: March 1954 (Script from printing)
I   LIKE   APPLE   PIE

April 1955 (Same patient one year later.)

D. Sixty-year-old right handed former postal clerk; right hemiplegic. March 28, 1957. Patient was given a pattern of a series of large circles for copy work. The therapist guided his hand in a tracing motion over the circles.

When the patient attempted the exercise unaided, he produced the following:

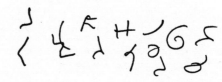

The therapist guided the patient's hand over a series of straight lines, but the patient persisted in making short random lines through the perpendicular lines:

Attempts to get the patient to copy his initials A. T.

Pattern:

May 2, 1957. (Copy work)

Pattern:

Pattern:

E. Excerpts from an autobiographical sketch written by a forty-six year old amnesic aphasic woman who had sustained a CVA in an aircraft factory where she was employed.

"I was born at Morrison, Okla. December 8, 1915. A Catholic. My Mother, Sophia Mary was thin, brown eyes, black hair, 5"-4' tall, good figure, nice personality, good cook, sews well and beautiful woman. My Father, Frank John thin, 6" tall, eyes brown, brown curly hair and happy determine personality. Nine children, four girls and five boys. So, I have brown eyes, cook & sew from mother—tall 5"-7' like father, curly brown hair and I have personality of each of them happy determine and nice personality.

"On May 12, 1941 I married Homer George at Sallison, Okla.—my first trip on airplane at Fort Smith, Arkansas—my first and last for me, I none like to be so high. Arrived on August 26, 1941 at Bellflower, California. May 5, 1952 my husband died.

"Bought 1955 Chevrolet on Nov. 1954 black and white. Bought my home in Norwalk, Calif., I like color so, I painted the house, my furniture are nice. . . . . Nov. 19, 1959 I had a Cerebral and my aching back at work. A woman can't talk, Ruth, I learn the A. B. C. at the hospital—I'm determined to talk again, I *will*. God had been good to me. Everyone has been nice to me. O yes! my hair is tinted light auburn and still a widow and I will always smile."

F. Letter written by a thirty-five year old traumatic case to his son. This patient made a complete recovery and returned to work in August 1960.

February 1959

Some times yuir desprecke to
has I umtuherd sower gheb
plint
I am going to be slow tos I
yet th quited
                    Love
                    Dallor

G. Examples of paraphasia heard in the Veterans Administration Aphasia Clinic.

1. Patient commenting on his pension: I think I should have more money before I am putting everything across to do.
2. Patient's answer to the question, Can you cook: Not now, I used to but since I'm killed I hurt so much I can't find it.
3. Referring to shaving before going on pass: I'm going to fix it before I take it up there.
4. Asking the therapist to write a lesson on the blackboard: Hold it up here so I can see it.
5. I want to ask you this before I say it.
6. You know how long I've been here? Way up in there before, I couldn't do it, right across.
7. Referring to mailing a Christmas package: I asked him and he took this time, otherwise he'd never make it; it is too fast.
8. Referring to his weight: Boy, I'm bigger than I used to have.
9. I'd like for Christmas—that's where I'd like to be. That's what hurts me around.

H. Examples of word formulation loss:
1. What do I want for Chrisunday? Sinty Clair (Santa Claus).
2. The guggy (puppy) is killed.
3. I like turset (turkey).
4. Will you rub the thirth (teeth).

I. Language formulation exercises.
Assignment: Write a sentence or two about the World's Series.
"I done care who whin's the word sires as long as they play on the square They play onec in a will to git a better score than the other team.
2. Assignment: Use these words in sentences. EVERYTHING ALIVE CRACKER POLE HOOK

Every thing Is going will.
Watch out for alive thing.
Watch out for the pole cracker.
Look out for the hook and ladder.
Look out for the pole.

J. Samples of writing of a patient with a homonymous hemianopia. **The** patient wrote across the entire page only when the therapist was helping **him.** When left to himself, he wrote only to the center of the page because that **was** the extent of his limited vision.

K. Lesson in advanced composition (written formulation).
Subj: Inter Catherization injection of the glorious sentation of my heart.
My intercession of my exploration was suggested by Doctor *J. I.* and *N. R.* in charge of D-2 of the word in charge. luckily corried on to their health of my so-for. success.
After numerous x-rays. I was elected for Catherization on a doubious introduction, but so san success & elated an old man of my age to be again possiable elected to further be, timing of my heart, the introduction of

further introduction of interjection of air, now, with a prayer to be carried furthr to be operated to be concludud with a fair operating mined in the future.

I am greatly, to all, for my make on failure to all.

L. Showing perseveration.
Dictated: He rides to class in his wheel chair.

He rediez ToToot in hes wheled ehriee

Dictated: Willie ate fish and pudding for dinner today.

Wille ate fish and pulamda for dimmmmmer ToD ay

Dictated: 192 x 8

100 92

Part Two

Aphasia in Children

ORIENTATION

Chapter 20

QUESTIONS COMMONLY ASKED REGARDING APHASIA IN CHILDREN

I. WHAT IS AN APHASIC CHILD?

T HE APHASIC CHILD is one who fails to *develop* adequate language or one who has sustained a loss of *acquired* language due to brain injury. In contrast to his non-verbal intelligence, his language[1] development is usually markedly retarded. Premature birth, congenital anomalies, birth injuries, incompatible blood diseases, altered blood chemistry, glandular disturbances, epilepsy, meningitis, encephalitis, tumors and trauma are some of the causes of brain injury.

Occasionally there is a child who has a marked language loss the etiology of which may not be revealed as organic through the usual neurological examination and E.E.G.[2] However a language and psychodiagnostic evaluation establishing defects in perceptual, conceptual and language areas[3] together with the syndrome of behavior characteristics[4] may classify this child as an aphasic. Aphasia in children is most easily distinguished when not accompanied by multiple handicaps such as hearing and visual defects and mental retardation. Brain injured children may have learning and behavior problems but not necessarily possess an oral speech defect.

II. HOW DOES ONE KNOW WHEN A CHILD IS APHASIC?

This is one of the questions most commonly asked by parents and teachers. The diagnosis is difficult and often lacks corroborating neurological findings. If other defects such as hearing and visual impairments, cerebral palsy, and mental retardation exist, the diagnostic picture becomes even more clouded. It is primary to an accurate diagnosis that modalities must exist through which the child may be tested. Again, the defects of aphasia often simulate symptoms of other handicaps. For example, the child with an auditory receptive[5] language loss may appear to have a hearing loss. A brain injured child may have behavior problems not unlike the emotionally disturbed child. A diagnosis requires the opinions of a team of experts made up of the

---

1. Language is used in this text to refer to oral speech and written speech (reading, writing and spelling), and the use of symbols as in arithmetic.
2. See Terms, Appendix.
3. See Evaluation of Defects, Chapter 24.
4. See Basic Concepts, Chapter 21.
5. See Chapter 24, Section IV.

neurologist, the psychiatrist, the psychologist, the pediatrician and the language therapist. Frequently the lack of speech development is the first objective symptom of aphasia that the family observes. In addition to a language problem, the child may be slow developing motor skills and adequate personal-social relationships. In children who have lesser degrees of brain injury, general growth and development other than language may proceed at a normal rate.

Aphasic disturbances occur in three general areas: (1) behavior, (2) learning and (3) language. *Behavior*[6] in the aphasic child may be characterized by any one or a combination of the following: hyperactivity, hypoactivity, short attention span, aggressiveness, inappropriate judgment, unusual fears, over gregariousness, severe to mild emotional problems, catastrophic reactions, unpredictable behavior, perseverative tendencies, and unusual compulsions.

Learning deficits constitute auditory and visual perceptual disorders which include confusion in body scheme, disturbance in foreground-background, poor eye-hand coordination, visuo-motor problems, undetermined handedness, lack of ability to distinguish the whole from the parts, and disturbance in spatial relationships. As a result there is a paucity of concept formation and abstract thought processes.

Language problems comprise auditory-verbal agnosia, visual-verbal agnosia,[7] motor speech (articulatory) problems, poor name association and language formulation, and an inability to acquire symbolic language (reading, spelling and arithmetic).

These problems are seen in isolation or in combination at the pre-school level or later. The child with the most severe problem will, in most cases, be the first to obtain an evaluation and diagnosis.

It is almost impossible to adequately assess a child's problem on the basis of a single contact. Many children do not respond to the testing situation and much is dependent upon clinical observation of behavior. Multiple contacts involving an extended period of time are often needed before a comprehensive evaluation can be made.

III. WHAT SPECIAL HELP DOES THE APHASIC CHILD NEED?

The aphasic child needs help psychologically, educationally, and physically. The pediatrician, the neurologist or the medical clinic often make initial referrals for special help. Since the initial diagnosis often produces a profound effect on the parents as well as on the child, early focus of psychological interest should be on the family. Once the problem is identified,

---

6. See Basic Concepts, Chapter 21.
7. See Terms, Appendix.

parents sometimes do not feel the same toward the child. The extent to which a healthy relationship can be present—or absent—for the child depends upon how drastically parental feelings have been altered. Problems arise continually with varying states of development as the full extent of the psychological and learning problems unfolds. It is important that frequent contact with the family be made so that any arising problems may be met by proper referral for psychological help which is often imperative to the success of any therapy. When the therapist recognizes that the child or parent has a problem not being resolved, he may help the parent to realize the need for psychotherapy.

Aphasic children frequently develop psychological problems that interfere with social adjustment and learning processes. They often react differently to love, hate, reward and punishment. Many reactions depend upon the child's involvement and the way his handicaps are regarded by those around him. Parents and others dealing with him should know that misbehavior is often not his fault but stems from his neurological involvement. Additional support, affection and attention from parents and teachers and from the team of medical advisors or therapists frequently serve to offset undesirable behavioral patterns. Though psychotherapy and psychological help are incorporated in many programs, it is frequently left to the language therapist or teacher in the situation to supply many of these needs.

Educational facilities must be found which offer special techniques for aphasic children. Many states are conducting experimental programs for the neurologically handicapped[8] which offer help to those not included in other school programs. A few states have classes in effect where therapeutic programs are now available, and some private schools[9] offer specialized help. Often the most available source is the individual tutor or the language clinic[10] where clinicians understand how to work with aphasic children.

If the aphasic child has physical involvements, the doctor often recommends physiotherapy and other therapies such as occupational therapy directed to aid physical development.

Drug Therapy. Some behavior problems (as described in Section II, How Does One Know When a Child is Aphasic) become sufficiently severe to interfere with social success and to deter general or specific learning. In such

---

8. Pilot Project for Neurologically Handicapped Children, John Howe, Coordinator, Los Angeles County Schools, 808 N. Spring Street, Los Angeles, Calif.
9. The Chicago School, Chicago, Ill.
   Bloomfield School, Denver, Colo.
   Dubnoff School, North Hollywood, Calif.
10. The Frostig School of Educational Therapy, 7257 Melrose Ave., Los Angeles, Calif.
   Hope Guild Clinic, St. John's Hospital, Santa Monica, Calif.
   Lakewood Speech Clinic, 4623 Harvey Way, Long Beach, Calif.

cases drug therapy has often been indicated by the physician and has been used with good results. The problem of choice of drugs and the response to them is varied because some aphasic children do not react to drugs in the usual way. Thus, the physician is often obliged to experiment for a time before the proper drug is found to suit the particular child. The success of the drug therapy is largely dependent upon the family's consistent participation in a rigid program controlled by the doctor.

IV. IS THE APHASIC CHILD MENTALLY RETARDED OR DEFICIENT?

Aphasic children who are retarded in language are not necessarily mentally retarded or deficient. Frequently their performance in areas not involving language is adequate or above average, as in cases of children with outstanding motor skills, with creative ability and other compensatory mechanisms. The total score or intelligence quotient as determined by conventional children's tests may not be valid because it fails to compensate for the aphasic child's language inadequacies. A child's performance on selected subtests and on specific non-language tests, together with observations of his reactions and general behavior during the testing situation may be more indicative of a potential. The aphasic child, like the aphasic adult, is often limited in his performance because of poor verbal expression, lack of good motor control, and reduced language comprehension; but when communication has been established such performances are improved.

V. HOW LONG WILL IT TAKE THE APHASIC CHILD TO ACQUIRE SPEECH?

There is, at present, no measure by which to indicate the length of time necessary for an aphasic child to acquire adequate speech. The degree of brain damage, the extent to which language areas are involved, basic intelligence and motivation play an important part. Some aphasic children need many years of specialized help. Others, provided with adequate training at the earliest indication of disability, will successfully enter a regular school program and do well.

VI. WHERE CAN ONE OBTAIN HELP FOR AN APHASIC CHILD?

Sources for qualified clinic help—neurologists, psychiatrists, psychologists, and speech therapists may be located through such agencies as the American Medical Association, the National Association for Crippled Children and Adults, American Speech and Hearing Association, universities, hospitals and individual physicians. Family counseling may often be secured through family service organizations, private psychiatrists and psychologists, and hospital and university clinics. Local and state rehabilitation programs sometimes provide help in securing specialized training and special schools. It is frequently necessary to obtain financial assistance from local, state, or national organizations to maintain the long and intensive training necessary. Sometimes service clubs and church groups will provide funds.

Chapter 21

BASIC CONCEPTS OF APHASIA IN CHILDREN

I. INTRODUCTION

APHASIA AND RELATED disorders in children exist as a result of damage to language areas incurred prior to birth, at birth or in early years. Lesions affecting language areas may result from such causes as anoxia (at birth), rubella (occurring in the mother prior to birth), cerebral hemorrhage (commonly a birth injury), encephalitis, meningitis and trauma in the childhood years.

There has been much confusion in the literature concerning the use of the term "aphasia" as applied to children.[1] Since the term, when applied to adults, indicates a loss of language already acquired, the term must have another connotation when applied to children who have never developed language. The common denominator in the case of both children and adults appears, then, to be the relationship of the language dysfunction to the brain damage. The term "childhood aphasia" may then be defined as a language dysfunction directly related to damaged areas of the brain. The term "language" implies in children, as well as in adults, areas of receptive, expressive and symbolic language.

The term "neurologically handicapped" child has appeared frequently in the literature of late.[2] This term has been used in an attempt to classify a type of child who has a "minimal" brain damage but who, because of learning and behavior disorders, presents a great problem in school and in society. This child may or may not have a language disorder.

Brain damage may be manifested in many different ways. Because of the present confusion in terminology,[3] it is helpful to think of the distinguishing characteristics of each defect. These defects resulting from brain injury may be viewed individually, but actually they are often overlapping.

Neurologically Handicapped	Aphasia	Cerebral Palsy	Mental Retardation	Epilepsy
Behavior and learning deficits	Language deficits	Coordination and muscle dysfunction	Lack of intellectual capability	Psycho-motor attacks

1. West, Robert (ed.) : *Childhood Aphasia*. (California Society for Crippled Children and Adults). page 2, San Francisco, California, 1962.
2. CANHC: California Association for Neurologically Handicapped Children, P. O. Box 604, Main office, Los Angeles 53, Calif.
3. A historical review of the problems pertaining to the concept of brain damaged children is presented in Chapter I, *Psychopathology and Education of the Brain Injured Child* by Strauss and Lehtinen.

II. CHARACTERISTICS OUTLINED

The behavior characteristics of the aphasic child must be examined since chiefly by these characteristics can he be distinguished.[4] For purposes of examination an arbitrary division of the characteristics into behavior problems and learning problems is established.[5]

A. Behavior Problems

1. Primary behavior problems
   a. Hyperactivity
   b. Hypoactivity
   c. Short attention span
   d. Disorganization (poor appraisal of situations; poor judgment)
   e. Catastrophic reaction (tantrums; rage; inappropriate fears)
   f. Mild motor incoordination: diffuse; fine finger
   g. Narcissism—autism
   h. Poor oral speech
   i. Epilepsy
   j. Need for highly structured situations
   k. Perseveration
   l. Compulsive behavior
2. Secondary behavior problems
   a. Hostility
   b. Aggression
   c. Withdrawal
   d. Apprehension
   e. Negativism

B. Learning Problems

1. Visual perceptual defects
2. Auditory perceptual defects
3. Difficulty in isolating items, i.e. foreground, background and in relating items in a picture to the picture as a whole
4. Difficulty in handling symbolic learning: reading, writing, arithmetic
5. Difficulty in establishing handedness
6. Poor eye-hand coordination
7. Difficulty in performing in areas of drawing, cutting, writing, and manipulatory play, buttoning and lacing

---

4. Strauss, Alfred and Lehtinen, Laura: *Psychopathology and Education of the Brain Injured Child*. Grune and Stratton, New York, N. Y., Chapter V, page 97.
5. Clark, Ruth: Language behavior of children with unsuspected brain injury. *Logos*, Bulletin of the National Hospital for Speech Disorders, Vol. 5. No. 1, April 1962.

8. Erratic innervation of motor movements
9. Disturbance of body scheme
10. Difficulty in assembling information
11. Short attention span
12. Inability to generalize

III. DESCRIPTION OF BEHAVIOR AND LEARNING PROBLEMS OF THE CHILD WITH MINIMAL BRAIN INJURY

In examining the behavior and learning characteristics of this child, it becomes apparent that there is much interchange of cause and effect. Many of the behavioral difficulties result in learning problems, and the difficulty in the assimilation of learning results in behavior problems. It also becomes apparent that the aphasic child is often the neurologically handicapped child with specific language deficits.[6] However, there is an overlapping in the terms since the aphasic child is any child whose language deficiency is related to organic brain damage; therefore multiple-handicapped children are also included in this category. The aphasic child who appears to have a potential of average intelligence is the most acceptable candidate for therapy.

A. Detailed Description of the Behavior Characteristics

These characteristics should be discussed in detail in order to indicate the relationship of the defect to language and learning problems. Furthermore, to do so highlights the relationship and the overlapping of the problems of the aphasic child and the neurologically handicapped child.

1. Primary behavior characteristics.

a. Hyperactivity. While many normal children are extremely active, hyperactivity of the brain injured child is characterized by purposelessness and incompletion of tasks, which may be closely related to erratic innervation. It is certainly a prime cause of difficulty in assembling information and of engaging in the learning process.

b. Hypoactivity. While seen less frequently, the brain-injured may show a pronounced lack of physical activity.

c. Short attention span. This constitutes an inability to sustain learning activities to completion. It is not necessarily characterized by physical hyperactivity.

d. Disorganization. The brain injured child cannot organize patterns of play or learning. He often appears to use poor judgment in very ordinary situations due to hyperactivity, short attention span, and perceptual and incoordination problems.

6. Clark, Ruth: Language Behavior of Children with Unsuspected Brain Injury. *Logos,* Vol. V, No. 1, April 1962, page 26.

e. Catastrophic reaction. Not infrequently one sees a brain injured child over-reacting to a rather commonplace occurrence. For example, a butterfly unexpectedly crosses his path and he screams and jumps in terror. When a situation becomes frustrating, or he is not permitted to do as he wants, the child exhibits a tantrum or an outburst of rage, intensified beyond the normal expectation of the situation.

f. Mild motor incoordination.

(1.) Diffuse: frequently it is noted that the brain injured child is awkward, or in some indefinable way, he does not function smoothly in motor ways and yet he runs, jumps, swings and rides a bicycle. It may be that there is a mild lesion of the motor strip which prevents fluent motor function or a smooth execution of the act, but does not completely interfere with the execution of motor patterns. This is a gross motor dysfunction.

(2.) Fine: another type of mild motor incoordination is noted in fine finger movements of manipulating pegs, small blocks, crayons, scissors, pencils, buttons and shoe laces. This would relate to a more specific lesion in the motor strip which controls the dexterity of these finger movements or to a break between the idea and the motor act comparable to the ideokinetic apraxia of the adult.[7]

g. Narcissism. Because of difficulty in performing and relating to the world he lives in, and perhaps also related to disturbance of body scheme, this child, almost of necessity, turns his attention inward and becomes concerned with himself in a narcissistic way. This in turn relates to some of the autistic-type behavior noted frequently.

h. Poor oral speech. This may be an articulation problem related to motor speech dysfunction. Since Broca's area[8] (which contains engrams for the memory of motor speech patterns) is closely related to the motor strip in the geography of the cortical areas of the brain, it is not difficult to see why both a motor speech pattern dysfunction and incoordination often exist simultaneously. Again, the problem may not relate to motor patterns but to involvement in association and recall. This may be part of the learning pattern difficulty or may indicate disturbances in other cortical areas.

i. Epilepsy. The presence of seizures and other epileptic manifestations, such as rage, psychomotor action and petit mal seizures, is not uncommon. This is discussed in the section on Special Problems, Chapter 22.

j. Need of highly structured situations. Because the brain injured child has difficulty moving freely from one situation to another (his defective

---

7. Nielsen, J. M.: *A Textbook of Clinical Neurology.* Hoeber, New York, N. Y., page 260.

———: *Agnosia, Apraxia, Aphasia.* Hafner Publishing Co., Inc., New York, N. Y., pp. 62, 268, 269.

8. See Chart, Chapter 2, Section III.

learning patterns do not permit a quick reorganization) , he becomes fearful of sudden change and of interruptions in routine. He is much more comfortable in a scheduled, organized routine to which he is accustomed.

k. Perseveration.[9] The repetition and continuance of activities to excess, either in language, learning or in behavior, is a common characteristic of the brain injured child. This is an exaggerated phase of the inability to shift from one situation to another.

l. Compulsive behavior. Because of the lack of organization in the world of the brain injured child he often over reacts with extremely compulsive behavior. His anxiety makes him withdraw from the unusual or untried, so that compulsive actions are a safer mode of behavior.

2. Secondary behavior characteristics.

Secondary behavior problems result as the brain injured child experiences the reactions of his peers and superiors to his primary behavior problems. As he meets with lack of understanding and criticism from those around him, he reacts in hostile, aggressive ways. He becomes apprehensive towards his efforts, constantly fears failure and may counteract by withdrawing from the world around him,[10] or he may be negative in his attitudes. It is notable that these secondary behavior characteristics are almost without exception found in the older child who has experienced many failures. The younger brain injured child is usually happy, sociable and shows little fear.

B. Detailed Description of Learning Characteristics

1. Visual perceptual defects. A visual perceptual defect is one of the most common problems of the brain injured child. It relates to the subject of visual agnosia which can be studied more accurately in adults than in children. Lesions in the occipital lobe (See Chart, Chapter 2, Section III) result in the visual perceptual defect. In children with minimal involvement, certain distortions and inaccuracies exist. They cannot easily distinguish between foreground and background objects, they do not recognize a variety of geometric shapes and they fail to see lines in their proper perspective. There is difficulty in eye-hand coordination (visuo-motor) . Not only do these perceptual defects present a problem in daily activities, but they are also the basis of many profound reading and writing problems.[11]

2. Auditory perceptual defects. As the visual perceptual defects exist, so do concomitant auditory perceptual defects. Sounds are not recognized and

---

9. See Terms, Appendix.

10. Clark, Ruth: Language Behavior of Children with Unsuspected Brain Injury. *Logos,* April 1962, Bulletin of the National Hospital for Speech Disorders, Vol. 5. No. 1.

11. Strauss, Alfred, and Lehtinen, Laura: *Psychopathology and Education of the Brain Injured Child.* Grune & Stratton, New York, N. Y., Chapter III, page 28.

frequently qualities of pitch, tone, loudness and timbre cannot be assigned. In extreme cases the child is often presumed to be deaf, but in actuality, he does not understand the spoken language he hears.[12]

3. Difficulty in isolating items. This pertains to distinguishing foreground from background and in relating items in a picture to the whole. It relates to a visual perceptual defect.

4. Difficulty in handling symbolic learning: reading, writing, arithmetic. Because this problem relates directly to the visual perceptual defect, children possessing this problem can frequently not learn in accustomed ways but must be taught with reinforcement in other modalities such as the tactile, kinesthetic and auditory.[13]

5. Difficulty in establishing handedness. Dominant areas for language, handedness, and eye movements are usually established rather early in life (between 2 and 6 years), but in the brain injured child handedness is often established late.

6. Poor eye-hand coordination. This results from incoordination of hand movements and visual guidance.

7. Fine finger incoordination. A lesion of the motor strip results in difficulties in handling crayons, pencils, scissors, drawing, cutting, writing and manipulatory play but does not necessarily interfere with larger movements used in running, in bicycle riding, in swinging, etc.

8. Erratic innervation of motor movements. This relates to motor incoordination and often appears as an aspect of hyperactivity.

9. Disturbance of body scheme. This may relate to lesions in the parietal lobe and interferes with recognition of the child's own body parts and therefore interferes with proper reaction to his environment. The child cannot use body parts effectively if he cannot first recognize their existence.

10. Difficulty in assembling information. It is difficult to assemble information that will lead to the forming of concepts,[14] if primary defects of visual perception, auditory perception and poor motor movements exist.

11. Short attention span. This is related to hyperactivity but may not manifest itself in any type of physical activity. The child is just not able to spend the necessary time in completing a learning process or a task.

12. Inability to generalize. Since the ability to generalize depends on

---

12. Mykelbust, Helmer R.: *Auditory Disorders in Children.* Grune & Stratton, New York, N. Y., 1954, Chapter I.

13. Fernald, Grace: *Remedial Techniques in Basic School Subjects.* McGraw-Hill, New York, N. Y., 1943.

14. Perception (as defined in Webster's New Collegiate Dictionary): Direct acquaintance with anything through the senses; awareness of objects.
Concept: A thought; an opinion; an idea of what a thing in general should be.

perceptual intactness, the assembling of information and development of concepts becomes difficult; therefore the child is not able to draw conclusions or place items in categories.

IV. SUMMARY

There are basic differences between aphasia in children and aphasia in adults. An aphasic adult has already established life patterns of speech, education, occupation, hobbies, marital status, and so on, so that much is known of the individual before the aphasia evaluation takes place. His retraining is directed towards reestablishing the known patterns. In the young child who has not established language, many questions must remain unanswered. Training must be directed towards establishing both concepts *and* language so that life patterns may yet be effectively established.

The determination of aphasia in adults is often more precise, since specific language losses are more easily recognized where mature language has existed. Adult aphasics have already developed non-language concepts, but have lost the language to express them, while children may fail to develop concepts in areas intimidated by injury.

A summation of the characteristics of the aphasic child may be one of the best indications of the presence of brain injury with resultant aphasia. Visually and auditorially the aphasic child may perceive but not recognize (i.e., he would be able to distinguish tones in an audiometric examination, but would not understand spoken words). There may be a hemiplegic involvement or a mild diffuse motor incoordination with symptoms of awkwardness and not infrequently a mixed laterality. Restlessness, inattention, distractibility, and perseverating behavior are frequently present. Psychologically there are often emotional outbursts, which show need of structured situations with the fewest possible distractions. Mental capacities are often marked by retarded concepts, by failure to integrate and usually by better physical performance than verbal response.

Compensating mechanisms are often observed in aphasic children. These may take the form of pictorial presentation of ideas, gestures and acting out, quick response to requests and a good physical performance. Aphasic children frequently demonstrate much love and affection, and show much dependence on parents or on the therapist, often requiring a close physical proximity of the latter.

An aphasic child must be regarded as having the same basic needs as all children: need of nurture, love, recognition, exploration and security. The basic differences in the aphasic child are the greater depths of need and the special ways in which he must be educated.

Chapter 22

SPECIAL PROBLEMS OF APHASIC CHILDREN

I. DIAGNOSTIC PROBLEMS

MANY OF THE complicating problems of the aphasic child arise from the fact that his difficulties frequently go undiagnosed. Not infrequently his symptoms are mistaken for mental retardation or for mental deficiency for deafness, for emotional problems or for prepsychotic states. The symptoms and problems attending this child are not observed in the infant or in the small child; consequently many problems arise before parents suspect that further examination is necessary. Often the diagnosis is confused with the symptoms of disease involvement as in the case of the multiple handicapped, the blind aphasic, the cerebral palsied aphasic or the epileptic aphasic child.

There are cases in which the aphasic child, who is multiple handicapped, is under observation at a comprehensive evaluation center and where an early diagnosis is made. When cerebral palsy or some other defect is evident, the child may be in the appropriate program for his primary disease but may need further evaluation and training for the accompanying aphasia. Often speech development is the first obvious symptom of the aphasic child; however many children enter school programs before serious learning problems present themselves. Many aphasics verbalize but present other symptomatology in symbolic language and in behavior areas. Psychological testing sometimes is necessary to detect conceptual and learning disorganization.

The importance of a comprehensive evaluation of the aphasic child cannot be over stressed. Complete and accurate diagnoses are best arrived at from a compilation of the following: psychological tests, medical history, pediatric and neurological examinations, an electroencephalogram[1] and an evaluation of learning problems. Psychological testing should be carried out by an experienced clinical psychologist alert to brain injury as a factor in behavior disorders. Since an I.Q. is not conclusive, psychological testing serves as a diagnostic tool rather than as a determination of potential. Selected subtests and special examinations, as well as observations of behavior, offer insight into areas for training.

The history of occurrence of related illness or of brain injury is helpful in furthering the diagnosis of aphasia. However, in many instances the damage may have occurred prenatally or may not even have been known by the family member informant. The parent's impression of the pregnancy,

---

1. See E. E. G. in Terms, Appendix.

the condition of the birth and the child's health and development during early life contribute much to total diagnosis. Behavioral history is revealing when symptoms of physical involvements are absent.

Pediatric and neurological examinations are helpful when positive findings are elicited, although the absence of positive findings does not preclude aphasia. In some cases behavior is the only discernible symptom during the early years before learning problems have become obvious.

The electroencephalogram (E.E.G.) has proved itself a valuable adjunct to making the diagnosis of brain injury; however, it is usually considered only as a supportive tool. Negative E.E.G.'s occur in some cases when a diagnosis has been made through other means.

An evaluation of the learning problems is usually considered after the diagnosis has been made. There are cases where the learning syndrome is the instrument which leads to diagnoses. In these instances, the learning problems help to confirm any further positive findings.

II. BEHAVIOR PROBLEMS

Behavior problems play an important part in the diagnosis of aphasic children. These neurologically handicapped have been characterized in a study made under the direction of John Howe,[2] as hyperactive, of short attention span, with poor impulse control, and frequently as stubborn and aggressive. Often these children are in interpersonal difficulty, when in their failure to perceive the structure of social situations, they digress from the accepted way. They have difficulty in arriving at individual values compatible with group values and, as a result, find themselves constantly at odds with those around them. They are often characterized as "naughty," "impossible," or "little terrors." Aphasic children develop secondary psychological symptoms when peers and those in authority show disappointment and anger when the children fail to integrate successfully. In their attempt to defend themselves against consequent anxiety, they withdraw into defeat or intensify their anger, aggression or indifference.

When parents seek advice they are often told that there is nothing wrong with their child, or that he'll grow out of it, or that he must be emotionally disturbed. This often results in increased confusion and guilt on the part of the parents. The aphasic child then reacts with emotional symptoms to his parents' confusion. Parents often find it necessary to seek help from outside sources before they can adjust to the child in a constructive way. The child's self adjustment, of course, depends upon the reaction of the parent

---

2. CANHC: Case Histories of Neurologically Handicapped Children (Los Angeles County Pilot Project) Mr. John Howe, Coordinator, L. A. County Supt. of Schools, 808 N. Spring St., Division of Research and Guidance, Los Angeles, Calif.

and on the many aspects of his own personality. The severely handicapped child is sometimes less able to cope with his own situation by himself and is in great need of emotional support from his parents and from those around him. If they are understanding and know the child's limitations, they can help him adjust to his environment and feel more secure within it.

Recommendations: Aphasic children, including the neurologically handicapped and the multiple handicapped, have a greater need than other children for structure in their lives. Parents of a handicapped child sometimes tend to be oversolicitous and to allow more freedom than such a child can handle. A simple home atmosphere, a planned day, regular habits and avoidance of confusion and excitement are contributory factors. Preparation for any new situation is a valuable consideration in handling these children.

III. SCHOOL PLACEMENT

Adjustment problems arise when the aphasic child is ready for school. The more physically involved will require a special school; some with adequate help, can enter a regular school situation if they are met with understanding. In a few communities special programs are in effect. Others find no program available. The entrance of the aphasic child into a school situation depends on his behavior and on the status of his learning capabilities.

Even though an aphasic child functions well in the sheltered situation of the home, the stimulation of children and activities in the classroom pose too great a problem for him and for those dealing with him. Behavior problems and personality disorganization become so exaggerated that learning becomes an impossibility. The hyperactivity, short attention span, and general behavior problems often forbid continued school attendance. Because he frequently does not learn as other children do, he is considered mentally retarded (and certainly he is retarded in some areas). Such an appraisal and the general lack of specialized facilities frequently are responsible for the placement of this child in groups where he does not belong. In such a situation he will seldom develop the concepts which will lead to the establishment of good language and learning.

In some states, programs and research projects for the neurologically handicapped child are in progress, and prospects for classes are under consideration. The growing awareness of the needs of the child who presents an organic learning syndrome will promote greater opportunities for him since at present educational facilities for the neurologically handicapped and aphasic child pose a major community problem. Small private schools are sometimes able to adapt to the special problems of the aphasic. Private clinics are becoming more plentiful and may be the stabilizer that will carry a child through other school programs. Whatever the school situation, the teacher who has some understanding of the language difficulty can contribute much towards providing necessary experiences and associations.

Recommendations: Recommendations concerning schools are as numerous as the problems that arise. Occasionally much unhappiness can be averted if the family prepares the way for the child to some extent. It should not be necessary for him to enter the school situation only to experience repeated failure and rejection in that environment. As a result of repeated failure, problems of a psychological nature relating to school and to learning, as well as to social relations, arise. When the diagnosis has been made before the entrance into school, the child may be allowed a period of nursery school experience to evaluate his performance in a group. If the nursery school situation proves to be unsuccessful, it may be helpful for the parents to approach the school with their problem rather than to allow the child to suffer a school experience in which he meets with failure. If there is not a special program available, the family must then look to other sources for their child's education. Occasionally brief trial periods in the school program have been successful. For instance, a period of an hour a day in kindergarten may be the greatest length a child can sustain the stimulation of the class-room. A gradual increase of time according to the child's ability to tolerate the situation is recommended. A frank discussion with the teacher and other school personnel is of paramount importance. Continued language and psychological guidance may mean the difference between success and failure in a school. Sometimes a psychological workup further serves to pinpoint the learning problems and to evaluate particular levels of function.

Ideally, the aphasic child learns better in a situation with minimal stimulation. If the number of children in the classroom is limited, the aphasic's opportunities for learning and succeeding on a competitive basis are increased. The teacher should be a person sensitive to the aphasic's language and learning problems so that he may be helpful in the specific areas indicated.

IV. PHYSICAL PROBLEMS

A. General Physical Aspects

The brain-damaged child may present physical problems particularly in the early years of growth. However, as he approaches the school years, these problems become increasingly controlled and he usually appears to be an essentially healthy child. He may be receiving physiotherapy or may be under drug therapy but for all intents and purposes the physical aspects have become secondary to learning, habilitation and social growth. Since the physical development of most aphasic children closely parallels that of other children, their habilitation assumes an equally important role which necessitates early control of physical problems.

B. Motor Incoordination

In the grossly involved aphasic child, one sees readily observable motor incoordination. However, many children are not involved in the motor sphere and seem to have only a mild, gross incoordination. This difficulty manifests itself in poor hand-eye coordination, in an occasional failure to perform small and specific motor tasks, in awkwardness in walking, running, and in general handling of the body. Usually by exercising greater efforts the child will compensate for this incoordination. As he approaches puberty, stabilization sometimes occurs.

C. Drug Therapy

Since drug therapy for aphasic children has proved an important aid in many aspects, it warrants discussion in this brief volume.

Anticonvulsant medication is usually prescribed for the aphasic epileptic. Consistent treatment will suppress most manifestations and therefore relieve the social restrictions associated with this disease. To interrupt or discontinue drug therapy will promote recurrence of the symptoms of the disease. Drug therapy is often a matter of experimentation in finding the appropriate drug for the particular child and his problem. After the inception of such a program, the epileptic child is usually able to enter school or some other training program. A wide variety of anticonvulsant drugs is now available to the medical profession. It is essential that these be administered only as directed by the physician.

Since the advent of tranquilizing drugs, aphasic children as well as others with behavioral problems have received much benefit. Increased attention span, more selective reaction to stimuli and diminution of emotional aspects are frequently evident following the inception of drug therapy. Increased learning occurs with the added ability to attend. Frequently the resolution of behavioral symptoms will aid in the placement of aphasic and neurologically handicapped children in school. Parents and teachers are grateful for the additional aid offered by this phase of therapy.

Chapter 23

PARENT COUNSELING

I. INTRODUCTION

PARENTS OF THE APHASIC child are usually confused and baffled by the many problems confronting them. Why do these parents find their problems so acute? Much of the trouble centers in the disturbed family relationships, the lack of social acceptance of the child by other children and adults, and the difficulty in education and school placement. Parents may find that their child is inattentive and awkward. He often fails to comply, cannot communicate effectively, and exhibits tantrums and aggressive behavior. In a household where high standards of behavior are expected from other children, the aphasic child is a disturbing factor. The hyperactivity present, especially in the younger child, is exhausting for the whole family. Often the mother's attention must be diverted to him when other family members are in need. This aggressive, hyperactive, "unusual" child is often not accepted by other children. He may be a constant troublemaker, and the parents of other children do not want him in their yard. He is not a child of whom parents, with their love of ego-extension, can be proud. Although his appearance, in many cases, may be most attractive, his actions override this favorable point.

As the child nears school age, the problem of education arises. Adequate placement is hampered by the lack of proper facilities. A few communities have established special classes for neurologically handicapped and aphasic children, but these do not begin to absorb the number in need of special training. Thus a fear that there will be no facility for educating their child grows in the parents. Much can be done to allay these fears and to help parents meet these special needs through individual and group counseling.

The term counseling is used here in a broad sense to encompass a wide range from generalized orientation to individual counseling. Counseling takes many forms, any and all of which have their place. The neurologist or psychiatrist undertaking the medical evaluation may have a series of interviews with the parents, as may a member of the medical team in a clinic or hospital. An evaluating psychologist often suggests psychotherapy as an aid in handling the difficult dynamics of the home situation. The individual therapist or educator who undertakes therapy or training usually includes counseling as a part of treatment. Clinics, both private and public, and those connected with universities and colleges, include counseling as an important part of therapy.

What then may be accomplished through counseling? It is considered sufficiently essential by some facilities to require a series of orientation lectures as a prerequisite to the enrollment of a child in the facility. Many clinics have a mandatory individual counseling session for parents each month, with the parents' organization meeting frequently for more generalized orientation.

II. PARENT GROUPS

An increased awareness of the advantages of organization has led to a growing number of parents groups.[1] These groups have been a valuable adjunct to counseling by providing a cathartic situation. Members avail themselves of specialists and of allied personnel in the field by inviting their participation at meetings to further parent orientation. The most important phase of counseling, however, is performed by the parents themselves. As a group of parents becomes well acquainted with the purpose of organization, it usually takes much pleasure in offering support to new members. Such organizations provide encouragement as well as opportunity to share problems and to gain strength from identification with a group. Parents often better the care of their child by improving services through group endeavor. Such groups provide means for organized action on a local and national level, and some offer funds for scholarships and research.

III. UNDERSTANDING THE APHASIC CHILD

The parents need to understand the basis of their child's behavior. Most of the symptoms are directly related to the brain injury and must be understood as part of the picture of the aphasic child. Failure to comply with requests is often misinterpreted as disobedience. Actually, a child may appear to disobey because he does not understand the verbal command or because he cannot answer appropriately, or he may not even have the concept of what is involved. This may be further complicated by a motor incoordination which prevents execution of the task. The fact that this child is subject to the same problems of other children cannot be overlooked. He is first of all a child and his behavior problems should not be overlooked on the basis of his aphasia even though his problems are accentuated by the syndrome of his brain injury.

As the parent learns to accept the aphasic child, he feels less resentful toward the attitude of others. Sharing the knowledge of common problems

---

1. One such organization is the ACPA—Aphasic Children's Parents Association, Lakewood Speech Clinic, 4623 Harvey Way, Long Beach, California.

with those in similar circumstances offers a denominator of stability and a bulwark against public opinion. While the school problem is not easily solved, professional advice and specialized therapy may contribute much to a successful solution.

As an outgrowth of counseling, parents can become aware of the necessity of building up language concepts, of understanding the reasons for behavior deviations, and of helping the child understand that they, the parents, understand. Further, much can be done to keep many situations at home simple and structured in order to reduce baffling, complicated experiences. A parent who understands that his child does not break things purposely, does not want to disobey, hits others because he has no other way of expressing himself, can face the situation much more equably. Increased ability of the family to cope with the situation is in itself therapeutic for the child.

IV. REFERENCES

Matis, Edward E.: Psychotherapeutic tools for parents. *Journal of Speech and Hearing Disorders,* Vol. 26, No. 2, May 1961.

Travis, L. E., Editor: *Handbook of Speech Pathology,* Appleton-Century-Crofts, Ch. 32, p. 1015.

Van Riper, Charles: *Speech Correction.* Prentice-Hall, New York, N. Y. Third Edition, pp 513 and 537.

References suitable to parents

1. *Case Histories of Neurologically Handicapped Children* compiled by CANHC, Main P. O. Box No. 604, Los Angeles 53, Calif.

2. Lewis, Richard, and Strauss, Alfred A.: *The Other Child.* Grune & Stratton, New York, N. Y.

3. Clark, Ruth: Language behavior of children with unsuspected brain injury. *Logos,* Bulletin of the National Hospital for Speech Disorders, Vol. 5. No. 1, April 1962.

TRAINING APHASIC CHILDREN

Chapter 24

EVALUATION OF DEFECTS[1]

I. INTRODUCTION

A TEAM OF SPECIALISTS contribute much to the evaluation of the defects of the aphasic child: neurologist, psychiatrist, pediatrician, otolaryngologist, audiologist and language therapist. General areas to be considered in these many tests include neurological evaluation, emotional status, motor performance, personality, mental capacities, hearing, language and learning. A neurological examination is of primary importance as a basis for establishing the organic basis and the need of a drug therapy program. In addition to the opinions of qualified professional people, a complete history from the family and from other interested persons is needed. Clinical observations and an appropriate language evaluation by the speech and language pathologist are important. This team of investigators can do much to determine the direction of an appropriate over-all therapy program for the child involved.

A Suggested Diagnostic Approach:

1. Information sheets filled out by the parents (Section II below)
2. A history taken by the speech pathologist (Section VIII C below)
3. A psychodiagnostic evaluation (Section III below)
4. Auditory and visual perceptual capacities test (Section IV below)
5. Motor abilities (Section V below)
6. Language capacity test (Section VII below)

II. INFORMATION FROM PARENTS

The Parent Information Record is a suggested outline of pertinent data which have been found necessary in working with brain injured children. While all of the information may not be needed at the outset, many occasions arise during the course of therapy, particularly when the parent may not be immediately available, wherein the data contained in the record are helpful.

---

1. Observations on testing the brain injured child are made in Strauss and Lehtinen: *Psychopathology and Education of the Brain Injured Child.* Grune & Stratton, New York, N. Y., Chapter 6.

Haeussermann, Else: *Developmental Potential of Pre-School Children.* Grune & Stratton, New York, N. Y., 1958.

Taylor, Edith M.: *Psychological Appraisal of Children with Cerebral Defects.* Harvard University Press, Cambridge, Mass.

PARENT INFORMATION RECORD

Date _____

Patient's name: _____ Birthdate _____

Age now _____

Name and address of person referring you to the clinic:

_____

_____

_____

Parents: mother _____

father _____

address _____

_____ Phone _____

Marital status of mother   M   S   D   W   (Circle)

(If remarried name of stepfather) _____

Other children (names and ages):

NAME   AGE

_____   _____

_____   _____

_____   _____

_____   _____

_____   _____

_____   _____

Other persons living in the home: _____

Religious affiliation _____

Occupation of mother _____

Occupation of father _____

Approximate annual income _____

1. EDUCATIONAL HISTORY

Present schooling: _____ Grade _____

address: _____ Phone _____

Teacher: _____ Principal _____

School attended last year: _____ Grade _____

address: _____ Phone _____

Teacher: _____ Principal _____

Previous speech therapy: _____

Therapist's name: _____

Other therapies: _____

2. MEDICAL HISTORY:

Family physician or medical clinic: _____

address: _____ Phone _____

Other doctors: _____

address: _____ Phone _____

Has your child seen a psychologist? _____

Name of psychologist _____

address: _____

Has your child seen a neurologist? _____

Name of neurologist _____ Address _____

Was an electroencephalogram (EEG) made _____ Date _____

Has your child had a hearing test? _____ Date _____

Name of person giving test: _____

address: _____

The following is a list of diseases, many of them associated with childhood. Please give the age of the child when the disease occurred, whether it was a mild, a moderate or a severe case, whether the child had a high fever, and any noticeable effects which may have followed.

tonsillitis   tonsils removed?   child's age at time of tonsillectomy _____
whooping cough   mumps
pneumonia   convulsions
scarlet fever   rickets
tuberculosis   enlarged glands
pleurisy   heart trouble
chicken pox   rheumatism
smallpox   thyroid disturbances
influenza   nervous trouble
diphtheria   infantile paralysis
measles   frequent colds
other:

Accidents such as severe falls, blows on the head, car accidents, etc. (Please give date of accident and child's condition at time of accident.)
Was there any medical procedure at the time?
Is epilepsy present? _____
        Is patient on medication? _____ If so what? _____
        Are seizures controlled? _____

3. COMMENTS

    Please comment in detail on the following items:
    a) Pregnancy: _____
            Birth history: _____

    b) Developmental history: (give approximate dates)
            Sitting _____
            Crawling _____
            Walking _____
            Self feeding _____
            Talking _____
            Toilet training _____
            Dressing self _____

    c) Coordination:
            Does your child have difficulty in walking, running, riding bike?
            Does your child have trouble in using crayons, scissors or pencil?
            Is your child right or left handed: _____. Has he always been consistent about
            handedness? _____. Describe any changes:

    d) Language or speech development:
            Has your child had difficulty in hearing? _____.
            As a baby did the child babble during the early months? _____.
            When did he begin to say single words _____; phrases _____;
                sentences _____?
            Is gesture language used? _____. To what degree? _____.
            Is child generally understood by his peers, the family and others? _____.
            Is another language spoken in the home? _____.
            Is there a marked speech problem present now? _____.

    e) Behavior:
            Tantrums
            Thumbsucking
            Bed wetting
            Other comments
            How does the child get along with the following people:
            Mother
            Father
            Other children in the home

Playmates
Other comments
f) Play and special interests
g) What do you feel your child's problem is:

III. PSYCHODIAGNOSTIC EVALUATION

A psychodiagnostic evaluation of the aphasic child includes items which assess:

(A) Behavior and social maturity
(B) Mental capacity
(C) Visual and auditory perceptual capacities
(D) Motor capacities

While the information on these tests is basic to the language therapist and his work, an additional language evaluation is needed. An overlapping takes place in much of the testing.

A. Behavior and Social Maturity

Behavior of the aphasic child is usually evaluated through observations during testing and clinical periods. Chapter 2, Basic Concepts, describes in some detail the behavior characteristics to be assessed. General descriptive comments should be made from actual observations of the child.

1. Characteristics of Primary Behavior Traits. Are any of the following characteristics present: (Make descriptive comments).

a. *Hyperactivity*—extreme physical activity characterized by incompletion and purposelessness.
b. *Hypoactivity*—pronounced lack of physical activity.
c. *Short attention span*—inability to sustain any kind of learning activity to completion.
d. *Disorganization*—inability to organize patterns of play or learning.
e. *Catastrophic reaction*—over-reaction to commonplace occurrence; tantrums; outbursts of rage; tears, crying.
f. Mild motor incoordinations:
   (1) Diffuse: awkwardness; inability to perform gross motor acts in smooth patterns (ride a bicycle, run, skip, swing, etc.)
   (2) Fine finger coordination (loss of dexterity of finger movements).

TEST—Mild Motor Incoordination (In testing consider developmental age.)
Materials: Crayon or large pencil, blocks, peg board, scissors, plain paper.
   (1) Can child manage crayons?
   (2) Can he draw lines and forms?
   (3) Can he draw an original picture?
   (4) Can he copy letters, names, words?

(5) Can he arrange a tower or a train with the blocks?

(6) Can he place the pegs in the board? Observe handedness as he performs.

(7) Can he manage scissors?

(8) Can he cut a disc, square, star?

g. *Narcissism*—An autistic-type behavior in which the child becomes chiefly concerned with himself in his own world to the exclusion of reality.

h. *Poor oral speech* (tested more fully in language test) —poor articulation; poor association in recall of words.

i. *Epilepsy*—Presence of any indication of epilepsy from marked to mild seizures; other indications as suggested in medical reports.

j. *Need for structured situations*—Inability to function outside the confines of an organized routine.

k. *Perseveration*—Repetition to excess in continuous activities.

l. *Compulsive behavior*—Inability to attempt new situations or insistence on performing in habitual ways.

2. Characteristics of Secondary Behavior Traits. (Comment on the presence of hostility, withdrawal, apprehension and negativism.)

3. Assessing Social Maturity. The best known instrument available for assessing social maturity is the Vineland Social Maturity Scale by E. A. Doll.[2] This is a standardized developmental schedule extending from birth to adulthood. The scale attempts to measure the increasing independence of the individual as he matures. It has a special advantage for use with aphasic children as the child does not participate. It depends instead, on the information given by a reliable informant, usually a parent.

B. Mental Capacity

One of the most difficult areas to assess in the aphasic child is that of mental capacity. Frequently public training programs demand a statement of intelligence level before admitting a child to the classroom. Examiners and clinicians feel that standard measurements are not applicable and that, at best, they can give only a subjective evaluation based on observation. Subjective evaluations from experienced clinicians are often invaluable. However, standardized tests do exist which can be used with aphasic children in part or in their entirety.

---

2. Doll, E. A.: *The Measurement of Social Competence.* The Educational Test Bureau, Minneapolis, Minn., 1953.

Myklebust, Helmer R.: *Auditory Disorders in Children.* Grune and Stratton, New York, 1954, pp. 292–297 offers a complete discussion of the Vineland Maturity Test.

1. Tests for Children Under Six Years of Age.

a. Cattell Test for Infants and Young Children.[3] This test requires a minimum of language and much opportunity for observation. It covers an age range of two years to thirty months.

b. "A Suggested Battery of Mental Tests for Use with Children Below Six Years of Age Who Present Problems of Auditory Disorder" (page 306 in *Auditory Disorders in Children* by Helmer Myklebust). This list suggests mental tests which have been found useful with aphasic children with auditory disorders.

2. Standard Tests of Intelligence Above Five Years of Age.

a. The Grace Arthur Point Scale of Performance Tests.[4]

b. Wechsler Intelligence Scale for Children.[5]
Frequently it is not desirable to use all items from a test, but rather only selected items.

3. Peabody Picture Vocabulary Test (Lloyd M. Dunn, George Peabody College for Teachers, Nashville, Tenn.).

Materials are obtainable from American Guidance Service, Inc., 2106 Pierce Avenue, Nashville 12, Tenn. This test consists of a series of plates, four pictures to a plate. The examiner names one picture: the subject points to the one he thinks is the correct one. No oral reply is necessary. The test has been standardized from ages 2 years 9 months to 18 years 5 months.

C. Psychomotor Evaluation

The psychodiagnostic evaluation will include a psychomotor evaluation which often provides the language and educational therapist with much of the basis of his work. These include many of the visual perceptual areas, tests relating to kinesthesia, to body scheme and visuo-motor areas. Many of these tests determine more than one defect and are overlapping in their design. An experienced therapist may wish to devise original simple tests; many prefer to use published materials. Suggested areas to be tested include the following:

1. Body Scheme. In this area an evaluation is made of the child's recognition of his body and its functioning in relation to the environment. This may be determined through the following:

a. Goodenough Draw a Man Test.[6] The child is scored on the details included in his drawing.

---

3. Cattell, Psyche: *The Measurement of Intelligence of Infants and Young Children.* The Psychological Corporation, New York, 1940.
4. Arthur, Grace: *A Point Scale of Performance Tests.* The Commonwealth Fund, N. Y., 1930.
5. Wechsler, David: *Wechsler Intelligence Scale for Children.* The Psychological Corporation, New York, N. Y., 1949.

b. Flannel board figures. Observe the child's ability to place body parts correctly.

c. Doll with realistic features. Can the child match his own body parts with the doll's?

d. The examiner may ask the child to imitate him as he holds up his hands, points to body parts, etc.[7]

2. *Figure-Ground Discrimination.* A simple test may be devised by the clinician in which the child distinguishes foreground objects from diffuse backgrounds.

The child may name the outlined object, match it, or trace it.

Such items are discussed in Strauss and Lehtinen, *Psychopathology and Education of the Brain Injured Child* and are included as part of the Frostig Developmental Test of Perception by Frostig, LeFever and Whittlesey.

3. *Visuo-motor Performance.* Testing in this area assesses visual perception through motor responses. The clinician may devise tests in which the child is asked to arrange peg-board patterns, or form-board[8] patterns, or copy figures such as the cross, circle and square.

Several excellent tests exist which evaluate this function:

a. Bender Gestalt: *A Visual Motor Gestalt Test and Its Clinical Use* by Lauretta Bender, M.D., Research Monograph #3 (The American Orthopsychiatric Association, New York, N. Y.) 1938. This test may be used with children from four to twelve years to assess visual perception through motor response. The test consists of nine designs presented (on cards in a sequence of difficulty) to the child who copies designs on plain white paper.

b. *Copy of Forms* by A. Gesell. The child is asked to copy from cards: a circle, a cross, a square, a triangle, a rectangle and a diamond. This is to be

---

6. Goodenough, F. L.: *Goodenough Draw a Man Test—Measurement of Intelligence by Drawings.* World Book Company, Yonkers-on-the-Hudson, N. Y.

7. This should be done facing the same way as the child to avoid confusion of laterality—J. M. Nielsen, M.D.

8. See 5. Spatial Orientation below.

used with children from three to six years. A description may be found in
The First Five Years of Life by A. Gesell *et al.* (Harper Brothers, New York)
1940, p. 163.

4. Laterality and Handedness.

A discussion of laterality is to be found in Kephart's *The Slow Learner in
the Classroom,* page 42. In testing, observations should be made as to right
and left hand preference and to the use of the body as a whole.

a. Does the child use his body bilaterally for unilateral acts? (Are there
mirror movements in drawing or in writing?)

b. Does he use the body unilaterally for bilateral acts? Does one side
appear paralyzed or useless as in walking? Can he insert pegs in the peg board
when directed to do so simultaneously from each side?

c. Observations should be made as to whether the child is left or right
handed or ambivalent in this matter. Crayons or peg board may be used for
testing.

5. Spatial Orientation.

In evaluating this area, observations are made as to the child's informa-
tion concerning his relationship to distances and space in the world around
him. This orientation must be developed through the use of various senses.
Often the information develops through kinesthesis of the muscle sense.
Newell Kaphart has an excellent discussion of this subject in Chapter 6 of
The Slow Learner in the Classroom.

Form boards such as the Binet-type or the Sequin-type may be used.[9] In
these tests the child is asked to insert the correct form in the board.

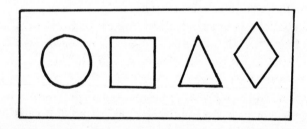

IV. AUDITORY AND VISUAL PERCEPTUAL CAPACITIES

Strauss[10] defines perception in the following way. "Perception can be
considered an activity of the mind . . . . intermediate between sensation
and thought. It is the mental process which gives particular meaning and

---

9. These form boards are described in *The Standard-Binet Scale, Manual for the Third Revision,*
   Psychological Corporation, 304 East 45th Street, New York 17, N. Y., and in *A Point Scale of
   Performance Test* by Grace Arthur, C. H. Stoelting Co. Chicago, Ill., 1930.

significance to a given sensation and therefore acts as the preliminary to thinking. It is the means by which the individual organizes and comes to understand the phenomena which constantly impinge upon him."

A. Auditory Evaluation

It is important to keep in mind that two types of impairment may exist: a peripheral hearing loss and a loss of auditory perception, recall and memory. A complete audiometric examination or PGSR (psychogalvanic skin response test) is of prime importance to help make the distinction between the peripheral and the central nervous system disorder. While this distinction is difficult to make, it is of great significance to the therapist. It is conceivable that both defects sometimes do exist in the same child.[11]

Informal tests[12] may be made which evaluate perception and discrimination of sound. (Auditory *verbal* tests are discussed under the language test.)

1. Perception of Sound

a. Environmental sounds: The clinician notes the child's reaction to common sounds in the environment such as a door slamming, a dog barking, a baby crying, water running.

b. Varieties of common sounds. The clinician introduces common sounds such as ringing a bell, shaking a rattle, the baby-doll cry, without allowing the child to observe. Later he is shown the objects in a group and asked to select the appropriate one.

2. Discrimination of Sounds

a. Several instruments such as a drum, a whistle and a rattle are used. The child is shown these and then asked to listen to the sounds of one instrument without looking. He then selects the one he thinks produced the sound.

b. Covered jars half-filled with various sound-making substances such as beans, nails, sand, etc. are used for this test. The clinician shakes one, shifts the jars around, then asks the child to try them until he discovers the appropriate one.

10. Strauss, Alfred A., and Lehtinen, Laura E.: *Psychopathology and Education of the Brain-Injured Child.* Grune and Stratton, New York, N. Y., 1947, Chapter III, Perception and Perceptual Disturbances of Brain-Injured Children.
   In this chapter the authors discuss perceptual disturbances in visual, in tactual, and in the auditory fields, and describe testing procedures which were used in each sensory area.
11. Myklebust, Helmer: *Auditory Disorders in Children.* Grune & Stratton, New York, N. Y., Chapter VII. Dr. Myklebust treats the entire subject of auditory evaluation extensively.
12. Barry, Hortense: *The Young Aphasic Child.* Alexander Graham Bell Association, Washington D. C., 1961, pp. 5–7.

B. Visual Evaluation

An evaluation of vision by a competent ophthalmologist must be made before visual perceptual areas can be evaluated. Brain injury which causes field defects is determined both by the ophthalmologist and the neurologist. Tests for visual perceptual capacities are included under the psychomotor evaluation. An outstanding test in the area of visual perception is the:

> Frostig Developmental Test of Perception (Marianne Frostig, Welty LeFever and John Whittlesey). The materials are available from The Frostig School of Educational Therapy, 7257 Melrose Avenue, Los Angeles 46, Calif.)

Subtests assess the following areas:

a) Eye-motor coordination
b) Figure Ground
c) Form Constancy
d) Position in Space
e) Spatial Relationship

V. MOTOR ABILITIES

A child's ability to perform motor functions grossly and in fine motor skills should be observed.

A. Gross Motor Skills

These may be observed as a child walks, skips, runs, swings, rides a bicycle, throws a ball or walks a rail for balance. A schedule of motor development is cited in Myklebust's *Auditory Disorders in Children* (Grune, Stratton, New York, N. Y.) 1954, page 308. A. Gesell includes a motor development scale in *The First Five Years of Life*. Gross motor movements are discussed throughout Kephart's *The Slow Learner in the Classroom* (Charles Merrill Books, Inc., Columbus, O.).

B. Fine Motor Skills

These may be evaluated by watching the child work with scissors, crayons, peg board, buttons, zippers, beads, etc. His dexterity in handling these together with his handedness should be observed. See III *Psychodiagnostic Evaluation*.

VI. SIMPLIFIED PSYCHOMOTOR EVALUATION

Below is a suggested procedure for the therapist or clinician who wishes to make a cursory examination in the areas of body scheme, figure-ground, visuo-motor, laterality and spatial orientation.

A. Body Scheme

1. The child is to imitate the examiner

    (a) hold up hand

    (b) put hand on head
    (c) hold up foot

  2. Draw-a-Man (Goodenough)

B. Figure-Ground Discrimination

Present the picture of this house. Tell the child to outline the house with crayon.

C. Visuo-Motor Performance

  1. Determine whether the child can copy these figures. Can he place form board figures (of same size and shape) on these outlines?

  2. Can the child copy these forms?

D. Laterality and Handedness

1. Ask the child to place 10 pegs simultaneously from each side of the peg board.

2. Ask the child to draw two lines on paper simultaneously (or on the blackboard with chalk).

E. Spatial Orientation

1. Ask the child to build a tower. (Hand him five blocks).

2. Ask the child to fit forms in the form board.

3. Ask the child to imitate a cross on the peg board using eight pegs.

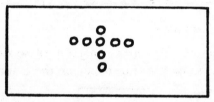

F. Other Visual Perceptual Items

1. Colors. Ask the child to match color discs.

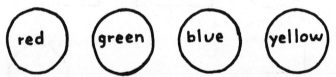

2. Similarities. Ask the child to match big circles, little circles.

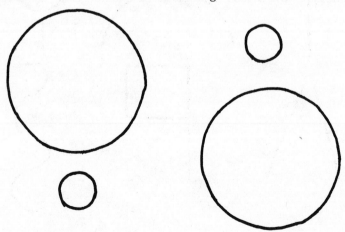

VII. EVALUATING LANGUAGE[13]

An evaluation of the language of an aphasic child should include areas of visual recognition, auditory recognition, naming, oral formulation, conceptualization and articulation. If the child is old enough, recognition of symbols such as those used in reading, writing and arithmetic should be evaluated, together with skills of reading, writing and arithmetic at appropriate levels. The development of language considered normal for the chronological age of the child must also be taken into consideration.

Basic to all therapy is the establishment, through testing and observation, of the level of function. Often the starting point is at a pre-language level. An evaluation of the language development of the child will determine the avenue of approach most effective in therapy. An excellent language test for *aphasic* children $2\frac{1}{2}$ to 9 years of age may be found in the "Illinois Test of Psycholinguistic Abilities" by McCarthy and Kirk, published by the Institute of Research on Exceptional Children, University of Illinois, Urbana, Ill. This test is available at ITPA, Incorporated, Box 2141, Madison 5, Wisc.

* * * * * * * *

LANGUAGE CAPACITY TEST

Instructions: The examiner must ascertain the reliability of the modality he is using. For example, he must not give oral instructions unless it has been determined that the child understands spoken language. He should not penalize a child in areas of drawing and manipulation if a paralytic involvement exists. The testing material must be evaluated in terms of the child's relationship to the environment and to the examiner. The test should not be administered until some degree of rapport between the child and the examiner has been established.

No attempt has been made to establish intellectual capacities (except indirectly) or to establish developmental criteria. The test assesses *only* how the child performs in language and in the perceptual and conceptual areas relating to language.

Materials: (1) Ball, cup, doll, bell, horn, blocks (six; two each of red, blue, yellow), rattle, comb
(2) Form board with circle, square, triangle
(3) 2 peg boards (use large pegs and limit holes to 16)
(4) Black crayon; plain paper
(5) Flannel board or cardboard face with separate eyes, nose, mouth
(6) Card with figure-ground drawing

---

13. This test is currently in use at the Lakewood Speech Clinic, Long Beach and Anaheim, Calif., and by the screening board of the aphasia classes in Garden Grove, Calif.

(7) Construction paper circles—two each of red, blue, yellow, green, purple, orange

(8) Single item pictures—2 balls, 2 girls, 2 kittens, 2 houses

(9) One set of action-sequence pictures from such a source as *We Read Pictures* or *Before We Read* (The New Basic Readers, Curriculum Foundation Series; Scott, Foresman and Company)

(10) Abstract figures from Section VI C, 2, above

(11) Pack of 3 x 5 cards for alphabet letters, numbers and words

LANGUAGE CAPACITY TEST

A. Visual Recognition

(This section precludes a competent ophthalmological examination for any defect in vision).

	The Test	Directions for Testing	Examiner's Remarks
Animate Objects	(1) Does the child recognize people such as mother, examiner, or any animals such as a dog.	(1) Observe the child's reaction to people or to animals in the testing environment.	
Inanimate Objects	(2) Does the child recognize the following objects: ball, cup, doll, several blocks, rattle. (Appropriate handling of the items indicates recognition)	(2) Place the toys before the child then observe his handling of the objects. If he does not touch the objects, he should be encouraged to play with them without being given any verbal clues as the names of the objects.	
Body Scheme	(3) Can the child imitate the examiner: a. put his hand on his ear b. touch his stomach c. touch his toes	(3) Face the same way as the child and demonstrate each action.	
	(4) Can the child place eyes, nose and mouth on a flannel board or cardboard face.	(4) Present the child with a flannel board or cardboard circle representing a face. (Hair and ears should be drawn in for orientation.) Eyes, nose, and mouth, cut out separately, are to be placed on the face.	
	(5) Can the child draw a person such as a man, woman, or child.	(5) Ask the child to draw "Daddy," "Mamma," or a boy or a girl. From	

*Examiner's
Remarks*

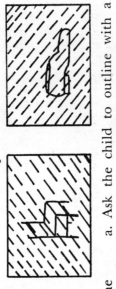

age 4, this may be scored by a Goodenough Draw-a-Man Test.

(6) Ask the child to point out what he
sees in the picture.

a. Ask the child to outline with a
black crayon what he sees.

(7) Ask the child to place the blocks of
the same color together (or show
him with one set).

a. Present 12 colored discs made of
cardboard or construction paper
(two colors of each and not in
paired order). The child is directed
to match them in pairs.

(8) Present the child with two cards, one
with two vertical dots, the other with
two horizontal dots. The child is

*Figure-
Ground*

(6) Can the child point out the figure on
the diffuse background.

a. Can the child draw around the
figure with a crayon.

Colors

(7) Can the child match by placing the
blocks together:

two red

two blue

two yellow

a. Can the child match several colors:

red   yellow   green

blue   orange   purple

*Spatial
Relationship*

(8) Can the child connect two dots verti-
cally and horizontally.

Visuo-Motor

a. The child is asked to place forms in a simple form board.

a. The child is simply directed to place the forms in the cut-out spaces in the form board.

(9) Can the child arrange four large pegs on a simple peg board to match the examiner's pegboard.

(9) The examiner has two peg boards for large pegs. He places a design on one made up of four pegs then directs the child to copy this design on his own peg board.

Shapes

(10) Can the child recognize basic shapes. (Refer to psychomotor test for further evaluation in visuo-motor areas.)

(10) Ask the child to match these forms.

directed to connect these dots with a crayon.

(11) Can the child copy abstract figures: found in Section VI,C,2 above.

(11) Present a card containing the abstract figures and ask the child to copy them with crayon on white paper.

Picture Items

(12) Can the child recognize pictured items:
ball
cup
doll
block

(12) Present the child with a series of four cards each picturing a single item. He is requested to match with actual items or name them.

	The Test	Directions for Testing	Examiner's Remarks
Non-Verbal Sounds	(13) Can the child recognize items in a picture.	(13) Present a picture showing a play scene. Ask the child to point out items or talk about the picture.	
Visual Verbal Recognition			
Letters	(14) Can the child recognize upper-case (capital) letters: A C M S X	(14) Present each letter printed on a separate 3 x 5 card. The child indicates recognition if he matches the letters, or if he points them out as the examiner names them.	
	(15) Can the child recognize lower-case (small) letters: a f p d e r	(15) Present each letter as in the directions above.	
Numbers	(16) Can the child recognize numbers: 1 5 3 2 4 6 7 8 9	(16) Present each number as in the directions above. The child indicates recognition if he shows the correct number of figures.	
Words	(17) Can the child recognize words from a standard preprimer list: look puppy apple come house	(17) Present each word printed in lower-case on a separate card. Ask the child to read the word. Or, place the five cards on the table, say one word, and ask the child to select the proper card.	

B. Auditory Recognition

(This section precludes a competent audiometric examination for defects in hearing.)

Voice	(1) Does the child respond to the examiner's voice.	(1) Observe the child's reaction to his voice, or to his mother's voice (*not as*

...a test of recognition of the actual language, but simply an awareness of perception of the sound).

Environmental Sounds	(2) Does he pay attention to the sounds in his environment, example: telephone ringing, dog barking, sound of a door closing.	(2) The examiner observes whether or not the child appears to recognize other sounds in the environment.
Specific Sounds	(3) Can the child recognize *specific* sounds: bell rattle small horn (type with a squeeze bulb)	(3) Behind a small screen so that the child cannot see the object, demonstrate one of the sounds. A set of the same instruments is placed before the child; he is to select the instrument which made the sound.

Auditory Verbal Recognition

Single Word	(4) Can the child select the objects named: ball block cup rattle doll	(4) Name an object and ask the child to point to it.
	(5) Can the child point to the correct body part: nose knee eye foot ear stomach	(5) Ask the child to point to the body part named.
Simple Commands	(6) Can the child follow a simple command.	(6) Ask the child to perform the given command.

The Test

    This further tests recognition of body scheme

a. Throw me the ball.
b. Drink from the cup.
c. Similar simple commands.

(7) Can the child follow commands involving the body.
    a. Hold up your hand.
    b. Put your hand on your head.
    c. Touch your toes.

Double Commands

(8) Can the child complete a more complicated command.
    a. Put one block on the table and one on the chair.
    b. Pick up the doll and place it on the chair beside you.

C. Naming

Objects

(1) Can the child name common objects:
    ball   cup   doll
    block   bell   rattle

People

(2) Does the child name people in his environment:
    his own name

Directions for Testing

(7) Give the oral request without any demonstration or gestures.

(8) Give the child the direction, being careful not to give any gesture clues.

(1) Hand the child each object and ask him to name it. With the very young child observe spontaneous naming and also question the parent regarding naming words the child uses at home.

(2) Observe how the child calls a parent by name. Supplement this by asking for information regarding naming in

Examiner's Remarks

Mama
Daddy
Sister
Brother

the home environment. (If the examiner has a set of family figures, he may ask the child to name them.)

Environment (3) Can the child name things in his immediate environment:

door   floor
window   table

(3) Ask the child to name these as he points them out.

Picture Items (4) Can the child name items from a composite picture.

(4) Present the composite picture. Ask the child to name items in the picture (both animate and inanimate).

Geometric Figures (5) Can the child name the figures on the form board:

circle (ball)
square
triangle

(5) Ask the child to tell what he calls the three geometric figures. Any descriptive name such as ball or block should be considered appropriate.

Colors (6) Can the child name the colors:

red   green   yellow
blue   orange   purple

(6) Present the colors used in the test on matching, then ask the child to tell the names of the colors.

(If the child has spontaneously given the names, omit this)

Letters (7) Can the child name the letters:

A C M S X
(and others if desired).

(7) Ask the child to name the letters.

Numbers (8) Can the child name the numbers:

1 5 3 2 4

(8) Ask the child to name the numbers.

Directions for Testing

(1) Note whether the child has any spon-
taneous speech.
   Ask the parent if he makes any re-
quests. Example:
      Go bye-bye
      Go potty
   Note the quality and extent of this.
   Is the speech telegraphic.

(3) Perform the indicated actions and
ask the child to tell what he is doing.

The Test

D. Formulation

Spontaneous   (1) Does the child have any spontaneous
Speech   formulation. Does he make any spon-
                     taneous requests.

Questions   (2) Does the child ask the examiner any
(This, of   questions spontaneously as they pro-
course, may   ceed to the therapy room.
be contingent
on child's
relationship
to the testing
situation.)

Action Words   (3) Can the child supply the verb or a
                     phrase containing a verb as the exam-
                     iner performs the following acts:
                        a. throw a ball
                        b. clap hands
                        c. jump

Play-scene picture
(Used in test item VII A, 13 above)

(4) Can the child describe what is happening in the picture.

(4) Ask the child to tell what is happening in the picture. Ask questions if necessary to elicit conversation from the child about what takes place in the picture.

Action-Sequence Pictures

(5) In a series of action pictures, can the child tell what is happening in each picture.

(5) Present the picture series (*We Read Pictures, We Read More Pictures,* and *Before We Read,* The New Basic Readers, Curriculum Foundation Series; Scott, Foresman & Co., 1956 contains appropriate pictures and picture series).

Story

(6) Can the child tell a simple story about something he does. *Example:* What did you do last Sunday.

(6) Ask the child to recount a recent day's activities.

Prepositions

(7) Can the child give the preposition or prepositional phrase as the examiner places the block in these positions:

a. *on* the table
b. *under* the table
c. *in* a box, or *in* his pocket.

* * * * * * * * * * * * * *

Other characteristics of oral speech such as descriptive words (adjectives and adverbs) belong to the refinements of speech with older children who may have mild residuals of aphasia. Language workbooks such as Webster Language Workbook and Textbook by Hartzog and Neeley, Webster Publishing Company, St. Louis, Mo., and other excellent books are available for such purposes.

The Test	Directions for Testing	Examiner's Remarks

E. Articulation[14]

Any Recognizable Oral Speech

(1) *Describe* characteristics of the child's speech:

(1) Does the child make any attempt at oral speech? If the words are not recognizable, is he consistent in his neologisms. (Reference is made here to the self-made word-forms children attach to people and things). If no speech exists, does the child have any sounds, does he do any babbling? Does the child have any vowel or consonant sounds which he uses consistently in his speech.

Articulation Test

(2) How does the child perform on an articulation test.

(2) The following articulation test may be administered or other available tests may be used.[15]

---

14. An articulation defect may be a motor speech problem as comparable to the adult with motor aphasia. It is also conceivable that the articulation defect may be entirely unrelated to the primary aphasia. Children with muscular disorders such as cerebral palsy may show evidence of a dysarthric type of speech (See Terms, *Appendix*).

15. Edmonston, William: *Laradon Articulation Scale.* 2090 Fir Drive. Thorton 29, Colorado, 1959. Schoolfield, Lucille: *Better Speech and Better Reading.* Expression Co., Boston, Mass., p. 141. Travis, L. E., Editor: *Handbook of Speech Pathology,* Milisen, Isolated-Word Articulation Test and Stimulability Test. Appleton-Century-Crofts, New York, N. Y., 1957.

1. Articulation Test

	Initial	Medial	Final
p	pig	apple	cup
b	ball	baby	tub
m	milk	hammer	gum
wh	wheel	pinwheel	
w	wagon	sandwich	
f	fish	telephone	knife
v	valentine	river	stove
th (unvoiced)	thumb	birthday	mouth
th (voiced)		mother	
t	table	letter	boat
d	dog	radio	bed
n	nail	penny	moon
s	soap	whistle	glass
z	zoo	scissors	rose
r	rooster	carrot	car
l	lamp	balloon	bell
sh	shoe	dishes	fish
ch	chair	kitchen	match
j	jug	engine	cage
k	kite	basket	clock
g	gun	wagon	bug
y	yellow	onion	
h	house	birdhouse	

F. Reading, Writing, Arithmetic

For older children of school age and experience more extensive testing is needed in each area. Standardized tests used in many school systems are available for this purpose. The following testing is simply to indicate defects which need further testing.

1. Reading

Word Similarities

(1) Can the child indicate the words which are alike:

look

look

come

see

(1) Ask the child to draw a line through the pairs of words which are not alike.

	The Test	Directions for Testing	Examiner's Remarks
Word Recognition	doll ball bed bed want want (2) Can the child circle the word which the examiner reads in a series of four: go up look bed two big puppy and home baby see down	(2) Present the child with the series of words. Ask him to circle the word he hears pronounced.	
Sentence Recognition	(3) Can the child recognize the sentence which the examiner reads: I see the ball. Run to me. Look at the puppy. The baby plays. Look at the book. I see mother.	(3) Present the child with the series of sentences, then read one sentence of each series. Ask the child to circle the sentence he hears.	

Sentence Comprehension	(4) Can the child complete the following:
	The boy (runs
	         (and
	         (up
	I see the (has
	         (baby
	         (to
		(4) Ask the child to draw a line to the correct word.	

Story *Compre-* *hension*	(5) Can the child read the following story with comprehension? Mother, Daddy and I went to the farm. I saw a horse. I saw a cow. I had a good time.	(5) Ask the child to read the story aloud, then ask: a. Who went to the farm? b. What did you see? c. What kind of a time did you have?

Many good reading tests exist which offer a complete analysis of the reading problem, such as *Survey of Primary Reading Development,* Harsh, Richard J., Soeberg, Dorothy, (Educational Testing Service, Los Angeles, Calif.) 1957.

California Achievement Tests (Primary, Elementary, Intermediate and Advanced) Tiegs, Ernest W., Clark, Willis W. (California Test Bureau, 5916 Hollywood Blvd., Los Angeles, Calif.)

Gates Reading Survey, Grade 3 (second half) through Grade 10, Gates, Arthur I. (Bureau of Publications, Teachers College, Columbia University, 525 West 120th St., New York 27, N. Y.)

2. *Writing and Spelling*

Copy Letters
in Printing
	(1) Can the child copy the following letters:
	
	   A C M S X
	    o p t n l
	If the child has defects in visual perceptual areas he may not be able to perform in this area.
		(1) Ask the child to copy upper and lower case letters in printing.

Print or *Write Letters* *Spontaneously*	(2) Can the child print or write his name?	(2) Ask the child to write or print his name.

Examiner's Remarks

(3) Can the child print or write letters spontaneously.

(3) Ask the child to print or write letters at request.

Copy Printed Sentences

(4) Can the child copy the sentence: See the puppy run.

(4) Direct the child to copy the sentence printed on one line of the paper.

Spelling

(5) Can the child spell (in writing) words as dictated:

go
I
Mother
and
to
see
house
like
me
ride

(5) Ask the child to write the words as they are dictated.

Sentence Formulation

(6) Can the child write any sentences of his own.

(6) Ask the child to write a sentence about something familiar. Example: your house, your puppy, your daddy's car.

3. Arithmetic

Counting

(1) Can the child count ten blocks (or any part of ten) or ten sticks.

(1) Ask the child to count blocks or sticks, making sure he is not counting by rote.

Copy Numbers

(2) Can the child copy numbers:

1 2 3 4 5 6 7 8 9 10

(2) Ask the child to copy the numbers 1-10.

Number Recognition

(3) Can the child match the correct number of blocks to printed numbers?

(3) Ask the child to match the correct number of blocks with the indicated numbers: 3, 5, 2.

Oral Arithmetic

(4) Can the child add numbers mentally when presented with blocks:

2 blocks + 2 blocks =
2 blocks + 1 block =
4 blocks + 1 block =

(4) Ask the child to tell how many blocks are in each group.

Written Arithmetic

(5) Can the child add the written numbers.

(5) Ask the child to do the following examples on paper:

$$\begin{array}{r} 3 \\ 1 \\ \hline \end{array} \quad \begin{array}{r} 2 \\ 2 \\ \hline \end{array} \quad \begin{array}{r} 1 \\ 4 \\ \hline \end{array} \quad \begin{array}{r} 2 \\ 1 \\ \hline \end{array}$$

Further analysis of spelling, written language, and arithmetic may be made through standardized tests such as the California Achievement Tests.

VIII. TEST SUMMARY AND INDEX FOR THERAPY[16]

Name   Age   Date
Diagnosis
Etiology   Handedness
Epilepsy

A. Summary Psychodiagnostic Evaluation
   Measure of Intelligence
   Emotional Status

B. Observations of Behavior Characteristics
   Primary Behavior Characteristics: Comments:
      1. Hyperactivity
      2. Hypoactivity
      3. Short attention span
      4. Disorganization and poor judgment
      5. Catastrophic reaction
      6. Mild motor incoordination: diffuse; fine finger
      7. Narcissism
      8. Poor oral speech
      9. Epilepsy
     10. Need for structured situations
     11. Perseveration

   Secondary Behavior Characteristics:
      1. Hostility
      2. Aggression
      3. Withdrawal
      4. Apprehension

C. Language and Related Functions

Language Function	Therapist's Comments	Training Reference Chapter Section
1. Visual Recognition	Chapter 28	
animate objects		II,A
inanimate objects		II,B
body scheme		II,C
figure-ground		II,D
colors		II,E

---

16. The therapist will find it convenient to make notations (following the actual test) on the test summary sheet. To do so provides a quick reference and a starting point for immediate therapy.

Language Function	Therapist's Comments	Training Reference Chapter Section
spatial relationships		II,F
visuo-motor		II,G
form		II,H
picture items		II,I
Visual Verbal Recognition	Chapter 28	
letters		III,A
numbers		III,B
words		III,C
2. Auditory Recognition	Chapter 29	
non-verbal sounds		II,A
voice		II,C
environmental sounds		II,D
specific sounds		II,B,E
Auditory Verbal Recognition	Chapter 29	
single words		III,A
simple commands		III,B
— body scheme		
double commands		III,C
3. Naming	Chapter 30	
objects		I,A
people		I,B
environment		I,A-3
picture items		I,A-5-6
geometric forms		I,E
colors		I,F
numbers		I,G
4. Formulation	Chapter 31	
spontaneous speech		I
questions		II
action words		III
play-scene picture		IV,A
action-sequence pictures		IV,A
story		V
prepositions		VI
5. Articulation	Chapter 32	

Language Function	Therapist's Comments	Training Reference Chapter Section	
any recognizable oral speech	————————	Chapter 24,	VII,E
articulation test	————————	Chapter 24,	VII,E,I
6. Reading, Writing, Arithmetic		Chapter 15 and	
a. Reading	————————	Chapter 33,	I
word similarities	————————		I,A
word recognition	————————		I,B
sentence recognition and comprehension	————————		I,C
story comprehension	————————		I,D
b. Writing and Spelling	————————	Chapter 16 and	
copy letters in printing	————————	Chapter 33,	II,A
print or write letters spontaneously	————————		II,B
copy printed sentences	————————		II,C
spelling	————————		II,D
sentence formulation	————————		II,E
c. Arithmetic	————————	Chapter 17 and	
counting	————————	Chapter 33,	III,A
copy numbers	————————		III,B
number recognition	————————		III,C
oral arithmetic	————————		III,D
written arithmetic	————————		III,E

IX. CONCLUSION

After the therapist has noted on the Test Summary Sheet the language and learning defects found in testing, he immediately wishes to turn to therapy which will develop the deficient areas. Basic areas of perception and conception must be developed as the level of achievement indicates. This means that many older children, even adults, will be working on primary levels, although the therapist may adjust the approach appropriately according to the age and interests of the patient. Material presented to the young aphasic child is usually extremely simple and repeated many times. The therapist will wish to extend the material presented in the training chapters with ideas of his own.

Chapter 25

ATTITUDES AND SPECIAL TECHNIQUES APPLICABLE IN TRAINING CHILDREN WITH APHASIA

I. GENERAL ATTITUDES AND TECHNIQUES

CHILDREN WITH APHASIA, like adult aphasics, respond to a variety of approaches and techniques. Yet the need of reenforcing the same concept over and over again often necessitates a great amount of repetition. The child himself will often seek out the same activity many times as though satisfying his own need of reenforcement. The imaginative therapist will find many different ways of teaching the same concept through varied approaches. If the child is enrolled in a school program for the aphasic child[1] or for the neurologically handicapped child,[2] the therapist may choose to develop the most defective areas or to strengthen an area of success as decided upon by the teacher and the therapist in consultation.

The "atmosphere" of therapy is referred to in many texts and is considered of great importance. It is often felt that an environment sterile and free from distraction is of prime importance. While lack of distraction is often helpful, it has been demonstrated that aphasic children can work successfully in an atmosphere of normal distractions, where the therapy is structured and the relationship with the therapist is close. Certainly a great deal of structure with aphasic children is indicated, at least until they are well integrated in their learning processes and personalities. They are often easily disturbed by changes in program and in environment. However, a certain permissiveness must exist within the structure in order to consider the individual differences and the personality of each child. While these children should not be presented with great confusion, they should be permitted simple choices.

The short attention span and hyperactivity of the aphasic child presents one of the greatest problems of early therapy. The therapist must be ready to offset this with a number of planned activities directed towards the same goal. The young child must often explore his environment before settling down to the work at hand. At times he will not respond to a planned activity but will engage in his own self-initiated interests. This may be an indication of

---

1. Bolsa Public School, Garden Grove, California; the Berkeley Program, Berkeley Public Schools, Berkeley, Calif.; Public School 158 School for Deaf and Aphasics, New York, N. Y.
2. Long Beach, Calif. and other cities have such programs.

needs, and the wise therapist will make use of these interests to extend therapy. Dr. Maria Montessori remarks on the child's development in *Dr. Montessori's Own Handbook*,[3] page 33:

> The aim is an inner one, namely, that the child train himself to observe, that he be led to make comparisons between objects, to form judgments, to reason and to decide; and it is in the indefinite repetition of this exercise of attention and of intelligence that a real development ensues.

If the child becomes perseverative in his activities, the therapist will have to intercept these activities and motivate him in other directions.

The relationship with the therapist or the teacher becomes one of the most crucial aspects of the child's academic and emotional growth. The young aphasic child often needs a close physical relationship with the therapist and will sit closely by him. The problems of each day, the extent to which pressure may be exerted in behavioral and academic ways, the allaying of anxieties, the meeting of emotional needs are all considered by the sensitive teacher and therapist.

Since the aphasic child is first a child, and secondly aphasic, his emotional problems take precedence. In addition to language therapy, play therapy is often indicated in alleviating severe emotional disturbances which grow out of the inhibited language situations. Play therapy is not unlike that used with any group of children. There is need of sand and water play and aggressive and regressive situations. Although the aphasic child may find it difficult to be creative, he should be encouraged to be so. Such mediums as clay and finger paint form a means of expression especially satisfying to these children who lack the ability to verbalize their feelings. In addition to language therapy, in extreme cases the skills of a trained psychiatrist or skilled psychologist are needed in meeting the emotional needs of the child.

Since the response to therapy is usually slow, the setting of feasible goals is important both to the therapist and to the child. Rewards in therapy must come from small gains. However, even the slightest advance can be very helpful in alleviating the frustrations which are a result of the child's lack of communication or from his behavior problems.

II. SPECIFIC TECHNIQUES

A. Specific Techniques for the Training of Language Functions

There are specific techniques which apply to the training of language functions of the aphasic child. These techniques are designed to establish auditory verbal recognition, visual verbal recognition, motor speech patterns,

3. Montessori. Maria: *Dr. Montessori's Own Handbook*. Frederick A. Stokes, New York, N. Y., 1914.

language association and language formulation. Often basic to this training are the development of perceptual areas and the establishing of non-language concepts. In the older aphasic child the use of propositional speech and symbols used in writing, reading and arithmetic may be used in therapy. The developmental level rather than the chronological age of the child is the prime factor to consider. Whatever the age of the child, development of any concept must follow the order of perception, integration and association of ideas, and an expression of the concept. This may be expressed in another way:

1. The child sees the object (e.g., a ball)
2. The child recognizes the object as a ball and establishes his concept of the ball through:
   (a) recall of other balls
   (b) recognition that the shape is round
   (c) selection of other round objects (circles, wheels, buttons, etc.)
   (d) realization of the purpose of a ball (the ball can be thrown, tossed, caught)
3. The child externally expresses the idea by:
   (a) placing a ball in a group of other balls
   (b) throwing the ball
   (c) drawing the ball
   (d) saying the word, BALL

All learning for the child must essentially follow these steps. Regardless of his age he must be able to recapitulate these steps of perception, conception, and expression.

Myklebust refers to this as internal and expressive language.[4] In the acquisition of language, Dr. Montessori refers to three steps. In the first step the teacher names the object for the child; in the second step the child is requested to recognize by producing the object as named; in the third step the child says the word as the teacher says, "What is this?" These steps she terms Naming, Recognition, and the Pronunciation of the Word.[5] While Dr. Montessori's system was not devised with the brain injured child in mind, the orderly introduction of concepts via many modalities prior to the presentation of language items, appears to be highly desirable in the teaching of the aphasic child. Under the Montessori method the children are placed in an environment completely scaled to their own use. They become familiar with carrying out many tasks pertaining to daily living in an orderly way. The "intellectual" material introduced begins with three series of cylinders,

4. Travis. Lee Edward: *Handbook of Speech Pathology*, Appleton, Century, Crofts, New York, N. Y., 1957, Chapter 15.
5. Montessori, Maria: *Dr. Montessori's Own Handbook*. Frederick A. Stokes, New York, N. Y., 1914.

each varying in size relationship which the child must arrange. Further materials consist of a graduated tower, steps, tactile material, rough and smooth, shades of color, textures, sound discriminatory items, all preparatory to the functions of reading and writing. When the child is finally presented with the symbols of the letters of the alphabet, he has been so thoroughly prepared in discriminating size and shape that the tools of language are more easily acquired.

B. Developmental Approach to a Concept

The following outline is presented as an indication of a developmental approach to a concept.

1. Perception is defined by Strauss (Psychopathology and Education of the Brain Injured Child) as "an activity of the mind, intermediate . . . between sensation and thought. It is the mental process which gives particular meaning and significance to a given sensation and therefore acts as the preliminary to thinking. It is the means by which the individual organizes and comes to understand the phenomena which constantly impinge upon him."

Perception in any modality may be considered as an awareness. Concepts involve relationship and understanding. For example, a child perceives a ball and realizes its presence. As he builds a concept of the ball, he realizes that it is round, it can be thrown or rolled, that it has depth, and that other things are round also. Several modalities should be used in presenting an object to a child with perceptual deficits.

The following outline is suggested:

   a. Visual perception or awareness
       (1) Show the object in several positions.
       (2) Show the object in relation to several other objects of the same shape or kind. *Example:* apple, orange, ball.
   b. Auditory perception or awareness
       (1) If there is any sound connected with the object, demonstrate it. *Example:* bouncing a ball.
       (2) Give the name of the object slowly several times.
   c. Tactile perception or awareness
       (1) Give the object to the child to handle and to feel.
       (2) Cover the child's eyes, have him feel the object and handle it for several minutes.
   d. Kinesthetic perception or awareness
       (1) Allow any motion connected with the object to be performed. *Example:* throwing the ball.
   e. Awareness of space relationship

(1) Show the object in motion: rolling, falling, so that the motion of the object may be seen.
  f. Outline study
      (1) Allow the child to trace the outline of the actual object, then trace a plane outline of the same figure on paper or a plane inset.
2. Concepts
   The Montessori order of procedure for the education of the senses is:
   a. Recognition of identities (the pairing of similar objects and insertion of solid forms in places which fit them).
   b. Recognition of contacts (presentation of the extremes of a series of objects). *For example:* Smallest and largest of a group.
   c. Discrimination between objects very nearly similar to one another (apple and orange).
3. Presentation of the concept of a circle (or disc)
   (Non-language Concepts)
   Materials: Several cardboard or wooden discs of various colors.

Remarks	Techniques
a. This is for perception and recognition.	a. Show the child a disc of cardboard or wood. Give it to him to handle.
	b. Show him a ball and let him handle it.
c. This is the introduction of concepts (other things are round).	c. Show him other things in the room which are round. *Example:* round pillow, buttons, top of can, glass top.
d. This is the introduction of size.	d. Show him several discs of varying sizes. Show him several balls of varying sizes.
e. The child is beginning to recognize shape and also to develop dexterity in insertion of plane figures.	e. Ask him to insert wooden discs in plane insets.
	f. Ask him to handle the wooden discs with his eyes closed, then handle the balls.
g. This develops the kinesthetic sense.	g. Ask him to throw the ball, then roll it.

h. Ask him to trace the outline of
the disc and the ball, and then
the plane insets.

i. See if the child can match the red
wooden disc with a red cardboard or paper circle.

(Language Concepts)

j. Suggested commands for auditory verbal training:
(1) Show me a circle (use the child's term: ball, "round," circle,
disc) .
(2) Show me a red circle.
(3) Show me the smallest circle.

k. Commands for oral speech:
(1) (Hold up the ball.)
What is this?   Child may reply: Ball. That is a ball.
(2) (Hold up the circle.)
What is this?

l. Commands for identification with oral response:
(1) (Hold up the *blue*
ball) What is this?   Child: That is the blue ball.
(2) (Hold up the *red* ball)
What is this?   That is the red ball.
(3) (Hold up a *large* ball)
What is this?   That is the big ball, or the
big red ball (as the case
may be) .

Chapter 26

GROUP THERAPY FOR CHILDREN

I. INTRODUCTION

IN ADDITION TO THE structured therapy of language training, many children with aphasia have a great need for play therapy.[1] Play is valuable both in alleviating the frustrations of children who cannot communicate in language and in providing a release of emotional tension. It also provides situations for concept building, naming, and developing relationships. The amount of time devoted to play therapy will depend to a great extent on the emotional needs of the individual child.

Some of the attendant frustrations may be lessened by allowing an opportunity to make use of aggressive and regressive toys. Children may display aggression through the media of sand, clay, water, and finger paints. Manipulation of family figures, hammering and pounding activities and puppet play further alleviate emotional stress. Because of their non-verbal communication, these children seem to have a greater need of expression of aggressive acts.

Other aphasic children have a greater need of dependence and of a close relationship with therapists and family members. They frequently choose regressive toys such as bottles, cribs, and play pens as an expression of their needs.

Expressive media assume a particular importance to aphasic children who cannot convey messages in language but who can spread bright paint across a sheet of paper. It is not unusual to see an aphasic child sketch out his idea on paper or mold a descriptive figure in clay. Many family relationships can be interpreted with family figures and doll-house play.

Constructive toys such as building sets, simple puzzles and blocks supply a mode of creation and accomplishment which supplant the verbal activities of children who can speak. (See Play Therapy Materials, Chapter 27.)

Another implication of play therapy is its relation to language building. Play therapy sessions can also be sessions for identifying objects in the home, the furniture for example, and family figures. As the child selects the activity or object, the therapist should relate language activities to it. Frequently aphasic children seem to be compulsive in their interests but, since much repetition is necessary to develop language in a given area, a great deal of

---

1. The techniques of play therapy as described here are not intended to be the same as those used by clinical psychologists and speech pathologists in treating functional speech problems.

time is well spent on a particular interest. This gives good opportunity to incorporate play therapy with group therapy activities.

II. GROUP THERAPY

Individual therapy is usually necessary with an aphasic child. Distractability, disorganization and inability to cope with competition at his own age level stress the need of a simple relationship between therapist and child. However, these factors do not preclude the use of group therapy. Sometimes, both group and individual therapy are indicated, especially as the child progresses and becomes more organized. Small groups of three or four children are usually the most effective.

Such activities as finger painting, clay, water play, blocks and sand can often be carried on in groups of three or four. Simple story telling, record playing, and the use of rhythm toys are suitable in a group. It is often possible for motor speech activities or other language skills to be carried on in small groups of children at a compatible level. Activities effective in small groups where a large indoor or outdoor space is available include rhythm band, simple dance patterns and gymnastics.

Increasingly more school systems throughout the country are adapting small classes for neurologically handicapped and aphasic children. These classes are comprised of a small group in the ratio of two to four children to one teacher. Learning is constructed along simple and concrete lines. The short attention span of the children is partly counteracted by introducing many physical-activity breaks during the day. These special classes have proved effective in dealing with aphasic children for whom regular school placement is often undesirable. It must be remembered that, to the aphasic child, his problems are often almost insurmountable and that, difficult as it is for him to cope with them individually, it is almost impossible for him to do so in groups until he has reached a level of development which will permit group activities. As aphasic children develop and grow older, they need the common denominator and socialization of a school situation.

III. GROUP PROJECTS

Several activities adaptable to the use of group work which have been used successfully with aphasic children are described below:

A. Finger Painting[2]

Finger painting has many desirable attributes for aphasics. It allows unrestricted movements in gross patterns which produce immediate and at-

---

2. Kephart, Newell C.: *The Slow Learner in the Classroom.* Charles E. Merrill, Columbus, Ohio, 1960, page 167–169.

tractive results. The child can constantly create new patterns and color combinations. The activity provides an introduction of color and experimentation with the blending of colors. It provides a release of emotion and tension which permit the child to enjoy this activity for a long period of time.

1. *Materials:* Powdered tempera paint and liquid starch, smocks or old shirts, newsprint, individual formica-topped boards (2 feet square). Provide each child with his own individual work area by placing his board on some larger work space such as a picnic table. It is most important that all materials be prepared before the group activity begins in order to minimize confusion and to assure an immediate starting point.

2. *Mixing of Paints:* Place liquid starch on each board. Add a small amount of the tempera to the starch.

   a. *Process:* Show the child how to mix his paint and how to make a design with two or three fingers or his entire hand. A design may be varied by using one finger to "draw" a lighter design through the heavier color mixture.

   b. *Music accompaniment:* Rhythmic music accompaniment to finger painting frequently suggests a pattern for the design, the accented beats calling for larger and firmer strokes. Tunes in 3/4 and 6/8 time are particularly suggestive of varied movements for design.

Sample 3/4 time design

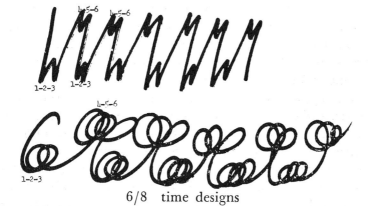

6/8   time designs

After a design is completed, place a piece of newsprint over the board to reproduce the pattern. The child may continue to make other designs with the same mixture or with another color added to produce different color combinations.

B. Collages

This activity affords another form of creative expression. It provides opportunity for the child to collect various materials and to plan their arrangement on paper. He learns form, shape and texture in collecting and placing material on background paper. The collecting in itself is a profitable activity for him: for example, collecting shells at the beach, small pebbles, colored leaves and flower petals. Coordination skill in pasting these objects on paper is developed.

   1. *Materials:* Colored paper, confetti, yarn, snips of material, peas, beans, rice, barley, small pebbles, coffee, alphabet soup, macaroni, leaves, rock salt. Heavy paper similar to cardboard, and liquid glue.
   2. *Process:* After the material has been assembled, glue each item separately on the heavy paper, or first cover a large surface with glue, then place the material on the glued surface. Some children may be able to follow an original design which they have drawn on the paper while others may need a design provided for them. Many prefer to create free-style designs as they go along.

C. Clay

The handling and molding of clay provides an outlet either for aggressive or regressive activity. Clay also provides a modality for creating shapes and designs and for strengthening coordination, and is another activity which often results in prolonged interest for the aphasic child.

   1. *Materials:*
      a. A home-made clay may be made by mixing 5 cups of flour, 1 cup of salt, 1/3 cup of cooking oil and enough water to form a bread-dough consistency. Food coloring may be added. This is not a permanent clay; a commercial moist or powdered clay is recommended for permanent forms.
      b. Rolling pins, cookie cutters, jar lids, rubber or wooden hammers.
   2. *Process:* Either commercial or home-made clay is easily molded into free forms or rolled out with a rolling pin or beaten into shape with wooden or rubber hammers. Give the child clay to free mold or roll out, or beat as he wishes. Provide a smooth surface such as formica or plastic-covered area. Designs can be made with cookie cutters and the like, then lifted out with a spatula. Favorite forms which the child wants to preserve may be hardened in the sun or in a moderately hot oven and then painted with powdered paints.

D. Gymnastics (Suggested by Gene Schroen)

Young children enjoy play such as running, jumping, climbing, tumbling, and twisting their bodies into all sorts of contortions, but urban living today gives them little opportunity to find an outlet for these motor activities. Seldom can they climb trees, roll on grassy slopes and jump and tumble in new mown hay. Activities which use the whole body are essential to physical growth and development. It is necessary, therefore, to include special physical activities in the therapy program which will help meet these needs. The exercises given here help develop coordination of the arms and legs while strengthening the large muscles. As coordination improves, the child be-comes more secure in handling his body in space.

This form of activity should be supervised by one skilled in its techniques and aware of its limitations. For the aphasic child, limited in physical activity, gymnastics provide therapeutic outlet and release of physical tension besides preparing him for the restrictions mandatory during language therapy.

Before starting any activity, a demonstration of the exercise should be given. This introduction will reduce any fear the child may have before participating in this new activity.

Materials needed: heavy tumbling mat or padded quilt, cushions or pillows.

1. *Bridge*

The child lies on his back with his knees drawn up close to his body. He places his hands under his hips and then using his hands he raises the hips off the mat and supports his body with his feet and head.

2. *Back Bend*

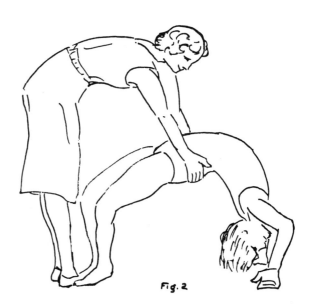

Fig. 1   Fig. 2

After the child experiences proficiency in doing the bridge exercise, the back bend can be tried. The child stands with feet apart, hands raised and palms skyward (Fig. 1). With the help of the therapist, the child's hands and head go back to touch the ground (Fig. 2). (A stack of cushions on the ground helps the child for the first few tries; later cushions are removed.) The child's back should be supported until he is able to do the exercises alone.

3. *Forward Roll (somersault)*

Place the head far down between the knees so that the forward roll is not done on the head. If the child shows a great degree of flexibility, he may put his hands on his knees, otherwise the hands should be placed on the ground with feet slightly separated. Pick the feet up and roll forward on the shoulders, turning a somersault.

4. *Back Lean*

The child kneels on both knees with hands at his sides. He leans backward until his hands reach the floor in back of him and supports his body in a leaning rest position.

5. *Rocking Horse*

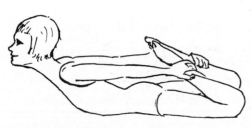

The child lies on his stomach, then arches his body up and away from floor, grasping his feet with his hands. He should try to lift the legs and head high so that the knees are raised from the floor; then the body forms a smooth, flexible arch.

E. Rhythm Band

Although bells, triangles, rhythm sticks, tambourines, maracas, castanets and other commercial percussion instruments are usually found in rhythm bands, interesting substitutes may be made from utensils found in the home. Children usually enjoy the surprise they experience when they are shown how to use common household objects in a rhythm band.

Music: rhythmic phonograph records, radio music, or someone at the piano.

1. *Instruments:*

    a. Glasses partly filled with water, spoons for tapping them

    b. Two wooden spoons or pairs of straight wooden sticks to be clapped together

    c. A pair of blocks with sandpaper thumb-tacked over them to be rubbed together

    d. Small pasteboard box containing a few grains of corn, Bb's or something which will rattle as the box is shaken

    e. Comb wrapped in one layer of tissue paper

    f. The resourceful therapist will think of other instruments convertible from articles in the kitchen cabinet or about the house.

2. *Procedure:* Allow the children to keep time to the music, varying the procedure in the following ways:

    a. Let the good singers "play" the tune on the tissue paper-covered combs while the percussion players rest.

    b. Let the good singers "play" the tune on the tissue paper then the rhythm-stick players or the sand-block players, the rattlers, the base drums etc.

    c. Let everyone play on the first beat of the measure and count aloud (or silently) on the remaining beats.

4/4 time —	1	2	3	4
	play	say "two"	"three"	"four"

    d. Let everyone play on the first two beats of the measure and be silent on the last beats.

    e. Let each group play on a selected beat only. (This takes some skill in coordination.)

4/4 time —	1	2	3	4
	only the	only the	only the	only the
	glasses	rhythm	sand	drums
	play	sticks	blocks	play
		play	play	

    f. Let the children take turns standing before the group as the leader or conductor.

F. Dance and Rhythm

Helpful references for simple dance steps and rhythm exercises for children include *Creative Rhythmic Movement for Children* by Gladys Andrews (Prentice-Hall, N. Y., 1954) and *The Dance in Elementary Education* by Ruth Lovell Murray (Harper Bros., N. Y., 1953).

IV. REFERENCES

Barry, Hortense: *The Young Aphasic Child.* Volta Bureau, Washington, D. C., 1961.

Carlquist, Maja, and Amylong, Tora: *Balance and Rhythm in Exercise.* The Viking Press, New York, N. Y., 1951.

Fraser, Ellen D., Bransford, Joan B., and Hastings, Mamie: *The Child and Physical Education.* Englewood Cliffs, N. J., Prentice-Hall, Inc., 1956.

Jackson, Lydia: *Child Treatment and the Therapy of Play.* Ronald Press, New York, N. Y., 1950.

Kephart, Newell C.: *The Slow Learner in the Classroom.* Chas. E. Merrill, Columbus, O., 1960.

Kepler, Hazel: *The Child and His Play.* Funk and Wagnalls, New York, N. Y., 1952.

Travis, L. E.: *Handbook of Speech Pathology.* Appleton-Century-Crofts, Inc., New York, N. Y., 1957, Ch. 23.

Chapter 27

THERAPY MATERIALS

I. TEACHING MATERIALS

A. Simple Household Furniture and Objects

Familiarizing children at all levels with their immediate environment is a big step in developing good communication. Actual furniture may be used. Doll house furniture has special appeal to many children.

B. Food and Clothing

Food, clothing, kitchen utensils and table service are used. This type of identification may be furthered through concrete objects and pictures of objects.

C. Toys, Dolls and Puppets

Representative dolls such as baby dolls, girl or boy dolls which can be easily dressed or undressed are good. These provide a medium for identification as well as for developing good rapport. They have a particular appeal for younger children. Puppets are invaluable as a basis for play therapy and for stimulating speech situations. Manipulative and constructive toys are also recommended.

D. Raised Figures

Some blocks have raised figures that are helpful in establishing kinesthetic concepts. Clocks and raised numbers are helpful at a more advanced level. Plastic letters and sandpaper letters may be used.

E. Records

Records have a particular appeal to some children. There are musical and story-telling records for relaxation and enjoyment. Those relating to specific sounds are available. Records relating to identification of farm sounds or the sounds around the home are particularly good for the aphasic child who is building concepts.

F. Tape Recorder

This device is excellent for auditory training as well as for home therapeutics at a more advanced level. Recordings serve as a good record of progress.

G. Mirrors

Working before a large mirror provides excellent training for motor-pattern development. Children enjoy working with their own image in a mirror.

H. Play Villages

Building this type of project will sometimes take several sessions but such projects help establish associations in several areas. For example, farm villages, Christmas villages, or a circus set-up may be fashioned from cardboard, wooden blocks, clay and odd materials as well as from commercial cut-outs. Occasionally it is necessary to limit the figures in order to avoid distractions. A typical village may be found in the commercial toy, Kinder City (Sifo Company, 353 Rosabel Street, St. Paul 1, Minn.).

I. Neighborhood Services in Story and Image Form

Visits to fire stations, airports, train stations, ship docks and the market are good. Stories and play figures may later be related to these visits. Postmen, firemen, milkmen, grocerymen and service station attendants are available in lifelike figures for identification and manipulation.

J. Seasonal Objects and Stories[1]

Seasonal interests are stimulating to most children and offer good possibilities for reinforcement in the every-day environment: holiday symbols (turkey, Christmas tree, jack-o-lantern, Easter eggs, May basket, valentine) ; autumn leaves, snowmen, icicle, flowers, birds.

K. Noise Toys

Noise toys are excellent auditory stimuli in early therapy. They include snappers, rattles, bells, music boxes, push toys with bells, toy telephones, and animal toys with noises.

L. Books

A wide variety of children's stories may be used in therapy. Texts at various levels can be used according to the individual needs. Naming dictionaries are excellent for building associations.

M. Games

Sound discrimination games are of particular value at early levels; matching games offer associative building. Innumerable special interest games, such as sports, should be taken advantage of.

---

1. Smith, Glenn L., and Call, Verne P.: Selected Creative Communication, Box 703, Santa Ana, Calif. Seven sets @ $1.65 per set or $8.95 for complete set which includes Hallowe'en, Thanksgiving, Christmas, Valentines Day, Easter, Spring, Listening (the train sound).

N. Live Animals

The presence of live animals in the home and clinic (if protected) are usually of interest. Zoos and animal habitats may be visited.

O. Blackboard, Bulletin Board, Flannel Board

See: Kephart, Newell, *The Slow Learner in the Classroom* (Charles Merrill Books, Inc. Columbus, O.).

II. PLAY THERAPY MATERIALS
(See Chapter 26, Group Therapy)

A. Expressive Materials

doll house	family figures	large drawing paper
farm figures	sand, water, clay	crayons
animal figures	blocks	finger paints
neighborhood figures	stuffed animals	puppets

B. Aggressive Materials

hammers and nails	family figures	blocks
soldiers and Indians	punch toys	bean bags to throw

C. Regressive Materials

baby dolls	baby carriage
baby bottles (plastic)	diapers and any other articles of
crib or play pen—realistic objects for play	clothing

D. Constructive Materials

large blocks or cardboard cartons	constructive put-together toys
small blocks	wooden puzzles
sand box	sand table

III. MATERIALS FOR BUILDING CONCEPTS

A. Visual and Motor Concepts

blocks for size and form relation	tying and lacing boards
form boards with geometric inserts	snaps, buckles, zippers
graduated stairs	color cards
poles (gradated)	beads to string
counting sticks	sorting board (Chapter 28, Section
peg boards	H)

B. Auditory Concepts

glass jars filled to various depths with water
opaque boxes partially filled with rice, sand, nails, or beans, etc.
xylophone
bells, other musical instruments

C. Tactile (Kinesthetic) Concepts

strips of material of varying textures such as velvet, burlap, sandpaper of several grades

IV. CATALOG FOR THERAPY MATERIALS

1. A. Nienhuis, Edison Straat 64, 25—Gravenhage, Holland (for Montessori materials).
2. Community Playthings, Rifton, N. Y.
3. Community Rehabilitation Industries, 1438 East Anaheim Blvd., Long Beach Calif.
4. Creative Playthings, 5 University Place, New York 3, N. Y.
5. Educational Playthings, 2301 S. Flower Street, Los Angeles 7, Calif. and San Mateo, Calif.
6. Educational Supply and Specialty Company, 2823 Gage Avenue, Huntington Park, Calif.
7. Go-Mo Products, Inc., P. O. Box 143, Waterloo, Iowa.

V. RECORDS

1. Children's Music Center, 2858 West Pico Blvd., Los Angeles 6, Calif.
   Scott and Wood: *Listening Time*—3 albums
   John Tracy Clinic: *Learning to Listen*
   Van Riper, Charles: *Fun with Speech*
   Mikelson, Elaine: *Speech Initiation*
   ——————————: *Babble Record*
   ——————————: *Listen and Learn, Vol. 1*
   ——————————: *Listen and Learn, Vol. 2*

2. Jeri Productions, 3212 Glendale Blvd., Los Angeles 39, Calif.
   Royer, Marie E.; Schelb, Henry; Jensen, Geraldine: *Time to Relax,* Albums 1 and 2
   Thompson, J. J.; Schelb, Henry; Jensen, Geraldine: *Say and Sing,* Albums 1, 2, 3 and 4

3. Jones, Morris Val: *Speech Correction at Home.* Charles C Thomas, Publisher, Springfield, Ill., pp. 27–31.

VI. TEACHING HELPS

1. Arnold, Genevieve: *Sound and Articulation Game.* Expression Company, Magnolia, Mass.

    —————————: *Sound Ladder Game.*

2. Cardozo, Peter: *A Wonderful World for Children.* Bantam Books, 25 West 45th St., New York 36, N. Y.

3. Dolch, E. W.: *Reading Games and Cards.* The Hart Vance Company, St. Louis 3, Mo.

4. Durrell, Donald D., and Sullivan, Helen Blair: *Look and Say.* World Book Company, Yonkers-on-the-Hudson, N. Y., 1950.

5. *Fun with Numbers,* Exclusive Playing Card Company, Chicago, Ill.

6. Gregory, Frederick K., *Alpha Book, People, Objects, Farm,* Timothy Gee's Tiny Textbooks, 1516 N. Gardner, Hollywood 46, Calif.

7. Ingram, Christine T.: *Education of the Slow Learning Child.* Ronald Press, New York, N. Y. 1960.

8. Jacob, Nina and Oftedal, Laura: *My First Dictionary.* Grosset and Dunlap, New York, N. Y.

9. Kephart, Newell: *The Slow Learner in the Classroom.* Charles Merrill Books, Inc., Columbus, O.

10. Miller, Marie B.; McCausland, Margaret; and Okie, Isabel: *Speech Through Pictures.* Expression Company, Magnolia, Mass.

11. Montessori, Maria: *Dr. Montessori's Own Handbook.* Frederick A. Stokes, New York, N. Y. 1914.

12. Nemoy, Elizabeth, and Davis, Serena: *The Correction of Defective Consonant Sounds.* Expression Company, Magnolia, Mass., 1938.

13. Nemoy, Elizabeth: *Speech Correction Through Story-Telling Units.* Expression Company, Magnolia, Mass., 1954.

14. Riess, Anita; Hartung, Maurice; and Mahoney, Catharine: *Numbers We See.* Scott Foresman Company, New York, N. Y.

15. Schoolfield, Lucille D: *Better Speech and Better Reading.* Expression Company, Magnolia, Mass., 1951.

16. Scott, Louise Binder and Thompson, J. J.: *Talking Time.* Webster Publishing Co., Pasadena, Calif., 1951.

17. Smith, Glenn L. and Call, Verne P.: *Selected Creative Communication.* Box 703, Santa Ana, Calif.

18. Stoddard, Clara B.: *Sounds for Little Folks.* Expression Company, Magnolia, Mass.

19. Utley, Jean: *What's Its Name.* University of Illinois Press, Urbana, Ill.

20. Walpole, Ellen W.: *The Golden Dictionary.* Simon and Schuster, New York, N. Y.

21. Warnock-Medlin: Word Making Cards. *Word Making*. P. O. Box 305, Salt Lake City 10, Utah.
22. Watters, Garnette and Courtis, S. A.: *The Picture Dictionary for Children*. Grosset and Dunlap, New York, N. Y.
23. *Winston Clock Face:* John C. Winston Co., Philadelphia 7, Pa.
24. Zedler, Empress Young: *Listening for Speech Sounds*. Harper Brothers, New York, N. Y., 1955.

Chapter 28

TRAINING FOR VISUAL RECOGNITION

I. INTRODUCTION

CHILDREN WITH DEFECTS in visual perception have deficits in many areas which relate to learning and to visual verbal language. They fail to recognize visually one or more characteristics of objects or symbols of language.

II. TRAINING FOR NON-LANGUAGE VISUAL RECOGNITION

REMARKS

A. This defect is not often seen even in very young children.

1. In identifying his own body the child becomes aware of the animate object with which he most closely identifies himself. It is easier for the child to transmit knowledge of his own animate body to other living things.

2. This provides a tactile and kinesthetic experience.

3. The child is now extending recognition from himself to another person in the environment.

4. Animals help show the child that life extends to animate objects other than people. The child comes to see that animate objects such as people and animals have the identity of names.

5. The concept of animate is

EXERCISES

A. Animate Objects

1. Take the child's hand and place it on each major part of his own body. As this is done, say, "This is your head, arm, stomach, legs, etc."

2. Have the child place his hand on his arm and leg as he swings them, feeling them in motion.

3. Place the child's hand on the therapist's head, arms, legs etc. again naming body parts.

4. Show the child other people or animals in the environment. If one is available, allow him to hold or pet the animal. Ask him to point out the puppy's or kitten's eyes, nose or tail. Ask the child his name. Tell him the animal has a name, "Blackie" (as the case may be) .

5. Take the child outdoors.

---

1. Reading readiness books provide many of these: *The New Basic Readers* and *We Read Pictures,* Curriculum Foundation Series, Scott, Foresman and Company, Chicago, Illinois, 1956.

extended to other than people or animals.

6. This provides pictorial representation and permits a wider range of examples of animate objects.

7. The child is beginning to associate animals in other forms.

8. Associations are made with groups of animate objects.

9. Self and family member photographs provide a good starting point of identification in therapy.

B. While many children appear to recognize common objects, further identification is often helpful in establishing recognition and concepts.

1. It is wise to start with one familiar object.

2. Allow the child as much contact as possible with the objects to utilize the tactile sense.

3. Tossing the ball utilizes the kinesthetic association.

4. As the child sees one object as compared with others, he begins to distinguish. He observes differences as he sees the special properties of each in appearance and purpose, e.g., a ball is round and you throw it, the blocks are square and you build with them, a rattle is a different shape and you shake it for the sound.

5. As the child matches the objects with pictures, he is learning to interpret the pictorial representation.

Show him flowers and plants and tell him these are "alive."

6. Show the child pictures of people and animals.[1] Ask him to point out "mama," "daddy," "brother," "baby" and "puppy."

7. Ask the child to place animal cut-outs on a flannel board.

8. Show the child pictures of farm animals, pets, family groups.

9. Ask the mother to provide snapshots of child, family and pets.

B. Inanimate Objects

1. Show the child a familiar object: ball.

2. Place the ball in the child's hand so that he may feel its roundness.

3. Toss the ball to the child. Ask him to toss the ball.

4. Show the child several objects: ball, blocks, rattle. Ask him to pick up the ball. Encourage him to handle and play with the objects. Ask him to show the object as named.

5. Show the child pictures which correspond to the objects: ball, blocks, rattle. Ask the child to match the object with the picture of it.

6. If the child has no speech, the foundation for motor patterns and auditory associations are placed.

7. Identification of common objects can extend to the child's entire familiar environment. Suggestions for doing this at home can be made to the parents.

8. Another concept of representation is introduced with the miniature objects. Children learn to recognize objects in another scale of dimension.

9. If the child is able to assume a more complicated task, introduce therapy to cause him to think in terms of categories in order to build concepts.

This may be presented in a number of ways. If the child has speech, he may be asked, "What do you like to eat?," "What toys do you like?"

Have an open box for each category with one item from each group pasted on it. Say to the child, "In this box put all the things we eat," etc.

6. Name the objects. Ask the child to name them.

7. As the child becomes capable, introduce many common objects in the environment, asking him to touch them, constantly supplying for him the name of each object.

8. As the child's sense of identification grows, introduce miniature objects: doll furniture, animals, cars, trucks, small dolls.

9. Present a sorting game in which the child is asked to place related objects or people together. Give him cards on which pictures of objects or people are shown. The following categories are suggested:

  a. people:

mother	farmer
father	postman
child	fireman

  b. transportation:

car	jeep
truck	boat
plane	

  c. animals:

cow	dog
pig	cat
chickens	

  d. food:

apples	cake
bread	soup
milk	eggs

C.

1. The concept of body scheme becomes the primary identification the child makes. His own body becomes his reference point. Kephart

C. Body Scheme

1. With the very young child or severely deficient child present the concept of the face. Ask him to put his hand on his eyes, nose, and

has an excellent discussion of this in *The Slow Learner in the Class-room*.[2] The concept of a face which is related to a generally round shape appears to be the simplest study to undertake. If the child does not understand oral directions, help him execute the act.

2. A round flannel-board circle is easy to construct. Eyes, nose and mouth may be cut out of felt.

3. The doll's features should be easily identified.

5. If the child cannot draw a circle for a face, do this for him, then ask him to draw in eyes, nose and mouth. (Any attempt would be acceptable.)

7. Commercial materials are available which may aid in this study. The important factor to be considered is the simplicity. Children with visual perceptual problems find coloring books, for example, much too complicated. *What's Its Name*[3] has a good repre-

mouth. Help him do this with verbal associations. Ask him to imitate the therapist's movements of touching eyes, nose and mouth.

2. Present the child with a simple flannel board face on which he may place felt eyes, nose and mouth. Show him how to place the parts and then ask him to do this independently.

3. Ask the child to identify eyes, nose and mouth of a large doll.

4. Use clay to help the child mold a head with eyes, nose and mouth.

5. Ask the child to draw a face on paper or on a blackboard.

6. The study of body parts is then extended to the entire body. The child learns to identify arms, legs, body trunk, hands, feet, etc. Ask the child to imitate the therapist in body movements. Ask him to execute simple commands, "Hold up your hand," "Touch your foot."

7. The following techniques suggest ways of furthering the concept of body.

    a. Use a large flannel-board figure on which felt arms, legs, trunk and head may be placed appropriately.

    b. Use a large doll for identifi-

---

2. Kephart, Newell: *The Slow Learner in the Classroom.* Charles E. Merrill, Columbus, O., 1960.

sentation of body parts. As many tactile and kinesthetic sensations as possible should be used. A good part of the child's knowledge of his own body comes through the movements he feels, tactile sensations, pain, heat and cold.

cation. Ask the child to dress the doll (simple clothes).

c. Ask the child to close his eyes. Touch his hand. Ask "What am I touching?"

d. Use large cardboard cut outs of a child or a stencil to outline. Ask the child to make features and draw in clothes.

e. Use directions to associate movement with body part, "Swing your arms," "Let's kick our feet."

f. Use a simple puzzle in which body parts form the pieces.

g. Ask the child to draw himself, mother, daddy.

8. All games and techniques must be related to the child's ability to perform in the given area. This is generally more important than the child's age level.

8. Play "Simon Says." This very old game is especially effective with a group of children. One child is chosen as Simon. Simon says, "Thumbs up" or "Thumbs down," etc. If the child omits "Simon says," the command is not to be followed.

D. Many children cannot distinguish the primary object or individual parts (in actuality or in a picture) against the confusion of background and detail.

1. This exercise may be made more complex as the child improves. If he has difficulty outlining the foreground figure, guide his index finger around the outline.

2. After some training, several figures may be superimposed on each other. If the child is capable, let him draw one figure on top of the other.

D. Figure-Ground

1. Present the child with a heavily outlined simple object against a figured background as in the testing (see Chapter 24, Sec. VI,B.) Ask him to trace the outline with his finger or with a crayon.

2. Present two simple objects, one superimposed on the other. Ask the child to outline one form in one color, the other form in a contrasting color.

---

3. Utley, Jean: *What's Its Name.* University of Illinois Press, Urbana, Ill., 1950.

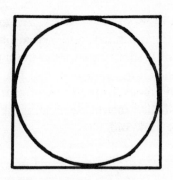

3. Both prominent foreground and more minute background items may be selected.

3. Ask the child to indicate items in a picture. "Where is the house?" "Where is the sky?" "Where are the trees?"

4. Ask the child to arrange items on a flannel board to make a scene.

5. Drawing a picture often represents a more advanced development of the child. As he progresses even more, the introduction of perspective will further strengthen foreground and background.

5. Ask the child to draw a simple scene with house, man and tree.

E.

1. The recognition of colors is frequently discussed in relationship to other phases of visual recognition; however, much specific training is often needed with children in this area. It forms an important part of their early school work.

Some children may need to start with only two colors to match. This can then be continued until all the basic colors are included.

2. Aphasic children often can not concern themselves with more than one problem at a time, so they may not be able to consider shape.

E. Colors

1. Present the child with two sets of the primary colors, red, blue and yellow, on large circles of construction paper. Ask the child to match these.

2. Give the child five large crayons: red, blue, yellow, orange and purple. Color some circles on a piece of paper. Ask the child to

Random marks are then acceptable.

4. The immediate environment provides an excellent source of color. It also provides opportunity for following oral commands. If the child does not understand oral language well, he may often get the idea of matching. Hand the child a yellow circle. Show him how he may find something else in the room which is yellow.

6. Children at a rather early stage of development appear to enjoy arranging colors of surprisingly fine differentiation of light to dark.

7. In presenting games or more complicated techniques, the child must be advanced enough to understand what is wanted.

make similar circles or balls, balloons, or any kind of mark.

3. Have the child match objects of the same color, for example, a red block with a red peg.

4. Have the child identify or match colors around the room or on his person.

"What color is your shirt?"

"Do you see anything in the room which is red?"

5. Ask the child to color simple figures with colors of his choice. Ask him to tell the name of the colors he has used or show by indicating color circles.

6. Ask the child to arrange color circles from light to dark.

7. Present a game such as "Old Maid" in which the object is to collect pairs of cards with the same color. Two or more can play this game.

F. Spatial Relationship

The child's concept of space and his relationship to it is based on his knowledge of himself in relationship to space. He builds this knowledge on the way he perceives things, on body movement and on all other perceptions.[4]

1. The child needs the movement of his body in relationship to points in space.

1. Draw chalk marks on the floor, the first, one foot from the child, and two or three more farther from the child. Ask him to walk first to the nearest one, then to the

---

4. Kephart, Newell: *The Slow Learner in the Classroom.* Charles E. Merrill, Columbus, O., 1960, Chapter 6.

2. From the circle the child learns that a point may be equidistant to the circumference.

3. A child visually develops ideas of distances in space. He learns to judge that certain things are near, others far. Later, the use of perspective in drawings becomes evident to him.

4. A "walking board" or plank teaches equilibrium as well as staying within confines.

5. Tossing horseshoes, bow and arrows, and other games of skill may be used with older children. "Tiddly winks" also teaches space relationship. All sports and physical activities augment the concept of spatial relationship.

6. In the use of form boards and puzzles, the child is seeing the relationship of shape as well as sensing the placement of the object.

At first a very simple form board may be necessary, with much help given to the child in placing the forms. Cardboard boxes may be used.

7. Younger children enjoy this play which involves much bodily activity.

8. Asking the child to perform tasks which set a definite limit helps

next one, always returning to the starting point. Say to him, "This mark is near, this one is farther away," etc.

2. Draw a circle on the floor. Put a large dot in the middle. Walk around the circle, then at several points walk to the center dot and back to the rim of the circle.

3. Place a toy barn before the child. Place the toy animals in various ways around the barn. Ask "Which animal is nearest the barn?," "Which animal is far away?" Ask the child to put the different animals in the barn.

4. Place a plank on the floor. Ask the child to walk down the plank, not stepping off.

5. Engage the child in ring toss. Place the stake near the child at first, then gradually move it further away.

6. Use form boards and puzzles as further training. Make up various exercises in matching shapes and forms. Have the child feel the cut-out of the form board before placing the piece. Later he may match paper forms as a more difficult task. This helps him gauge the necessary space it takes to place the piece in limited spaces.

7. Use barrels, hoops and obstacle courses for the child to climb through and over.

8. Ask the child to do such tasks as the following:

him establish boundaries in space. Coloring to the edge of a stencil is a simpler task than observing a line. The concept of space is developed as the result of many other concepts.

    a. Outline stencils
    b. Color within stencils
    c. Color within lines

9. Strauss observes that number concept is based on spatial relationship.[5]

9. Use various aspects of number concepts (see Arithmetic, Chapter 33, Section III.)

G. Visuo-Motor Defects

Children with visuo-motor (eye-motor) defects have difficulty in completing a motor act primarily because of a defect in perception.[6] In order to determine this defect any motor problem must be excluded.

1. With the child having a severe visual perceptual defect, first attempts at visual perceptual tasks are made with large objects which he may follow with his eyes. As he improves, the objects may be reduced in size or the task made more complicated.

1. Ask the child to look at a large colored ball or a brightly colored puppet.
    Move the puppet back and forth before the child's line of vision; then move the ball to various distances from the child. Constantly remind him to watch the object.

2. In moving an object from left to right before the child he is learning to use lateral eye movements.

2. Ask the child to watch a bright object on a string which is allowed to swing from left to right.

3. As the child observes objects in the distance, tell him that they appear small and far away. Later show him pictures which emphasize perspective.

3. Ask the child to look at objects in the environment. Indicate some objects near at hand and others far away. Take him outside and show him a street or road. Ask him to look at something far up the road.

4. The child needs to learn direction and to move his body from his visual cues.

4. Draw paths on the floor or on a sidewalk with colored chalk. Ask the child to walk following the

---

5. Strauss and Lehtinen: *Psychopathology and Education of the Brain Injured Child.* Grune and Stratton, New York, N. Y., 1947.

6. A complete discussion of many aspects of this problem is found in *A Visual Motor Gestalt Test and its Clinical Use*, Bender, Lauretta. The American Orthopsychiatric Association, New York, N. Y., 1938.

5. As the child performs some of the grosser tasks, he may then be asked to coordinate hand movements with visual cues.

6. It is important to emphasize that a motor involvement such as a right hemiparesis will cause failure in eye-motor tasks, but that the failure will be due to the motor involvement.

8. The child will often find these steps logical ones:
   (a) Trace the form board inserts with the finger.
   (b) Trace a stencil form.
   (c) Trace with crayon a heavily outlined figure under tracing paper.
   (d) Copy the figure from another drawing.

To these steps may be added recall by removing the figure and asking the child to draw it from memory.

9. Stopping within lines or boundaries presents a problem to children with visual perceptual defects. Many other activities may be introduced such as asking a child to move a toy car to a given spot. Double lines such as the following may be used.

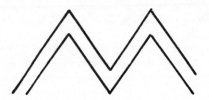

path. Draw a hopscotch pattern and show the child how to play.

5. Draw a road on a table or large sheet of paper (or help the child draw a road). Give him a small car to move up and down the roads.

6. Place a simple pattern on a peg board with the pegs. Ask the child to make such a pattern on his pegboard.

7. Give the child simple form boards and puzzles to complete.

8. Ask the child to trace simple geometric forms such as a circle, half circle, square and triangle; then ask him to copy these forms. Ask the child to copy many forms.

9. Give the child activities which emphasize limits. For example, draw heavy lines on the right side of the chalk board. Ask the child to start at the left, then draw a line just to the heavy line on the right. Draw heavy lines around small circles. (The child may want to call these balloons.) Ask him to color the circles just to the heavy line.

Ask the child to draw a line within these lines without touching the sides.

10. It is necessary for the child to develop a bilateral sense of his own body before he can establish positions in space in relationship to it.

11. Since right handedness is often considered more convenient, sometimes attempts to direct a child toward use of the right hand are made. If a therapist is able to recognize dominance, he may then discourage use of the minor hand, but it seems more successful to allow the child to show a preference of hand dominance. It may be important to establish a writing hand before learning to reproduce symbols. Some children do better at strength tasks with one hand but prefer to write with the other.

H. The recognition of form, form constancy and shape is related to all aspects of visual perception and may be developed by the therapist in conjunction with many practices in this entire section.

1. The tactile and kinesthetic modalities may be used constantly to aid in the perception of thickness and depth. Incidental training may be used constantly. "Draw your finger around the edge of the table. It is square." "Do you see something round in this room?"

Most children enjoy the geometric names of forms, square,

10. Play games with the child which emphasize both sides of the body. "Hold up your right hand, hold up your left hand, swing both hands together." "Hop on one foot, hop on the other foot, jump with both feet together."

11. Ask the child to trace the outline of a human figure. Ask him to point to one hand, the other hand, to one ear, and to the other ear so that both sides of the body are emphasized.

H. Form and Form Constancy

1. Ask the child to handle objects with different shapes such as a ball or a large block. Tell him "This is square. This is round."

circle, triangle, and rectangle. They also appear to learn these names readily.

2. A child should be able to recognize shapes and forms in all aspects of his environment. Series of figures and shapes may be found in many reading readiness books.

4. A sorting board may be used for this purpose. This is a board with pockets stitched across it where cards or pictures may be placed. The circles, squares and triangles may vary in size while the form remains consistent.

5. Stencils of increasing complexity may be added to this practice.

6. As the child's ability to see and categorize forms improves, ask him to distinguish forms in more complex pictures.

7. Many reading readiness books provide forms such as this in preparation for recognition of forms of letters and words.

2. Show the child a series in which two shapes or figures are alike. Ask him to circle those which are similar.

3. Carry out the same exercise except ask the child to circle the forms which are different.

4. Give the child many circles, squares and triangles cut out of cardboard or construction paper. Ask him to sort these according to their shape.

5. Ask the child to trace around the square, circle and triangle of the form board; then ask him to draw a circle (ball or balloon) and a square.

6. Show the child a picture scene. Ask him to point out something square (a house), something round (a ball), something tall (a tree), something small (a doll).

7. Ask the child to make forms which look like these:

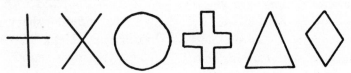

I. Pictures present another aspect of visual perception which relates to other visual perceptual defects rather than being a specific deficit itself.

I. Picture Items

1. The first pictures used with the child should be individual items which can be easily matched with the individual item.

2. Many reading readiness books present action pictures in series which provide a wide source of picture training material.[7]

3. As children develop in visual perceptual areas they become more capable of handling complicated pictures. The reading readiness books present many familiar childhood scenes. It seems wise to avoid the impressionistic drawings observed in some of the children's books until the child is well developed in visual perception. As he proceeds into reading areas he will frequently use the device of matching words and pictures.

4. It is important that the child recognize what is appropriate in a picture and what is not.

1. Present the child with several clearly drawn pictures of familiar objects. Have the actual objects and pictures.

2. Ask the child to look at a series of action pictures. Then have him tell the story or indicate what is happening in the pictures.

3. Show the child a picture of a familiar scene. Ask him to tell or indicate what is taking place. Ask him to point out individual items.

4. Show the child pictures in which one or more inappropriate items are included. For example in food items, a hammer or toy might be the inappropriate item. Ask the child to cross out or point out the items which do not belong.

III. VISUAL VERBAL RECOGNITION

Dr. J. M. Nielsen believes there is some indication that small children learn to recognize letters as objects. When they become symbols for language they are then stored in the angular gyrus.[8]

7. Bond, Guy; Cuddy, Marie: *Stories in Pictures.* California State Series, State Department of Education, Sacramento, Calif., 1954.
Durrell, Donald; Sullivan, Helen: *Look and Say.* World Book Co., New York, N. Y., 1950.
Gray, William; Monroe, Marion; Artley, A. S.: *Before We Read.* Scott Foresman Co., New York, N. Y., 1956.

8. Nielsen, J. M.: *A Textbook of Clinical Neurology.* Paul B. Hoeber, New York 16, N. Y., Chapter X, 1951.

REMARKS	EXERCISES
A.	**A. Letters**
1. Letters may be presented in these forms:	1. Show the child a letter whose shape is easily identified, for example O.
(a) raised block letters	
(b) sandpaper letters	
(c) felt flannel-board letters	
(d) letter cut-outs	
(e) blackboard	
	a. Help him identify the shape of O by showing him a large ring, the rim of a saucer, the circle the mouth forms when O is sounded.
b. Children should have these stimulations:	b. Present the letter on a raised block; have him feel it.
(a) Tactile (raised block) (sandpaper)	
(b) Kinesthetic (large arm movements or blackboard writing)	
	c. Have the child trace a sandpaper letter O.
	d. Have him trace the O on paper, then make an O on paper.
	e. Have him make an O on the blackboard.
	f. Have him select the O from several blocks or anagrams.
2. Reasons may exist for giving priority to certain letters such as the letters of the first name. In the interest of self identification, it is often wise to start with these letters regardless of basic shape or sequence in the alphabet.	2. Choose another letter whose shape is easily identified, as the 1. Give the child many associations with this letter in the same manner as the O.
	Place a row of 1's and O's on the paper. Ask the child to identify the O's and then the 1's.
3. Amusing associations are often forceful. The therapist can make these up: such as the P is the	3. Give the child constant vivid associations so that he will have much reenforcement.

big man with the nose going this way →; the B has two fat stomachs.

4. Such a presentation is entirely arbitrary and not necessarily to be followed. However, children who have worked with the basic forms of ◯ ☐ △ can

often relate these letters to basic shapes.

5. Much has been written[9] and discussed concerning the order of presentation of letters. The therapist may find associations which will indicate an individual organization for the child. There has also been much discussion as to the advantage of cursive writing. The advantage of using manuscript letters lies in the fact that it may be in keeping with public school usage.

4. Present letters in a related sequence. Letters may be presented in relation to a basic form:

Circle: C G O Q
Straight line: E F H I L T
Straight line, slant line: A K M N V W X Y Z
Straight line, curve line: B D J P R U
Curved line: S

5. Lower case letters may be presented in similar sequence.

6. Commercial games may be used which teach letter recognition.[10]

B. The recognition of numbers is difficult for many aphasic children.

1. In approaching numbers it is wise to start with very simple concepts involving numbers one to five.

2. A great deal of time may be spent on the concept of 1 and 2 before advancing. Body parts may be helpful here—two ears, one nose, etc.

B. Numbers

1. Present the numbers individually with the concept they represent.

1—1 stick
2—2 sticks

2. In early practices ask the child to make simple observations.
(a) "Show me one stick."
(b) "Give me two blocks."

---

9. Strauss, Alfred A. and Lehtinen, Laura E.: *Psychopathology and Education of the Brain Injured Child.* Grune and Stratton, New York, N. Y., Chapter XII, 1947.

10. ABC Game: *First steps in Reading*, No. 2162, Kenworthy Educational Service, Inc., Buffalo, N. Y.

3. By constantly showing the child the numbers associated with the concept, he may learn to recognize the numerals long before he can make them.

3. Continually show the child the number associated with the concept, i.e., as two sticks are discussed show him the numeral 2.

4. The counting of beads (ten on a wire) is a convenient device.

4. Ask him to place the correct number of blocks or sticks in a little box with the corresponding number on it.

5. Fingers have the advantage of convenience and also association with body parts. A highly distractable child may be able to use his fingers before he can attempt counting by any other means.

5. Use fingers for counting as the most natural counting device.

6. Children with a visual-motor defect (eye-hand coordination) especially need much practice prior to the actual writing of the numbers.

6. Use these training methods before asking the child to attempt to write the numbers.

(a) Trace sandpaper number cut-outs.

(b) Connect dotted lines forming the numbers (see Chapter 17).

(c) Use stencils of the numbers.

7. Numbers may be given association comparable to those used in letters. These may be individualized for each child. For example, 8 may be a "crooked road," or 9 a "big nose."

7. Ask the child to make the numbers after he has had sufficient practice in tracing them.

C. Words

Some mention of recognition of words is made in this section simply because some words, as letters, appear to be recognized individually before they are integrated into the reading process.

1. Many of the work books accompanying reading series used in the public schools provide a practice similar to this.[11] It cannot be overemphasized that practices in areas of visual recognition (non-

1. Present the child with words on a pre-primer level. Choose words which relate to his interest or to letters he already recognizes. Have him fit these into general shapes of the words:

mother

home

boy

apple

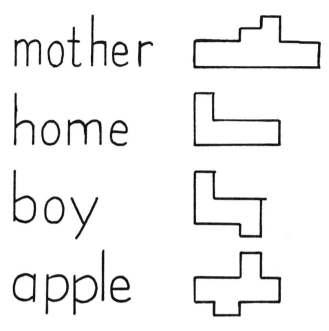

verbal) are essential before attempting any associations on the verbal level.

2. Many authors[12] of reading-method texts stress a phonetic approach to reading. This will be mentioned again in the chapter on reading. Ideas presented by such authors may be used. However, it must be remembered that it is necessary to adapt these to the brain-injured child. For example, a child with an auditory perceptual defect may have great difficulty assimilating a phonetic approach.

3. This practice may be extended in many ways. Words may be scattered over a board or printed on cardboard.

These may be presented on written cards and the shapes (on the same size card) presented for matching.

2. If the child recognizes letters, present him with a family such as *an*. Have him place consonants such as *c d f m p* before the *an*. Tell him the words he has made.

3. Ask the child to match words. Give him two sets of like words for the matching exercise.

| cat | home |
| dog | car |

11. Russell, David H., *et al.: Fun with Tom and Betty*. Ginn and Company. New York, N. Y.. 1961, p. 52.

12. Hay, Julie and Wingo, Charles E.: *Reading with Phonics*. J. B. Lippincott Co., New York, N. Y., 1954, is an excellent text.

Ask the child to select the words which are alike.

4. In any technique such as this, the stimulus items should be restrained to a very few.

5. Simple line drawings or uncluttered pictures cut from magazines may be used.

4. Ask the child to tell whether words are the same or not.

the	them
mother	mother
car	cat
home	home

5. Picture and word matching may be used as a game. Pictures of such words as *dog, baby, home, ball,* and *car* may be used for matching with printed cards.

6. The child can be helped to see and recognize the letters in many forms and positions on the paper.

6. Ask the child to match letters of upper and lower case.

A	R	T	D
a	r	t	d

7. Ask the child to make words of his own with anagrams or flannelboard letters, copying from words on printed cards.

Chapter 29

TRAINING FOR AUDITORY RECOGNITION
(Non-verbal and Verbal)

I. INTRODUCTION

LACK OF AUDITORY recognition of non-language sounds is rarely seen in aphasic children, although occasionally they may have difficulty in interpreting the sound. Auditory *verbal* agnosia is much more commonly observed. The presence of a peripheral hearing defect may complicate[1] the diagnosis and treatment of both auditory agnosia and auditory verbal agnosia.[2]

II. NON-VERBAL SOUNDS

A. Animal Sounds

Materials: Actual pets in the environment or a tape recording of animal sounds, dog's bark, bird's chirp, cow's mooing, cat's meow. (Clinician may imitate these sounds.) Pictures of the animals.

1. Ask the child to listen to the sounds of one of the animals. Show him the matching pictures. Do this several times. Say "dog," for example, with the sound of his bark, at the same time showing the picture. Introduce other pictures in the same manner. Ask the child to listen to the sound and choose the appropriate picture to match the sound.

B. Music Sounds

Introduce a bell or a horn. Proceed in the same manner as in A, allowing the child to match the sound with the actual item or a picture of it.

C. The Voice

(An interpretation of what is said is not important in this exercise; the child is only to recognize that it is a voice.)

Someone is to hum a tune, or call "hello," or speak a phrase. Make a game by asking the child to point to the producer of the sound: the therapist, the child or someone else. When possible, use children's voices and masculine and feminine adult voices with accompanying pictures to aid in distinguishing the various voice qualities.

---

1. A study is currently underway at the Kennedy Foundation, Santa Monica, California, of diagnostic differences among peripherally deaf children, aphasic children with receptive defects, and aphasic children with a partial peripheral hearing loss.
2. Myklebust, Helmer: *Auditory Disorders in Children.* Grune & Stratton, New York, N. Y., 1954, pp. 139–140.

D. Environmental Sounds

The sounds include the telephone, door bell and knocking at the door, car sounds, kitchen sounds, a slamming door, foot steps, etc. Have the child knock at the door; the therapist answers the door. Change positions. Carry out the same procedure with the telephone, the horn of the car, etc.

E. Sound Qualities

1. Use a xylophone or piano to help the child distinguish between high and low sounds. As he hears the high sound, have him indicate this by word or gesture. Ask the child to play high and then low notes.

2. With a piano, toy drum or other instrument make loud and then soft tones to distinguish between loud and soft. Ask the child to clap his hands loudly, then softly.

3. Fill opaque jars or boxes with various materials (rice, nails, sand, etc.). Ask the child to shake each box. Have the material in the box ready to show him so that he will know what has caused the sound. Children usually enjoy experimenting with the boxes and the sounds they make. If a dual set is provided, the children may match the containers.[3]

III. AUDITORY VERBAL RECOGNITION

A. Single Words

Materials: Blocks, doll, rattle, bell.

Since many children who have not been able to recognize words often do not have speech, they may be trained to offer physical responses to auditory stimuli until speech is developed.

1. Using the doll, make the verbal identification "doll" and show the child how to respond by lifting the doll. Repeat this action several times. If the child can imitate by pronouncing the word doll, encourage him to do so.

Use the same technique in identifying the rattle.

Call for first one item and then the other. Add a block and the bell, then other items using the same technique. When the child can choose the items as he hears them named, broaden his auditory verbal recognition with additional words and corresponding items.

2.	2. Using object and picture
a. The therapy environment, play activities, games and incidental activities of any kind, provide opportunities for the	a. Offer the child the ball to explore and play with. Say "ball," repeat "ball" several times as he plays with the object.

---

3. Montessori, Maria: *Dr. Montessori's Own Handbook.* Frederick A. Stokes Co., New York, N. Y., 1914, following page 58.

development of auditory rec-
,ognition.

The experience of placing
the child in contact with his environment and allowing him
tactile and kinesthetic exploration along with repetitive naming is the simplest way of reenforcing auditory stimulation.

b. One technique includes
using objects which begin with
the same initial sound for sound
discrimination. This also provides reenforcement for the
child with motor speech defects.

Introducing pictures and
associating them may further
extend the concept of an object.

c. When it is felt that the objects can be identified by auditory recognition, games of
choice and matching can be
played.

b. Show the child a picture
of a ball.

Say "ball," show him the ball
again and say "ball."

Do the same with the "bell"
and picture of a bell.

c. Choice game. Show the
child how to choose the item
when hearing the single word
"ball" or "bell."

Show the child how to choose
the picture by saying "ball" and
pointing to the picture of a ball.

3. Adding the word for visual
stimulus.

a. Show the child that the
word "ball," the actual object,
and the picture of the ball are the
same.

b. Allow him to choose each
object on single-word request.

c. Introduce a "block," for
example, using the same techniques as above. Other words: bed,
toy barn, baby doll, bank.

c. The number of objects
may be increased with successful recognition of the various
objects.

4. When a few objects are
recognized, offer action words.

4. Teaching auditory recognition of action words.

a. Use simple pictures showing a child running and a child
walking.

b. Ask the child what is going on in the picture.
"The boy is running."
or
"The girl is walking."

B.

1. Throughout the therapy period the therapist asks the child to comply with a simple direction.

2. Children who are confused in body scheme may need much demonstration in learning both auditory recognition and identification of body parts.

3. As the auditory-verbal agnosia clears, the child is able to carry out commands of a more complex nature.

Many appropriate pictures can be found in illustrated fiction magazines and in children's periodicals.

B. Simple Commands
1. A game of simple directions:
    a. See the ball.
    b. Get the ball.
    c. Bounce the ball.
    d. Throw the ball.
2. Using body scheme:
    a. Hold up your hand.
    b. Close your eyes.
    c. Where is your toe?
    d. Open your mouth.
    e. Shake hands.
3. Single commands:
Show a picture such as a person closing the door. Ask the child to carry out a similar command.
"Close the door."

4. Complex commands.
As the child improves, give more complex commands such as.
"Bring me two books from the table in the corner of the room."

C. Double Commands
1. Ask the child to fulfill more complicated commands:
"Take the bear from the table. Put it in the little chair."

1. As the child proceeds in therapy and academic work, most activities will include forms of auditory verbal training.

Chapter 30

NAMING

Eʙₐ... ARLY IN LANGUAGE development, children attempt naming common objects and people. If the child has no word language, he will often assign a consistent gesture or sound to the familiar object.

I. TECHNIQUES

REMARKS

1. Opportunities for naming objects and figures in the therapy situation are many. If the child cannot orally name the objects, say *each* name so that he may make the auditory association. His attention should be directed towards the therapist as he names the objects. At this point the moto-kinesthetic method may be used so that the motor patterns of the word may be sensed. Even the association of an initial sound is helpful.

2. As the child progresses, more complicated units can be chosen for naming, such as items from a doll house. At times during the therapy, the therapist may present the name of the object.

"This is a chair." Ask for identification.

"Show me the chair." Ask for the name.

"What is this?" (pointing to the chair).

3. Much naming can be accomplished in an incidental way, thus saving the child from constant pres-

EXERCISES

A. Objects

1. Present a few common objects for naming: doll, ball, shoe, apple, bottle. Ask the child to name the articles as they are handed to him.

2. Present a unit from a doll house: "What room shall we put these things in?" As the child places toy furniture, ask for the names, "What is that?"

3. Take a walk with the child around the house, yard or neighborhood. Name as many items as possi-

275

sure of many questions. If the child does not comply with the request, say the name, but do not insist that he should do so.

4. Many inexpensive miniatures are available. They must be easily recognized.

5. Utley, Jean: *What's Its Name* (University of Illinois Press; Urbana, Ill.) 1950. Also see references at close of this chapter.

1. Ask the parents to tell you what is commonly used in their family such as "Mama," "Daddy," and nicknames. The child's own name is his first achievement and identity.

2. Photographs provide a good substitute for actual people in the therapy situation.

ble. The child should also take the therapist on a "naming walk."

4. Use a collection of miniature articles for naming. Play a game with these in which the child sees how many he can name for his points.

5. Use pictures for naming.

6. Ask the child to match items or pictures.[1]

B. People

1. Ask the child to name himself, then family members.

2. Use family photographs for naming.

3. Use family figures[2] obtained in toy models for naming.

4. Use pictures of familiar people: fireman, policeman, milkman, postman, etc. for naming.

C. Environment

(See 3 under Objects above.)

1. Dolch, E. W.: *Match*. The Garrard Press, Champaign, Illinois, 1953.
2. *Creative Playthings*. P. O. Box 1100, Princeton, New Jersey.

D. Picture Items

(See *5* and *6* under Objects; *4* under People.)

E. Geometric Forms

1. Present common forms for naming: square, circle, triangle.

1. These may be presented from the form board, in wooden forms, cardboard forms, or on the blackboard. Children may use such terms as "round," or "ball" for identification. However, most children *enjoy* the words square, circle, triangle, rectangle.

2. Present other forms: diamond, star, ellipse, rectangle. Ask the children to match forms, insert them in the form boards, and color these forms on paper, using name associations as the material is presented.

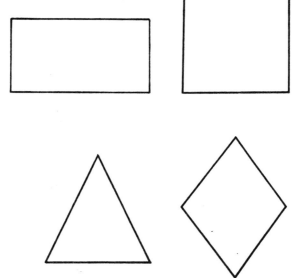

F. After colors are recognized, children begin to learn the names.

1. These may be presented as color discs from cardboard or con-

F. Colors

1. Present a few colors at a time: red, blue and yellow. As the child

struction paper. Because of the difficulty of initial consonant sounds in color names, the orders of presentation will have to be developed individually with each child.

    2. Many children enjoy naming less common colors: pink, grey, aqua. Crayons are produced in so many shadings today that it is necessary to recognize many variations of color.

    1. In addition to recognizing the concept of numbers, names must be associated.

    2. Fingers often are the most useful and available tool for naming. This also adds to the body concept.

learns the names others may be added.

    2. Use crayons to make colors on the paper. Ask the child to name each color.

G. Numbers

    1. Use two or three numbers at a time for naming, presenting one to five, then gradually adding six to ten.

    2. Use finger games, poems, and songs to aid the process of naming. For example:

    "One-two—buckle my shoe."

II. MATERIALS FOR NAMING

A. Cards

    1. *Match,* a picture-word matching game by Edward W. Dolch, The Garrard Press, Champaign, Ill.

    2. *Picture Words* (teaches 95 most common nouns) Pre-school and 1st grade. One of a series of Dolch Play-Way Learning Games. Gelles-Widmer Co., St. Louis 17, Mo.

    3. *Warnock-Medlin Word Making.* W. M. Productions, P. O. Box 305, Salt Lake City 10, Utah.

B. Books

    1. Durrell, D. D. and Sullivan, H. B.: *Look and Say.* World Book Company, Yonkers-on-the Hudson, N. Y. 1950.

    2 Oftedal, Laura and Jacob, Nina: *My First Dictionary,* The Beginners Picture Word Book. Grosset and Dunlap, New York, N. Y.

    3. McCausland, Margaret; Miller, Marie B., and Okie, Isabel: *Speech Through Pictures.* Expression Co., Magnolia, Mass.

    4. Utley, Jean: *What's Its Name.* University of Illinois Press, Urbana, Ill., 1950.

Chapter 31

Pilgrim Psych. Center
Speech & Hearing Clinic
Bldg. 23-6
West Brentwood, N.Y. 11717

FORMULATION

FORMULATION IN SPEECH and writing constitutes the highest development of language. After reception and assimilation of language, comes the expression of language in spoken and written formulation.

Aphasic children often have a tendency to respond in one word answers. When the therapist is sure that a child has the ability, he should encourage oral sentence formulation by various methods. Correct articulation is not necessarily a prerequisite to oral formulation.

I. SPONTANEOUS SPEECH

Spontaneous speech develops around daily school, therapy, and home situations. Frequently these are best expanded at the time of occurrence rather than in studied situations.

REMARKS

1. Particularly helpful in oral formulation is general conversation. Sentences may be simple or complex according to the child's ability.

2-3-4. The participation of the child in art activities such as finger painting or clay is often stimulating. See Chapter 26, III. Listening to music may also stimulate conversation.

EXERCISES

A. Oral Formulation

1. Conversation with an interested party or with the therapist is stimulating.

2. Use puppets to stimulate speech in make-believe situations.

3. Act out familiar stories such as Little Red Riding Hood.

4. Use stimulating pictures. If the child simply names the picture, ask questions to provoke more conversation.

II. QUESTIONS

A. The formulation of questions is often most difficult. Before the child learns how to ask questions, much practice may have taken place in which he has answered questions or followed commands. In early stages of question formulation the form-

A. Pictures

Present pictures or objects which can serve as a stimulation for questions. The child may ask such questions as:

1. Who is the boy (in the picture)?

ing of the question by the child may be very incomplete.

2. What is his dog's name?

3. How old is he?

B. Guessing Game

Play a guessing game in which each participant may ask three questions concerning a hidden object. The child who guesses the object wins.

III. ACTION WORDS

A. Many of the reading readiness books contain action words.[1] Other excellent sources are picture dictionaries and speech books.[2]

A. Pantomime

Ask the child to tell what the therapist is doing. The therapist may act out:

1. brushing his teeth
2. combing his hair
3. patting the dog
4. setting the table
5. playing the piano

B. Using Puppets

1. Using a family puppet group, allow the child to play through a circumstance in which he has participated. Encourage him to tell something about each manipulation of the puppet.

1. The use of puppets to re-enact activities aids in relaxing the child.

2. Pass several stick puppets from child to child in the group. As one formulates the action, he may use the puppet for demonstrating it.

1. Stauffer, Russell G. and Burrows, Alvina T.: *Ready to Go.* John C. Winston Co., 383 Madison Ave., New York 17, N. Y., 1960.

2. Utley. Joan: *What's Its Name.* University of Illinois Press, Urbana, Ill., 1950.

IV. PICTURES

A. Play-scene Pictures

1. Action-sequence Pictures. A most excellent source for these pictures to be used as a basis for stimulating description of the sequence of action is to be found in the reading readiness books[3] and workbooks accompanying pre-primers and primers.

2. Ask the parent to supply photographs of family activities. Make a scrapbook of them to use as a basis for story telling or action sequence.

3. Ask the child to describe the actions depicted in a series of pictures such as these:

4. Show the child a composite picture. Ask him to describe what he sees. If he does not formulate in sentences, reflect his ideas in simple sentences. *For example:* The girl is cooking.

She is making cookies.

5. Encourage the child to build a town with blocks. The Kinder City Blocks may be used for this purpose.[4] Have him place the buildings in the appropriate places and encourage him to talk about each with such simple sentences as the following:

3. Bond, Guy L. and Cuddy, Marie C.: *Stories in Pictures.* California State Series, State Department of Education, Sacramento, Calif., 1954.

4. Kinder City, Sifo Company, 353 Rosabel Street, St. Paul 1, Minn. A 37" x 40" layout of business buildings, a factory, houses etc. centered around the child's everyday environment. It features such familiar characters as the policeman, mailman, grocer etc. Blocks and layout can be stored in the draw-string bag.

"The house goes here."
"The post office goes here."

When the buildings are placed, identify a house and family. Create a story about the coming and going of a family:

"The mother goes shopping."
"The father goes to work.'

Continue to reflect the child's ideas in sentences until he is able to do so himself.

6. Use specific events such as a family vacation.

V. STORY

A. Story Telling

1. Simple story telling is an effective method for encouraging oral formulation.

2. Groups are adaptable to oral formulation activities and are worthwhile in stimulating a structured social situation or interaction.

3. Oral reading is an aid to building patterns for oral formulation.

1. The therapist initiates a story, then the child and the therapist take turns retelling it.

2. Seat several children in a circle. The therapist starts a story then directs the children to carry through with their ideas.

3. Use reading by asking the child to read orally at a comfortable level. Discuss the content of the story following the reading.

4. Examine the contents of a bag of three or four toys and associate each with a story. Summarize the story in a few brief points. Ask the child to tell the story or draw a picture of the story.

5. Past happenings, play activities, vacations or specific events of interest to the child always lend themselves to story telling.

5. Ask the parents to write a brief resume of a specific activity for use in story telling. *For example:* special holidays, a trip, birthday party.

6. Play a "what's next" game. Start by helping the child become familiar with the events of the activity by mentioning people and places. If family figures are avail-

7. Visual clues provide re-en-
actment of the story.

able one may re-create the story
with figures.

7. Pictures of similar happenings are helpful. The child may
draw pictures to describe an activity. When the sequence is complete,
a brief summary of several sentences
may be offered the child. Ask him
to repeat the sequence.

B. Recommended Stories:

The Cat in the Hat—Dr. Suess, Random House, New York, N. Y.
The Beginner Books Series (Random House) ; limited vocabulary
Seeds and More Seeds—Milicent E. Selson, Harper Bros., New York, N. Y.
Danny and the Dinosaur—Syd Hoff, Harper Bros., New York, N. Y.
The Munro Leaf Series (J. B. Lippencott, Philadelphia, Pa.)
  Manners Can Be Fun
  Geography Can Be Fun
  Lucky You
  John Henry Davis
Whistle for the Train—McDonald and Weisgard, Doubleday, New York,
  N. Y.

VI. USE OF PREPOSITIONS[5]

The child who has difficulty in using prepositions may have problems in
understanding them. This may relate to spatial concepts training as well.

A. Simple games may be played to
encourage the idea of up, down,
under, on, into etc.

A. Placement of Objects

1. Using a block and a box, show
the child how to place the blocks *in*
the box, *on* the table, *under* the box,
under the table. Reverse the procedure having the child act as
teacher.

2. Using a group of animals
(wild and farm) have the child
place them "*in* the zoo" and "*on* the
farm."

B. Following Oral Commands

Ask the child to sit *on* the chair,

---

5. Noon, Elizabeth: *The Instructor Basic Phonics Series, Set Three*, Advanced Consonants and
  Prepositions. F. A. Owens Publishing Company, Dansville, N. Y.

to get *under* the table, to run *out* the door, to sit *between* two other children, to sit *beside* the therapist, to come *into* the house.

Chapter 32

ARTICULATION

I. INTRODUCTION

Many aphasic children have a marked motor speech disorder which is sometimes characterized by severe articulation defects. The moto-kinesthetic[1] approach is particularly effective in working with a motor speech problem. Methods for dealing with articulatory defects are well covered in several texts.[2] Some of these techniques may be amended and simplified for the aphasic child.

II. BASIC TECHNIQUES

REMARKS

A.

1. Children usually will attempt vocalization after a concept has been established. In the beginning any response should be accepted.

Motor speech patterns can be presented effectively before a mirror. Some children enjoy this technique while others prefer to work with the therapist directly.

2. Moto-kinesthetic[2] reenforcement in motor speech problems is of prime importance. This technique has been shown to be most effective in establishing motor speech patterns.

A tape recording is useful in de-

EXERCISES

A. Severe Motor Speech Defect

1. Encourage the child to make any possible oral response to a given stimulus. Occasionally the therapist may be able to provide a feeling of success for the child by imitating the syllables initiated by the child. Slight modifications of the child's own syllables often lead to new sounds. A child, for example, may be able to say Ma-ma. The therapist may suggest my-my, me-me, oh-oh, and then mo-mo.

2. Present sounds of m, p, b, using effective suggestions to elicit them:

    m—hum a song
    p—puff out a match
    b—(baa) this is what the sheep
        says

---

1. See Chapter 11, Section IX for moto-kinesthetic method.
2. Nemoy, Elizabeth and David, Serena F.: *The Correction of Defective Consonant Sounds*, Expression Company Magnolia, Mass., 1954.
   Schoolfield, Lucille D.: *Better Speech & Better Reading*. Expression Company, Magnolia, Mass., 1951.
   Zedler, Empress: *Listening for Speech Sounds*. Harper & Brothers, New York, N. Y., 1955.

veloping sound discrimination. A child is often rewarded at hearing the play back of his more successful attempts.

Puppets can often be used to show formation of some sounds: o, m.

3. The therapist may use pictures, flannel board cut-outs or toy figures to illustrate sounds. Farm animals are excellent. The therapist proceeds to present sounds in the order of their development or as the child shows an inclination to say them.

Present toys which represent the same initial sounds:

mamma	baby
moo (cow)	ball
man	book

The child is to try these words with the therapist. If he does not complete the entire word but produces the initial sound, it should be regarded as success.

3. Play a sound game.[3] Therapist asks, "What makes these sounds?"

s	ch – ch	t – t – t
z	r	sh

4. As the child improves he may continue to show residuals of faulty rhythm and of defective sound production. Imitation continues to be a good technique and gives the child

4. Say a sound or phrase and ask the child to repeat it.

2. Young, Edna Hill and Hawk, Sara S.: *Moto-Kinesthetic Speech Training.* Stanford University Press, Palo Alto, Calif., 1955.

3. Scott, Louise B. and Thompson, J. J.: *Talking Time.* Webster Publishing Co., Pasadena, Calif., 1951.

a feeling of accomplishment. A phonetic approach is helpful in establishing sound associations. Moto-kinesthetic techniques should be continued.

B. Mirror practice is of particular importance in working with residual motor defects.

B. Use of Story Material

Choose stories in which the child may participate for practice of difficult sounds. For example: "Whistle for the Train" by Leonard Weisgard. This story contains the repetitive phrase, "clickety clack, clickety clack."

C. Reading words in groups and with appropriate expression should be encouraged. Nursery rhymes are often helpful.

C. Working for Rhythm and Inflection

Lists of sentences such as those found in *Better Speech and Better Reading* by Lucille Schoolfield should be read with varying inflections. Imitation of the therapist's inflections may contribute to more appropriate rhythm and speech patterns.

D. Recordings of the child and/or the therapist further develop discrimination, and help reenforce motor patterns.

D. Use of a Tape Recorder[4]

Record the child's speech. Have him imitate the therapist on the tape; play back for listening.

E. Many techniques listed in Chapter 11, Motor Speech Patterns, will be found helpful for articulation problems.

---

4. See Chapter 8, Sections II and III, for suggestions on using the tape recorder.

Chapter 33

READING, WRITING, ARITHMETIC

I. READING

THE ABILITY TO READ depends almost completely on the visual perceptual areas. Prognosis for success in reading is very poor if basic skills in visual perceptual areas have not been developed. There is a close correlation between defects found in tests for visual perceptual defects and for reading difficulties.[1] Some tests for reading comprehension should be made.[2] Starting with easy material and progressing slowly makes a safer situation for the child. It is helpful to offer words for identification and/or association prior to a new reading lesson. Tests of content following reading are important.

REMARKS

A. A combination of auditory, visual and kinesthetic methods is often helpful. The following are suggested approaches:

Auditory: (1) Phonetic association
        (2) Similar sounds
        (3) Different sounds

Visual: (1) Associate printed words with their sounds and meaning.
        (2) Use pictures and movement.

Kinesthetic: (1) Oral: perceive letters by muscle and lip movement particularly in initial sounds.
        (2) Manual: Use the Fernald Method — air writing (large

EXERCISES

A. **Word Similarities**
    (Refer to section on Visual Verbal Recognition: Words, Chapter 24, Section VII, A (14) .

---

1. Frostig, Marianne; Lefever, Welty; and Whittlesey, John: *Developmental Test of Visual Perception.*
2. See Testing Section, Chapter 24, Section VII, F.

arm movement),
sandpaper writing,
blackboard writ-
ing, paper writing.

2. Strauss, Alfred A. and Lehtinen, Laura E. (*Psychopathology and Education of the Brain Injured Child*, Grune & Stratton, New York, New York. 1947) present a chapter on teaching reading to the brain-injured child.

Fernald, Grace M., *Remedial Techniques in Basic School Subjects* (McGraw-Hill, New York, 1943) Part 2.

(b) house:

B. Word Recognition

(Refer to Visual Verbal Recognition, Chapter 28, Section III).

1. Present the child with words having a phonetic association such as a similar initial consonant:

(a)	*ball*	(b)	*man*
	boy		*mama*
	boat		*money*
	bag		*meat*

2. Present words from a sound "family"[3] such as *at* or *an*.

(a)	*bat*	(b)	*man*
	cat		*can*
	hat		*fan*
	mat		*pan*

3. Ask the child to point out words with different initial consonants: *pat, mat, bat, fat.*

4. Help the child make many associations between written words and pictures. *Examples:*

(a) Match words and pictures.

(b) Draw pictures of words (house, man, car, etc.).

(c) Show printed words naming objects in the room. Ask the child to point them out as he reads the words.

---

3. Hay, Julie and Wingo, Charles E.: *Reading with Phonics.* J. B. Lippincott Co., New York, N. Y., 1960.

Sister Mary Caroline, I.H.M.: *Breaking the Sound Barrier*, A Phonics Handbook. The Macmillan Company, New York, N. Y., 1960.

5. Present objects in categories such as fruits, eating utensils, articles of clothing. Ask the child to match the printed cards and the articles.

6-7. Offer a combination with and without the picture and color.

6. Associate picture and object starting with the child's name.

7. Use colors: grass (green)
                  house (yellow)
  action words: go (green)
                  stop (red)

8. Use the following kinesthetic devices:

(a) Trace sandpaper letters.

(b) Write words in large movements on the board, on a desk, or in the air.

(c) Present words or phrases printed on the board or on flashcards which the child may demonstrate. *Examples:* Run, stand-up, sit-down, walk, sing.

C. The child is to carry out the word, not merely read it aloud.

1. Ask the child to carry out the action indicated in the phrase.

C. Sentence Recognition and Comprehension

1. Increase the difficulty of the phrases to be read. *Examples:*

Close the door.

Raise your hand.

Put your hand on your head.

2. Many excellent workbooks contain exercises for developing word and sentence recognition and story comprehension.[4]

2. Present the child with sentences to be matched. Have him tell whether the sentences are alike:

I have a cat.   I have a dog.

I went to   I went to
school.   school.

3. Ask the child to complete the sentences by selecting the appropriate word from the right hand column:

I went   apple
I ate an   bike
I ride a   home

D. There are many books on the market under *Beginner's Reader* or *I Can Read it Myself* which contain controlled vocabularies with vivid pictorial associations. To note some of these:

Chandler, Edna: *Cowboy Andy*

Eastman, P. D.: *Go Dog Go* (75 words)

Lopshire, Robert: *Put Me in the Zoo* (100 words)

Dr. Seuss: *The Cat in the Hat*
        The Cat in the Hat Comes Back
        Green Eggs and Ham (50 words)
        One Fish, Two Fish, Red Fish, Blue Fish

(These are all listed under a series called Beginner Books, ˙Random House, 457 Madison Ave. New York 22, New York.)

The Developmental Reading Series: *Stories in Pictures* by Guy L. Bond and Marie C. Cuddy (Lyons and Carnahan, Pasadena, Calif. and Chicago, Ill. 1953).

D. Story Comprehension

1. Ask the child to tell a simple story relating to himself or to a picture series. Write this as the child tells it, then use it for reading material.

---

4. Bruechner, Leo J. and Lewis, William D.: *Diagnostic Tests and Remedial Exercises in Reading* John C. Winston Co., Chicago, Ill., 1947.

II. WRITING AND SPELLING
(Refer to Chapter 28, Section III, A)

The sequence suggested in Chapter 28, Section III, A may be followed, or any other which the therapist devises in working with an individual child. With the aphasic child especially, letters must be presented slowly. Often endless repetition must be used before success is achieved.

A. The child will be interested in printing or writing his own name; often these letters become the most important to acquire first.

2. Large sheets of paper may be used with single letters presented in dotted forms.

The child may practice one letter many times.

B. Much diversity exists in current school systems concerning the use of manuscript versus cursive writing. Some systems use upper case letters entirely, others start immediately with upper and lower case. It seems wise to adhere to the system in which the child may be enrolled for school.

A. Copy Letters in Printing

1. Ask the child to trace letters.
2. Ask him to form letters from dotted lines.

3. Direct him to trace letters from a stencil form.

B. Print or Write Letters Spontaneously

As the child gains competency in copying letters, ask him to print letters such as:
1. his name
2. the first letter of pictured items: apple, cat, boy, etc.

C. Copy Printed Sentences

1. Ask the child to copy short printed sentences. These may be some he has made up or those related to pictures or objects of interest.
2. Ask the child to copy his address.

D. Words chosen for the aphasic child must usually be selected individually. Spelling texts often present too many words for the child to absorb in a given time. If the child is in school, arrangements may be made with the teacher to take fewer words than the other members of the class.

D. Spelling

Refer to Chapter 16, Section V for a description of remedial techniques by Grace Fernald.

1. Present words from graded or standard lists or from a standardized spelling list.[5]

2. Have the child make a scrapbook of his own words.

3. Present the words individually on cards so that they may be traced.

4. Ask the children to spell the words with anagrams or block letters.

5. Use large arm movements in the air to spell words which are difficult.

E. Individualized notebooks and material designed for the child are often more appropriate. These may also be used as the basis for reading. Workbooks which require the child to complete sentences are useful.

E. Sentence Formulation

As the child improves in spelling words, help him write simple sentences. Help him formulate simple sentences with familiar words.

III. ARITHMETIC
(See Visual Recognition, Chapter 28, Section III, B)

Many commercial games now exist which involve counting or sorting.[6] Children's books[7] provide

A. Counting

1. Use blocks or counting sticks for counting.

---

5. Dolch cards, Gelles-Widmer Co., St. Louis 17, Mo.
   O'Donnell, Mable; Townes, Willmina, and Brown, Carl S.: *Reading Road to Spelling.* Rowe, Peterson & Co., Evanston, Ill., 1955.

6. Dolch Arithmetic Learning Series: *First Arithmetic Game.* Garrard Press, Champaign, Ill., 1957.

7. Doisneau and Gregor: *1 2 3 4 5.* J. B. Lippincott Co., Philadelphia, Pa., printed in Switzerland.

further practice. The therapist can devise many simple counting practices with pegs, blocks, counting sticks, colored paper and stickers. It should not be forgotten that fingers provide a natural counting device. For many children with disordered learning patterns, it is simpler and more effective to use fingers as part of the self image. One of the early concepts as stressed by Kephart[8] is the development of the bi-body image (two eyes, two ears, two arms, two feet, etc.)

B. It sometimes helps to arrange the numbers according to ease of formulation as in the letters.

    1, 7, 4 (straight lines)
    2, 5, 9 (straight lines and curves)
    3, 6, 8 (curved lines)

D. Many of the texts in use in the schools have material for this purpose such as Knight, F. B.; Gray, Wm. S.: *Number Stories,* Book 2, Scott, Foresman and Co., New York, N. Y., 1947.

2. Use sorting boxes in which to place sticks or blocks. Mark each box numerically with the number of blocks to be placed in each. stickers to match an indicated number.

   3. Ask the child to place colored stickers to match an indicated number.

B. Copy Numbers

Ask the child to trace or use connecting dots to make numbers initially.

C. Number Recognition

Match numbers with pegs, blocks or sticks.

D. Oral Arithmetic

1. Ask the child simple problems in counting *first* such as:

(a) How many fingers do you have?
How many ears do you have?
(b) How many windows in this room?
(c) How many books on the table?

8. Kephart, Newell C.: *The Slow Learner in the Classroom.* Charles E. Merrill Co., Columbus, O., page 43.

E. Many flash card series[9] have been manufactured which allow practice in the four basic processes.

E. **Written Arithmetic**

(Refer to Chapter 17, Section VI for suggestions in this area.)

IV. REFERENCES FOR THE THERAPIST

Figurel, J. Allen, editor: *International Reading Association Conference Preceedings,* **VI,** 1961, Report by Albert J. Harris: *Perceptual Difficulties in Reading Disability in Changing Concepts or Reading Instruction.* University of Chicago Press, Chicago, Ill.

Goins, J. T.: *Supplementary Educational Monograph #87.* University of Chicago Press, Chicago, Ill., 1958, "Visual Perceptual Abilities and Early Reading Progress."

Gray, Lillian and Reese, Dora: *Teaching Children to Read.* Ronald Press, New York, N. Y., 1949.

Harris, Albert J.: *How to Increase Reading Ability.* Longmans, Green and Co., New York, N. Y., 1956.

Robinson, Helen M., Editor: *Supplementary Educational Monograph.* December 1953, University of Chicago Press, Chicago, Ill. "Corrective Reading in Classroom and Clinic."

Wepman, Joseph M.: Auditory Discrimination, Speech and Reading, *The Elementary School Journal,* LX, March 1960.

Zoepfel, M. M.: Auditory Discrimination in the Learning Difficulties of Children with Neurological Disabilities. *The Reading Teacher,* Vol. 15, Nov. 1961.

---

9. *Super Speed Flash Cards:* addition, subtraction, multiplication, division (Visual Speed Card Company, 4111 Berryman Avenue, Los Angeles 66, Calif.).

Fun with Numbers, addition, subtraction, multiplication, division (Exclusive Playing Card Co., Chicago 5, Ill.).

Chapter 34

SAMPLES OF CHILDREN'S WORK

A.

W. T.: expressive aphasia. W. T. was saying a few words at an early age suffering a regression at about 4½ years. Therapy started shortly after. He had less than a ten-word vocabulary. Below are two fireplaces and a person he drew at 4½ years.

At six years, ten months, W. T. had integrated into a normal classroom after spending two years in kindergarten. Although he had residual speech and language problems, he was readily understandable and could perform writing and reading functions in the lower group of his class.

He was asked to draw another fireplace and a person.

B.

E. D.: marked motor-type distortions in speech; no receptive aphasia. Behavior was autistic in many aspects and there was little interaction socially. The first drawing, done at age 6 in an unstructured situation, was disorganized.

E. D.'s drawing at age 7½ years. He was reading at a second grade level at this time. Arithmetic performance was also at an appropriate level. There had been only minimal changes in behavior over a period of 18 months consequently he had been unable to attend school. Education was tutorial only.

"This is a station wagon with no driver."

E. D.'s drawing of a family at 7½ years of age.

E. D.'s printing at 7½ years.

C.

D. F.: Learning problems related to severely reduced visual perception. Though speech was excellent, a severe stuttering pattern existed. Ambidexterity dated from a badly burned right hand in a camping accident. Electroencephalogram was abnormal; periodic psychiatric observations were made. He attended a special training class in public school.

Printing made at age eight as special therapy was initiated.

Scores on expressive verbal scales were within normal limits. Performance scores were low. This Draw-a-man is at a five-year level.

D. F. is doing well in special training classes at ten years of age. Occasional stuttering is still in evidence and psychiatric help has been continued bi-annually since general adjustment has been satisfactory. Reading ability is at upper second grade level and cursive writing has been undertaken.

Copy work of the word *called.*

Most noticeable in this case is the child's grasp of ideas. The story below was recorded by the therapist.

"Our Christmas Eve"

We don't watch television on Christmas Eve. We go to Auntie "O's" or gramma's or grampa's. We have to get home by 10 o'clock P. M. I have to brush my teeth every night, but on Christmas eve, I have to brush in a hurry.

"Eleven O'clock P. M."

"Mom and Dad stay up until 11:30 on the nose. Everybody has to be in bed at midnight. Santa Claus doesn't want to be disturbed while he puts the toys out. Then he has to get more toys delivered and get back by 6:30 A. M. in the morning.

D.

T. E.: mild receptive aphasia with moderate expressive aphasia and dysarthria; severe behavior problems.

Drawing at five years of age.

T. E. one year later after individual therapy and periods of attendance in school. Speech became intelligible although mild articulatory defects of a motor type existed. Behavior improved to the extent that one hour of school was permitted daily.

Below is a self image at 6 years.

"me"

E.

D. A.: expressive aphasia of a motor type with minimal receptive involvement. Speech limited to a few animal sounds and "mama" and "dada."

Drawing at 4 years.

Following a period of six months in nursery school with good adjustment speech improved somewhat.

Drawn at $4\frac{1}{2}$ years.

D. A. at $5\frac{1}{2}$ years. Speech was fairly intelligible and consisted of four- and five-word sentences.

Drawn at $5\frac{1}{2}$ years.

F.

J. F.: mild receptive and moderate expressive aphasia; speech limited to gutteral sounds and screams during periods of frustration.

His only attempt at drawing at $3\frac{1}{2}$ years of age.

J. F. at five years, eleven months of age. Speech had improved to the extent that he could use three- and four-word sentences although some of his communication was not always understandable. His frustration tolerance excluded him from school.

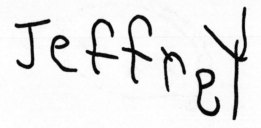

J. F. at six years, ten months. Communication was readily understandable with moderate articulatory residuals. He was now performing in a first grade classroom at an early first grade level in reading.

G.

T. N.: a fifteen year old boy with a severe auditory perceptual defect. An original diagnosis of severe peripheral hearing defect had been made, but training classes for the hard of hearing had proved ineffective. Behavior was autistic at times although he related briefly from time to time. Educational opportunities were limited to individual tutoring.

T. N. could make remarkable copies of stamps, maps, coins and paper bills in detail. Below is an illustration of a letter copied in code.

TXYPCAAY, Cutcbep 15 b9,1959
Aæp Uонин e AнA famnnyǫ

Tot Чoxp Jettep Oøко.Maybe Gpyɩɛ Peuornnзa My Jettæpc 6y Тx/c Тнme Co Jetc you XaBe Tem. Y GyM XaBe Tomoppuчy Тo Гo Co Txoxгxt Thnc A Бoя Тнme To 4upnte. Epнне AнR Jaỵле Ape Бøtx At Xome мↅ JↄAↄ Pop Бany Aↄᶙⅎↄ↔.Txea Ape Бⅎ꜀нer Txat Tↄ/o Uatc Q↔ Tↄↄ Tнↄ Poobc.Txey Ape Tbↄ꜀нↄr To Get Гe Cxatгtчнг Uↄ↔tep Tↄↄↄ꜀, AↄⅯ Apͅe Uⅉↄ pknr Qↄ A Jↄace Ulntx Гↄe XↄⅯↄ↔ Oↄ꜀ Pↄp Txeↄↄ꜀tepↄ꜀ FↄↄC Gↄatↄↄↄↄ꜀,

T. N.'s speech was paraphasic most of the time; nevertheless he often attempted to read some of the most difficult geographical names or scientific terms listed on the numerous graphs and maps he produced. He was able to say two- or three-word sentences within limits; for example, "What's 'at. Take one."

APPENDIX

BIBLIOGRAPHIES

GENERAL BIBLIOGRAPHY

Agranowitz, Aleen; Boone, Daniel; Ruff, Marion; Seacat, Gloria; and Terr, Arthur: Group Therapy as a Method of Retraining Aphasics. *Quarterly Journal of Speech*, Vol. 40, No. 2, April, 1954.

Aronson, Manuel, and others: Socio-Psychotherapeutic Approach to the Treatment of Aphasic Patients. *Journal of Speech & Hearing Disorders*, Vol. 21, No. 3, September, 1956.

Baker, A. B.: *Clinical Neurology.* New York, N. Y., Paul B. Hoeber, Inc., 1962, Chapter 8, Agnosias, Apraxias, Speech and Aphasia, by J. M. Nielsen, M. D.

Berry, M. F., and Eisenson, J.: *The Defective in Speech.* New York, N. Y., Crofts and Company, 1942.

————: *Speech Disorders.* New York, N. Y., Appleton-Century-Crofts, Inc., 1956.

Boone, Daniel R.: *An Adult Has Aphasia.* Cleveland 6, O. Cleveland Hearing and Speech Center, 11206 Euclid Avenue.

————: Communication Skills and Intelligence in Right and Left Hemiplegics. *Journal of Speech and Hearing Disorders*, Vol. 24, No. 3, August, 1959.

Boyle, D. G., and McKeown, Milfred: Case of Alexia and Visual Agnosia for Objects. *Bulletin of the Los Angeles Neurological Society*, Vol. 23, No. 2, June, 1958.

Brock, Samuel (ed.): *The Basis of Clinical Neurology.* Baltimore 2, Md., Williams & Wilkins, 428 East Preston Street, Chapter 17, The Brain; Its General Structure and Functions.

Brown, Joe R., and Simonson, Josephine: A Clinical Study of 100 Aphasia Patients, Observations on Lateralization and Localization of Lesions. *Neurology,* Vol. 7, No. 11, November, 1957.

Brown, Keene C., with Cadden, Vivian: A Winding Road, *Redbook Magazine,* December, 1959.

Corbin, M. L.: Group Speech Therapy for Motor Aphasia and Dysarthria. *Journal of Speech and Hearing Disorders,* Vol. 16, No. 1, March, 1951.

Fernald, Grace M.: *Remedial Techniques in Basic School Subjects.* New York, N. Y., Mc-Graw-Hill Book Company, 1943.

Freud, Sigmund: *On Aphasia, A Critical Study.* New York, N. Y., International Universites Press, Inc. First published in 1891; translated by E. Stengel and copyrighted by International Universities Press in 1953.

Fidler, Gail S., OTR, and Fidler, Jay W., M.D.: *Introduction to Psychiatric Occupational Therapy.* New York 11, N. Y., Macmillan, 60 Fifth Avenue.

Goldstein, Kurt: *Language and Language Disturbances.* New York, N. Y., Grune and Stratton, 1948.

Head, Henry: *Aphasia and Kindred Disorders of Speech.* Cambridge, Mass., Cambridge University Press, 1926.

Horwitz, Betty: An Open Letter to the Family of an Adult Patient with Aphasia. *Rehabilitation Literature.* Chicago 12, Ill., 2023 West Ogden Avenue, May, 1962.

Huber, Mary: Phonetic Approach to the Problem of Perception in a Case of Wernicke's Aphasia. *Journal of Speech Disorders,* Vol. 9, 1944.

————: Re-education of Aphasics. *Journal of Speech Disorders,* Vol. 7, 1942.

Jones, Morris Val.: *Speech Correction at Home*. Springfield, Ill., Charles C Thomas Publisher, 1957.

Kirkner, F. J.; Dorcus, R. M., and Seacat, Gloria: Hypnotic Motivation and Vocalization in an Organic Motor Aphasic Case. *Journal of Clinical and Experimental Hypnosis*, Vol. 1, No. 3, July, 1953.

Leutenegger, R. R.: Bibliography of Aphasia. *Journal of Speech & Hearing Disorders*, Vol. 16, No. 3, September, 1951.

Levin, Nathaniel M.: *Voice and Speech Disorders*. Springfield, Ill., Charles C Thomas, Publisher, 1961. Chapters 23 and 24.

Longerich, Mary C., and Bordeaux, Jean: *Aphasia Therapeutics*. New York, N. Y., Macmillan Company, 1954.

Longerich, Mary C.: *Manual for the Aphasia Patient*. New York, N. Y., Macmillan Company, 1958.

Marks, Morton; Taylor, Martha, and Rusk, Howard A.: Rehabilitation of the Aphasic Patient, A Survey of Three Years' Experience in a Rehabilitation Setting, *Neurology*, Vol. 7, No. 12, December, 1957.

Martin, Blanche R.: *Communicative Aids for the Adult Aphasic*. Springfield, Ill., Charles C Thomas, Publisher, 1962.

Mason, Charles F.: Hypnotic Motivation of Aphasics. *International Journal of Clinical and Experimental Hypnosis*, Vol. IX, No. 4, October, 1961.

McDaniel, Myra L.: The Role of the Occupational Therapist in the Re-Education of Aphasia Patients. (Master's Thesis, University of Southern California, 1953.)

Nielsen, J. M.: *Agnosia, Apraxia, Aphasia*, Second Edition. New York, Hafner Publishing Company, Inc., 1957. An epitome of this monograph may be found in the *Journal of Speech and Hearing Disorders*, Vol. 14, No. 3, September, 1949.

————: *Memory and Amnesia*. Los Angeles, Calif., San Lucas Press, 1958.

————: *A Textbook of Clinical Neurology*, Third Edition. New York, N. Y., Paul B. Hoeber, 1962, Chapter 10, Clinical Cerebral Localization.

————: The Cortical Motor Pattern Apraxias. *The Frontal Lobes*, Association for Research in Nervous and Mental Disease. Baltimore 2, Md., Williams & Wilkins Company, Vol. 27, 1948.

————: Motor Aphasia with Recovery. Report of Case with Autopsy Verification. *Bulletin of the Los Angeles Neurological Society*, Vol. 22, No. 3, September, 1957.

Nielsen, J. M.; Agranowitz, Aleen; Boone, Daniel; Ruff, Marion, and Terr, Arthur: Aphasia Rehabilitation—A Report of Nine Successful Cases. *Military Surgeon*, Vol. 114, No. 6, June, 1954.

Nielsen, J. M.; Amyes, E. W., and Mee, J. L.: Visual Agnosia and Irreminiscence for Animate Objects. *Bulletin of the Los Angeles Neurological Society*, Vol. 26, No. 2, June, 1961.

Nielsen, J. M., and McKeown, Milfred: Dysprosody. Report of Two Cases. *Bulletin of the Los Angeles Neurological Society*, Vol. 26, No. 3, September, 1961.

————: Summary of a Decade in the Aphasia Clinic of a Veterans Hospital. *Bulletin of the Los Angeles Neurological Society*, Vol. 25, No. 3, September, 1960.

Page, Irvine H., and others: *Strokes, How They Occur and What Can Be Done About Them*. New York, N. Y., E. P. Dutton and Company, 1961.

Penfield, W. G.: *Epilepsy and Cerebral Localization*. Springfield, Ill., Charles C Thomas, Publisher, 1941.

Penfield, W. G., and Roberts, L.: *Speech and Brain-Mechanisms*. Princeton, N. J., Princeton University Press, 1959.

Pfeiffer, John: *The Human Brain*. New York, N. Y., Harper and Brothers, 1955.

Robbins, S. D.: *Dictionary of Speech Pathology and Therapy.* Cambridge, Mass., Sci-Art Publishers, Harvard Square, 1951.

Rose, Robert H., M.D.: A Physician's Account of His Own Aphasia. *Journal of Speech and Hearing Disorders,* Vol. 13, No. 4, December, 1948.

Schuell, Hildred; Carroll, Virginia, and Street, Barbara S.: Clinical Treatment of Aphasia. *Journal of Speech and Hearing Disorders,* Vol. 20, No. 1, March, 1955.

Sharpe & Dohme, Medical Department (editors): Rehabilitation of the Hemiplegic, *Seminar.* Philadelphia, Pa., Sharpe & Dohme, Inc., 640 N. Broad St., January-February, 1952.

Silverman, Milton, and Holliday, Kate: Half Your Brain is a Spare. *Saturday Evening Post,* December 11, 1948.

Stokes, Maurice, with Paxton, Harry T.: I Woke up Helpless. *Saturday Evening Post,* March 14, 1959.

Subirana, Antonio (Barcelona, Spain): The Relationship Between Handedness and Language Function. *Logos,* Vol. 4, No. 2, October, 1961.

Swartz, Harry: *Intelligent Layman's Medical Dictionary.* New York, Frederick Ungar Publishing Company, 1955.

Taylor, Martha L.: *Understanding Aphasia: a Guide for Family and Friends.* New York, N. Y., The Institute of Physical Medicine and Rehabilitation, 400 East 34th Street, 1958.

Travis, L. E. (ed.): *Handbook of Speech Pathology.* New York, N. Y., Appleton-Century-Crofts, Inc., 1957.

Weisenburg, T., and McBride, K. E.: *Aphasia—A Clinical and Psychological Study.* New York, N. Y., Commonwealth Fund, 1935.

Wepman, Joseph M.: *Recovery from Aphasia.* New York, N. Y., Ronald Press, 1951.

————: Selected *Bibliography In Brain Impairment Aphasia and Organic Psychodiagnosis.* Chicago, Ill., Language Research Associates, 950 East 59 St., 1961.

West, Robert; Ansberry, Merle, and Carr, Anna: *Rehabilitation of Speech.* New York, N. Y., Harper & Brothers, 1957.

Wood, Nancy E.: Helping the Aphasic Adult. *Journal of Rehabilitation,* January-February, 1956.

Young, Edna Hill, and Hawk, Sara Stinchfield: *Moto-Kinesthetic Speech Training.* Stanford, Calif., Stanford University Press, 1955.

Rehabilitation Literature—*Selected Abstracts of Current Publications of Interest for Workers with the Handicapped.* Chicago 12, Ill., The National Society for Crippled Children and Adults, Inc., 2023 West Ogden. Published monthly.

* * * * *

APHASIA FILMS (made in the Veterans Administration Hospital Aphasia Clinic).
Part I—Diagnosis of Aphasia
Part II—Testing and Individual Therapy for Aphasics
Part III—Social Adjustment for Aphasia
Available at: Churchill-Wexler Film Productions, 801 N. Seward, Los Angeles, Calif.
May be purchased or rented. Rental fee is $7.50 each plus postage.

       Medical Research and Education Service, Department of Medicine and Surgery, Veterans Administration, Washington 25, D. C. There is no rental charge except postage.

BIBLIOGRAPHY REGARDING APHASIA IN CHILDREN

Agranowitz, Aleen: The Brain-Injured Child: Behavior, Learning and Language. *The Voice, Journal of the California Speech and Hearing Association,* Vol. XI, No. 3, November, 1962.

Anderson, Arnold S.: Behavior Problems and Brain Injury in Children. *Bulletin of the St. Louis Park Medical Center Research Foundation,* Vol. 4, No. 2, February 9, 1960.

Axline, Virgil A.: *Improving the Child's Speech.* New York, N. Y., Oxford University Press, 1947.

Backus, Ollie, and Beasley, Jane: *Speech Therapy with Children.* Boston. Mass., Houghton Mifflin Co., 1951.

Barry, Hortense: *The Young Aphasic Child: Evaluation and Training.* Washington, D. C., Volta Bureau, 1961.

Berry, Mildred F., and Eisenson, Jon: *Speech Disorders.* New York, N. Y., Appleton-Century-Crofts, Inc., 1956, Chapter 17.

Clark, Ruth: Language Behavior of Children with Unsuspected Brain Injury. *Logos, Bulletin for the National Hospital of Speech Disorders,* Vol. 5, No. 1, April, 1962.

Cruickshank, Wm. M.; Bentzen, Frances A.; Ratzeburg, Frederick H.; Tannhauser, Marian T.: *A Teaching Method for Brain-injured and Hyperactive Children.* Syracuse, N. Y., Syracuse University Press, 1961.

Eisenson, Jon: *Examining for Aphasia.* New York, N. Y., Psychological Corporation, 1954, Chapter 4, Testing the Congenitally Aphasic Child.

Gallagher, J. J.: *The Tutoring of Brain-Injured Mentally Retarded Children.* Springfield, Ill., Charles C Thomas, Publisher, 1960.

Gens, George W., and Bibey, M. Lois: Congenital Aphasia: A Case Report. *Journal of Speech and Hearing Disorders,* Vol. 17, No. 1, March, 1952.

Ingram, Christine T.: *Education of the Slow Learning Child.* New York, N. Y., Ronald Press, 1960.

Johnson, Wendell: *Speech Problems of Children.* New York, N. Y., Grune and Stratton, 1950.

Jolles, Isaac: Some Helpful Techniques for the Education of Brain-Injured Children. (Staff Psychologist, Dept. of Education of the State of Illinois, Springfield, Ill.)

Kephart, Newell: *The Slow Learner in the Classroom.* Columbus, O., Charles Merrill Books, Inc., 1960.

Lewis, Richard; Strauss, Alfred A., and Lehtinen, Laura: *The Other Child.* New York, N. Y., Grune and Stratton, 1951.

Montessori, Maria: *Dr. Montessori's Own Handbook.* New York, N. Y., Frederick A. Stokes, 1914.

Murray, Don: Children of the Empty World. *The Saturday Evening Post,* September 13, 1958.

Myklebust, Helmer R.: *Auditory Disorders in Children; A Manual for Differential Diagnosis.* New York, N. Y., Grune and Stratton, 1954.

Parker, William R.: *Pathology of Speech.* New York, N. Y., Prentice-Hall, 1951.

Spencer, Steven M.: The Priceless Gift of Speech. *The Saturday Evening Post,* January 3, 1959.

Standing, E. M.: *The Montessori Method of Revolution in Education.* Fresno, Calif., The Literary Guild.

Strauss, Alfred A., and Lehtinen, L.: *Psychopathology and Education of the Brain-Injured Child.* New York, N. Y., Grune and Stratton, 1947.

Sugar, Oscar: Congenital Aphasia: An Anatomical and Physiological Approach. *Journal of Speech and Hearing Disorders,* Vol. 17, No. 3, September, 1952.

Thorpe, Louis P.: *Child Psychology and Development.* New York, N. Y., Ronald Press, 1946.

Travis, L. E. (ed.): *Handbook of Speech Pathology.* New York, N. Y., Appleton-Century-Crofts, Inc., 1957, Chapters 15 and 16 by Myklebust, Helmer R.

Van Riper, Charles: *Speech Correction, Principles and Methods.* Englewood Cliffs, N. J., Prentice-Hall, Inc., 1954, Chapter 6, Delayed Speech.

West, Robert; Ansberry, Merle, and Carr, Anna: *The Rehabilitation of Speech.* New York, N. Y., Harper and Brothers, 1957, Chapter V, Chapter XI.

West, Robert (ed.): *Childhood Aphasia, Proceedings of the Institute on Childhood Aphasia.* San Francisco, Calif., California Society for Crippled Children and Adults, 1962.

Young, Edna Hill, and Hawk, Sara Stinchfield: *Moto-Kinesthetic Speech Training.* Stanford, Calif., Stanford University Press, 1955.

TERMS

1. ACALCULIA: A disturbance in arithmetic resulting from a loss of the significance of numbers or an inability to perform mathematical functions.
2. AGNOSIA: A loss of the function of recognition not due to an involvement of the sense organs themselves, but due to the association pathways. For example, an individual with auditory-verbal agnosia fails to recognize or to understand the words he *hears;* an individual with visual agnosia fails to recognize the objects he *sees,* and one with visual-verbal agnosia fails to recognize or to comprehend the *words* he sees.
3. AGRAPHIA: A disturbance in writing. This may result from a loss of memory of the movements used in writing (motor agraphia) or may result from a symbolic or formulation loss (amnesic agraphia). Paragraphia results in garbled spelling due to faulty recall.
4. ALEXIA: A disturbance in reading which may result in an inability to recognize letters or words, in an inability to comprehend simple written statements, or in an inability to comprehend the semantics of complicated written material.
5. AMNESIC APHASIA: An inability to recall appropriate words, phrases and language in general.
6. ANOMIA: An inability to recall and to express the names of objects, people and places.
7. APHASIA: A term in common use for all disturbances of language, motor or sensory, due to a lesion of the brain but not due to faulty innervation of the musculature necessary for speech or to involvement of the sense organs themselves or to general mental defect.—J. M. Nielsen in *A Textbook of Clinical Neurology,* page 276.
8. APRAXIA: An inability to perform voluntary or intended movements because of loss of memory of how to perform. In aphasics, apraxias are seen in motor speech defects and in writing defects. (See Ideational and Ideokinetic apraxia.)
9. ASTEREOGNOSIS: (Tactile agnosia) A loss of ability to identify an object by touch only.
10. AUTOMATIC SPEECH: Language which comes forth automatically without having to be thought out; often an interjection, profanity, exclamation, or repetitive phrase.

11. CVA: An abbreviation for cerebral vascular accident; commonly referred to as a stroke.

12. DYSARTHRIA: An inability to pronounce or to articulate accurately. A patient with dysarthria has difficulty in using the organs of speech for other purposes such as chewing and swallowing. (A patient with motor aphasia has difficulty in pronouncing or in articulating even though he can use the organs of speech for functions such as eating, drinking, etc.)

13. EEG: The abbreviation for electroencephalogram: a tracing of brain waves used as a possible indication of the foci of lesions.

14. GLOBAL APHASIA: A severe involvement in all areas of language, virtually depriving the patient of all communication both receptive and expressive.

15. HEMIANOPIA: Blindness in half of each eye, the right half or the left half of each eye, or the inner half of one and the outer half of the other.

16. HEMIPLEGIA: A weakness or paralysis of either the left or the right side of the body.

17. IDEATIONAL APRAXIA: An inability to combine several correctly executed elements of an act into the final larger intended act. (This is like extreme absent-mindedness wherein the patient successfully puts his pipe in his mouth and even lights the match, but forgets to light his pipe.)

18. IDEOKINETIC APRAXIA: An inability to connect the motor movements needed to carry out an act with the ideation which is attempting to promote the action. (The ideation may dictate that the patient is to remove his hat, but the hand does not receive the message and consequently goes through other gyrations in its attempt to comply. Both the idea and the hand are intact in themselves, but they cannot connect to carry out the order.)

19. LESION: A pathological change in the structure; or traumatic discontinuity of tissue.

20. MOTOR APHASIA: An inability to speak (even though the words are recalled) because of a loss of the motor patterns needed to guide the speech musculature in forming the words.

21. PARAPHASIA AND PARAGRAPHIA: The use of inappropriate and garbled words and phrases. If this defect is severe, the resulting language will be a jargon. Written garbled words and phrases due to faulty recall is called paragraphia.

22. PROPOSITIONAL SPEECH: The formulation of an idea into intelligible language.

23. PERSEVERATION: The constant and persistent repetition of a word or phrase as a substitute for other language. The patient is usually un-

able to say any other words at the time of the perseveration. Aside from language, perseveration also takes place in behavior and in learning.

24. TELEGRAPHIC SPEECH: A type of speech in which connectives, prepositions, modifiers and refinements of language are omitted.

25. TRAUMA: wound; injury.

INDEX

(Page numbers in Roman type refer to Adults; those in *Italic type*, to children.)